HELLENIC STU⸻⸻⸻ ⸻⸻⸻ /5

THE TEARS OF ACHILLES

Recent Titles in the Hellenic Studies Series

http://chs.harvard.edu/chs/publications

THE TEARS OF ACHILLES

Hélène Monsacré

translated by
Nicholas J. Snead

Center for Hellenic Studies
Trustees for Harvard University
Washington, D.C.
Distributed by Harvard University Press
Cambridge, Massachusetts, and London, England
2017

The Tears of Achilles
Hélène Monsacré
Copyright © 2017 Center for Hellenic Studies, Trustees for Harvard University
All Rights Reserved.
Published by Center for Hellenic Studies, Trustees for Harvard University,
  Washington, D.C.
Distributed by Harvard University Press, Cambridge, Massachusetts,
  and London, England
Production: Nancy Wolfe Kotary
Cover design: Joni Godlove

EDITORIAL TEAM

Senior Advisers: W. Robert Connor, Gloria Ferrari Pinney, Albert Henrichs,[†]
  James O'Donnell, Bernd Seidensticker
Editorial Board: Gregory Nagy (Editor-in-Chief), Casey Dué (Executive Editor),
  Mary Ebbott (Executive Editor), Scott Johnson, Olga Levaniouk, Leonard
Muellner
Production Manager for Publications: Jill Curry Robbins
Web Producer: Noel Spencer
Multimedia Producer: Mark Tomasko

Originally published as *Les larmes d'Achille. Le héros, la femme et la souffrance dans
la poésie d'Homère* (Paris: Editions Albin Michel, 1984).

*Ouvrage publié avec le concours du Ministère français chargé de la Culture-Centre
national du livre.*
This work has been published with the assistance of the French Ministry of
  Culture—Centre national du livre.

Library of Congress Cataloging-in-Publication Data

Names: Monsacré, Hélène, author. | Snead, Nicholas J., translator.
Title: The tears of Achilles / by Hélène Monsacré ; translated by Nicholas
  J. Snead ; with a foreword by Richard P. Martin.
Other titles: Larmes d'Achille. English | Hellenic studies ; 75.
Description: Washington, D.C. : Center for Hellenic Studies, 2017. | Series:
  Hellenic studies ; 75 | Includes bibliographical references and index.
Identifiers: LCCN 2017005164 | ISBN 9780674975682 (alk. paper)
Subjects: LCSH: Achilles (Mythological character)--In literature. |
  Homer--Knowledge--Psychology. | Epic poetry, Greek--History and criticism.
  | Women and literature--Greece. | Suffering in literature. | Emotions in
  literature. | Sex role in literature. | Heroes in literature. | Crying in
  literature. | Tears in literature.
Classification: LCC PA4037 .M6613 2017 | DDC 883/.01--dc23
LC record available at https://lccn.loc.gov/2017005164

Contents

Part III: Sobs of Men, Tears of Women

Foreword

RICHARD P. MARTIN
STANFORD UNIVERSITY

Warrior, hero, super-male—Achilles should not cry. Not, that is, in the contemporary understanding of the categories he seems to personify, categories that (one might at first assume) have always dominated the imagination of our cultural forefathers, from the earliest epics, through John Wayne westerns, to the latest *Star Wars* film, the protagonist of which, Luke Skywalker, was scornfully dubbed by some moviegoers "Luke Crywalker" for displaying an unacceptable sensitivity.

Of cultural foremothers, Western tradition has transmitted much less. What we do have—for instance, fragments of poetry attributed to Sappho (late seventh/early sixth century BCE)—tends to undercut easy assumptions that early Greek society was totally in the grip of patriarchal machismo. In contrast to the "finest" things that others praise on earth—an army of foot soldiers or horsemen, a fleet of ships—the poetess of Lesbos opts for "that which one loves" (fr. 16.1-4). Of course, one could argue that Sappho's bold preference for the erotic over the martial was a minority view, a "veiled sentiment" confined to women's quarters, safely marginalized, never a threat to glorious male ambitions. But we should remember that it was primarily *men* in their elite drinking parties who re-performed and disseminated Sapphic songs and sentiments, men who seemed to need deeply this mirror of the Other, to order and express their own moods and yearnings. The figure of Sappho, like Socrates' female instructor Diotima two centuries later (topic of another elite male symposium), possesses a deeply experienced form of wisdom not ordinarily accessible to men. So does the realm most associated with women in Greek thought: grief and mourning.

Hélène Monsacré's path-blazing study demonstrates how this same psychic dynamic is at work already in our earliest preserved Greek poetry, the epics attributed to Homer. Heroes weep. Not only do warriors break down and cry under the weight of battle, amid the slaughter of companions. The most heroic—Achilles, "best of the Achaeans"—cries most. We see him in tears in the very first book of the poem (*Iliad* 1.347–363):

> He led forth from the hut Briseis of the fair cheeks and gave her
> to be taken away; and they walked back beside the ships of the
>   Achaians,
> and the woman all unwilling went with them still. But Achilleus
> weeping went and sat in sorrow apart from his companions
> 350   beside the beach of the gray sea looking out on the infinite water.
> Many times stretching forth his hands he called on his mother:
> "Since, my mother, you bore me to be a man with a short life,
> therefore Zeus of the loud thunder on Olympos should grant me
> honor at least. But now he has given me not even a little.
> 355   Now the son of Atreus, powerful Agamemnon,
> has dishonored me, since he has taken away my prize and keeps it."
> So he spoke in tears and the lady his mother heard him
> as she sat in the depths of the sea at the side of her aged father,
> and lightly she emerged like a mist from the gray water.
> 360   She came and sat beside him as he wept, and stroked him
> with her hand and called him by name and spoke to him: "Why
>   then,
> child, do you lament? What sorrow has come to your heart now?
> Tell me, do not hide it in your mind, and thus we shall both know."
>
> (trans. Richmond Lattimore)

Why does the *Iliad* (and in a slightly different manner, the *Odyssey*) represent its protagonists as prone to tears? How, especially in light of later tradition, could weeping be conceived as a signal, rather than betrayal, of manhood? Hélène Monsacré's meticulous explanation gets to the heart of Greek conceptions, not just of heroism, but of society, divinity, and gender. One of the most striking conclusions of her analysis is that the later ideal of stoically inexpressive manhood runs contrary to the poetic vision of the *Iliad* and *Odyssey*. The epic protagonists, instead, are larger-than-life figures who transcend simple gender stereotypes. That is why they are *precisely* the men most likely to weep. In order to articulate this counter-intuitive position, the paradox of the tearful fighter, Monsacré expands her view to take into account all aspects of relations between men and women in the Homeric imaginary. The resultant new horizon blooms into a meditation on the nature of emotion and its depiction. Into such unfamiliar interpretive territory we are led by a guide who grounds in lucidly argued explication her deeply-felt intuitions. *Les larmes d'Achille* is thus more than a display of exegetical skill; it is a compelling message for anyone touched—like Achilles—by a world of grief.

To appreciate fully the achievement of the book, it is important to develop a sense of its full scope, lest we mistakenly pigeonhole it in too narrow a critical slot. In construction, it is a triptych, with three major sections devoted, respectively, to men; to women; and to interactions between the genders. In movement, it is more circular than linear, avoiding some easy Hegelian thesis-antithesis-synthesis, because it respects the complexities and essential asymmetries in the poetic materials. Running through the book, as through the poem, is a constant fascination with the body, with its movements and gestures, tactility and expressivity—far beyond the shedding of tears.

Somewhat surprisingly, Monsacré begins with eroticized bodies: in particular, the Trojan warrior Paris, more lover than fighter, whose marked affiliation with Aphrodite (and because of her, with Helen) sparked the entire conflict. His depiction in the *Iliad* demarcates one side of the broad field of heroic action. Hector, his brother, holds the middle ground, resistant to his wife's plea that he keep away from the midst of battle, placing the winning of immortal fame (*kleos*) before family relations, but all the while acutely conscious of the claims of non-combatants. At the other extreme from Paris is the Greek warrior Diomedes, a killing-machine with the help of Athena, untouched by *eros* and—appropriately—the only hero who does *not* cry in war (his only tears coming at his defeat in a chariot race: *Iliad* 23.385). While the body of the Homeric fighter functions in all its parts as a burnished mirror for male heroism, it also excites the desire to gaze. Epic poetry can feminize it, highlighting the tenderness of skin, making war look like an amorous encounter, an intimate battle-dance. Through poetic imagery and fictional devices, even death is eroticized. Cities are seized in the way that women are taken, both having "veils" that are ripped away. Dead, the fortunate fighter turns into aesthetic object, frozen in *la belle mort*. But there is also the chilling parallel between women who care for men—dead and alive—and vultures who just crave the warrior's corpse.

The final chapter of Part One, in which Monsacré carefully observes the role of mothers and images of the maternal in the *Iliad*, forms a bridge to Part Two, a richly detailed section devoted to women in epic. Eschewing the simplifications of positivist historians, Monsacré quickly moves beyond the obvious (that women occupy domestic spaces, for example) to focus on the interesting liminal scenes, where the sphere of women impinges on that of men—for example, the walls of Troy, from which wives become spectators of their doomed husbands and Helen is led away by Aphrodite to confront Paris in their bed-chamber. This initial overview, which stresses female mobility within the spaces of epic, then carries us into a fine-grained analysis of the poetic techniques whereby women are represented as individuals—or, as happens most often, are described within the system of conventional epithets that frames the world view shared by audience and poets. "Beautiful in face"; "with fine hair" (or, "lovely cheeks" or "white arms" or "slender ankles")—at first, we might think that the Homeric *"occultation du corps"* underwrites a suspect and essentializing commodification. But as Monsacré notes, Homeric men reside within a similar system of expectation. It is not that diction is destiny; rather, both the poetic semiotic system and the cultural codes of the heroic age (at least, as the age is imagined in epic) align. Paradoxically, there are definite horizons for male and female ambition, but these can only come into clearest view when there is a character (an Achilles or Helen) who threatens to transgress the bounds. What is more, the deployment of epithets and type-scenes makes explicit some striking parallels between the gendered worlds, as women's veils echo men's armor, in a shared appearance of brilliance and luster.

Like a skilled veteran ethnographer, Monsacré finds no detail of this representational system to be without interest. She is sensitive to all the senses, colors, appearances. And, like the self-aware cultural anthropologist, she pays attention as well to the contingent, fluid nature of her material. The *Iliad* and *Odyssey* are not historical accounts of static "cold" societies but warmly imagined, teleologically directed narratives. A critical account of the epics, therefore, will best resemble more a series of snapshots, candid as well as posed, than a continuous film. At heart, it is this modern anthropological attitude that guides Monsacré. She writes in a series of swift and incisive critical perceptions, thematically linked, rather than under the weight of some ponderous thesis that would have required propping up in the implausible parts. (It is worth noting in this regard that native-speaker reviewers of the original French volume praised the clarity and appeal of her prose style: e.g. Bouvier 1985.)

In their mastery of speech, as well, women can rival or outperform men, though more often by using speech-genres that are traditionally their own domain (such as lament). Goddesses and nymphs—Aphrodite, Calypso, Circe—may be more likely to speak out against male discourse (as when Calypso complains about being commanded to release Odysseus in Book 5), but the epics also feature powerful voices belonging to mortal females, like Hecuba, who gets the most lines of speech by women in the *Iliad*. Monsacré's point, that the most acceptable female speech interactions with men (in the sense that they neither deceive nor berate them) are those by Helen, corresponds with the findings of other scholars regarding the close proximity of the poetic narrator to this figure, as if Helen speaks to an audience beyond the immediate interlocutors, the generations to come for whom, as she self consciously asserts, she will be a subject of song (*Iliad* 3.125–130). Once more, the role of Homeric women cannot be disentangled from the fates of men. The final chapter of the book's second movement illuminates the episodes in which we see women operating from a superior authoritative status: queen Arete taking charge of the Phaeacians, Andromache advising Hector, Cleopatra successfully supplicating her husband Meleager or—most memorably—Penelope, who can be compared to a king whose fine reputation has spread far and wide (*Odyssey* 19.108). That such women are depicted in poetic terms also appropriate to warriors is not the result of some proto-feminist attempt to promote gender equality. Instead, the epics embody a deeper realization of the ways in which roles intersect and the genders interact—not unlike the complex play of forces that alternately unites and separates Homeric mortals and the gods.

In the book's third and final movement, Monsacré returns to the "tears" of her title, scrupulously comparing the moments and manners in which heroes and women weep, while contrasting these behaviors in the *Iliad* and *Odyssey*. In the former poem, weeping marks the deaths of beloved companions—most dramatically, but not exclusively, the death of Achilles' alter ego, Patroclus. In the *Odyssey*, it is the memory of war and home that haunt the hero, prompting his sighs and silent lament. Odysseus, meanwhile, displays the essence of his character as *polutlas* 'much-enduring' by his attempts to suppress and control weeping. The subcurrent of tears that flows through the poem eventually touches most figures in it, from Peisistratus, the son of Nestor recalling his dead brother killed at Troy, to Laertes, the aged father of the homecoming hero, crying at the mention of his son's name by Odysseus, hiding to the last his true identity (*Odyssey* 24.280). Odysseus' tears, unlike those of the *Iliad*, are never simple, but, like the poem's plot, occur among divagations and disguises.

If the epics diverge in the emotional coloration of their respective tears, they are united in another way. Andromache and Penelope both weep out of a sense of helplessness in the face of war and its consequences. Unlike the male heroes who can react to overpowering sadness, whether through devices of cunning or manic revenge, the leading female figures possess only their tears as a response—but these, coupled with expressive verbal lament have their own powerful communicative weight. Monsacré merges an analysis of the language constituted *by* tears with the poetic language *about* tears, the vivid comparisons of weeping to black-watered springs, or melting snow, and of cries to the sounds of predatory birds. Her meticulous observation of the fine points of Homeric diction surrounding grief uncovers startling cross-overs and parallels: tears (warm, flowing, tender) metonymically resemble the warriors who shed them (regularly described by the poetry in terms of plants, leaves, or trees bound to wither and dry up).

One warrior in particular embodies in all his parts this world of tears: Achilles, whose very name, as a compound, has been linked to *achos* 'grief' for the fighting group (*laos*)—grief *felt* passively as well as grief actively *caused*. It is striking, but appropriate, that the hero's final consolation for Priam, his slaughtered enemy's father (itself a surreal reversal) hinges on overwhelming grief, the story of the legendary Niobe, a mother endlessly weeping for her slaughtered children, even when she is turned to stone, like a spring in a mountain landscape. Monsacré sees in this ethical *exemplum* recalled by Achilles a confluence of themes—memory, maternity, nourishment—that have run throughout the *Iliad*. This association spells out a reading of the epic that counterpoints its brutality and suffering with another vision, an extremely slender shaft of light at the ultimate edge of the bleak picture. As in later Aeschylean tragedy—but, in Homeric poetry, with more restraint and less didactic dramatization—suffering brings knowledge. It offers the consolation that, for mortals while alive, grief can be, if not ended, at least diminished and contained. In the terms of the *Iliad*, the means for channeling the flood of emotion into a stream of tears are two: ritual and poetry, which is to say funeral rites and epic itself. In this way, Achilles becomes more than just a metonymy for the tragic situation of the *Iliad*. His deep comprehension of the aetiology of grief is summed up in the realization that one can find satiety even in tears, the sort of satisfaction provided by having eaten and drunk enough. Monsacré names this relief through sorrow *la jouissance-souffrance*. It is fair to say that exactly this effect is what epic song aims to achieve.

וו

This rapid overview of the book's sonata-like structure provides only a brief glimpse of the illuminating, at times brilliant, interpretations that will reward slow, careful reading. Since even the most brilliant critical analyses, however, emerge from a specific intellectual context, it is worth mentioning two important approaches to literature and culture with which Monsacré's writing engages. Neither is specific to Homeric studies, but in various ways, both have affected them in recent decades. Their adroit intertwining contributes to the overall impact of this volume.

First, the book has a close relationship with "structuralist" interpretation. Although now on the ebb, this theoretical approach to language, literature, and culture was at its height for roughly a quarter-century, from 1955 to 1980. "Structuralism" was never a monolithic approach. It drew from, and influenced in turn, work in linguistics, anthropology, and the broader study of sign-systems ("semiotics"). Among its leading proponents was the Russian linguist Roman Jakobson (1896-1982), whose work with Nikolai Trubetzkoy, a fellow member of the informal Linguistic Circle of Prague, laid the foundation for an approach to language as a system in which basic elements, like phonemes, possess meaning only through a systematic and contrastive relationship to other elements. During the Second World War, Jakobson taught at the New School in New York City. There, another émigré scholar, the French anthropologist Claude Lévi-Strauss (1908 –2009) attended his lectures on structural phonology, and with Jakobson's encouragement began work on what would become his landmark 1949 study *The Elementary Structures of Kinship*. This, and such later work as *Structural Anthropology*, developed the notion that all human cultures are patterned on underlying, often unconscious structures of thought, built around fundamental binary oppositions (like those evident in the structure of language). For Lévi-Strauss, such oppositions included hot vs. cold, raw vs. cooked, culture vs. nature, and male vs. female. Clearly, Monsacré's analysis relies on and extends the anthropological thinking about this lattermost category. Lévi-Strauss himself was more interested in complicating his identification of binary oppositions by investigating the role of mediating categories or figures, in which seemingly irreconcilable poles were brought together or transformed into other, more malleable sets of oppositions (as in his famous study of the myth of Oedipus). In the same way, Monsacré shows much more interest in the unexpected cross-over, the short-circuiting of seemingly stable oppositions, the *brouillage* ('blurring' or 'scrambling') that brings together joy and grief, real and fabulous worlds, and most of all, that plays with any and all oppositions of gender.

It is noteworthy, however, that the name of Lévi-Strauss comes up only once in the book, and then only in a footnote concerning the low regard in which the Greeks held archery in war, citing the 1979 piece "Lévi-Strauss en Brocéliande," a *tour de force* structuralist analysis of a twelfth-century French chivalric romance, written by the medievalist Jacques Le Goff (1924–2014) together with the historian of ancient Greece, Pierre Vidal-Naquet (1930–2006). Le Goff, a foundational figure of the *Annales* school of anthropologically-inflected historical studies, headed the École des hautes études en sciences sociales (EHESS) in the mid-1970s. Vidal-Naquet, who began teaching at EHESS in 1969, directed Monsacré's doctoral thesis, on which her book is based.

It is the application of Levi-Straussian structuralism to literature and history by the group of scholars sometimes known as the "Paris School" that has most immediately shaped Monsacré's work. Along with Vidal-Naquet, the Hellenists Jean-Pierre Vernant, Marcel Detienne, and Nicole Loraux, with a number of other colleagues and students from several subdisciplines (historical psychology, study of law and institutions, philosophy), produced highly influential studies from the mid-1960s through the 1990s, a body of work that fundamentally changed modern studies of ancient Greek culture. What ties together their diverse works is the shared tendency to balance broad structural analyses with the telling particularities of detail, often drawing on neglected myths, cults, legends, and lore. Sustained interpretation of a single text was not the preferred method of this group, although its members often made use of textual analysis as they articulated larger mindsets and structures within Greek culture. In Monsacré's book, the constant reference to macroscopic oppositional sets (men and women, gods and mortals) is consistently balanced by micro-level readings of individual episodes, lines, and words. In sum, hers is a solid structuralism, but one refracted through poetry, at a slant to the elucidation of binaries, explored with nuance and a light touch.

The second influential approach, also subtly deployed in the book rather than blazoned across it, is the systematic study of the techniques of oral-traditional heroic song initiated by Milman Parry (1902–1935) and developed by his collaborator Albert B. Lord (1912–1991). This approach, like structuralism, combines American and Parisian lines of development. Parry, a native of Oakland, California, began his doctorate at the Sorbonne soon after obtaining his MA from Berkeley with a thesis on the diction of early Greek epic poetry, directed by George Calhoun. In Paris, Parry engaged on a comprehensive analysis of the formulas in Homeric poetry, with a focus on recurrent combinations of proper nouns and attached epithets. He attempted to account for why, for example, at certain moments Achilles is "swift-footed" and Odysseus "of much cunning" but in other lines the same heroes are described, respectively, as "shining" or "of many devices." His major thesis, published in 1928 as *L'épithète traditionnelle dans Homère*, demonstrated for the first time that formulaic phrases provided, for each major character throughout the epics, one and (with very few exceptions) *only* one adjective to accompany any given proper noun, varying with the standard metrical segments of the epic hexameter line. Such an economical and extensive system, Parry concluded, could only have arisen over generations of poetic production, developed by epic poets who passed down their art within a continuing tradition.

The discovery of the metrically-sensitive and systematic nature of the Homeric "art-language" (*Kunstsprache*) had previously been noticed at the level of individual word-endings or pronoun usage: for example, the existence of five different forms of the genitive case for the word *ego* ("I") had been explained by earlier scholars as the reflex of necessity imposed by the hexameter (each form having a different metrical shape). That the epics consisted almost entirely of formulas—lines and phrases re-used in whole or part, involving all kinds of words, not just proper nouns—had been proposed but not demonstrated in

1923 by Antoine Meillet (1866–1936) in *Les origines indo-européennes des mètres grecs*. Parry's path-breaking work eventually brought the analysis of Homer to a new level. Briefly (since to recount the whole story would mean describing in detail Homeric studies of the last ninety years), the demonstration of the traditional nature of the formula enabled interpreters to claim access to deeper structures of thought and shared cultural knowledge (thus, in effect, connecting with the later project of structuralism). If the diction of Homeric epic results from multiple generations of transmission, we can hypothesize that it preserves concepts and meanings of deep and enduring importance to the audiences for epic. In short, the epics are not the one-time artististic inventions of a single person whose relationship to any broader culture is impossible to determine. Homeric poetry *is* the broader culture.

By the time that Monsacré began her thesis, a half-century after Parry, further refinements of the approach had largely overcome earlier objections that by acknowledging the formulaic nature of Homeric verse we obliterate any traces of individual genius, or deny intentional artistry. On one hand, the formula was now considered a highly flexible, adaptive, and creative device (as demonstrated by such scholars as J. B. Hainsworth, Mark Edwards, Michael Nagler and Arie Hoekstra). On the other, its deep-rootedness in Greek tradition, extending back even to the era around 3000 BCE when the language had not yet separated from the larger Indo-European family, had been re-affirmed and articulated. Here, the work of Gregory Nagy, in particular, was essential for showing that the central themes of the *Iliad* and *Odyssey*—the nature of the hero, the importance of "unwithering fame" (*kleos aphthiton*)—were foregrounded and thematized precisely by means of the traditional formulaic language of the poems. Although even now there are a few scholars who insist that "Homer" must have been a literate and "literary" artist like Vergil or Milton, a specific time-bound individual who innovated upon, resisted, or even tried to break out of his tradition, it is more fruitful to treat Homeric verse (as also Hesiodic and the so-called "Cyclic" poems) as a systematic narrative expression of larger cultural concerns.

Monsacré in her introduction acknowledges the key findings of Parry, but, as her concern is not primarily with the formula and its meanings, she does not devote extended sections to exploring formally the mechanics of traditional poetics. Yet her programmatic statement at the beginning of Part 2, Chapter 2 recognizes that it is *"le répertoire des formules et des épithètes"* which best represents communally shared ideas concerning women in epic. Furthermore, her sensitive appreciation of the aesthetics of Homeric diction, the way in which precise fixed expressions embody the poems' major themes, stands out in every chapter. Among numerous examples one should notice her discussion of the words for "withering" and "melting" in speaking of the "language of tears" and Penelope; the distinctions she draws among words for crying and lamenting (e.g. the verbs *klaio* and *kokuo*, the noun *goos*); her analysis of the rich semantics of the epithet *thaleron* 'blooming, fertile' in relation to the word for "tear" (with which it is formulaically bound); and her extended remarks on the expressions for groaning in pain or sorrow—the formulaic variations involving the verb *stenakhizo* and several different adverbs. The texture of every discussion is enriched by this attention to dictional detail; in addition, it is exactly the evidence of diction—for instance, the complex semantics of *thaleron*—that grounds a number of Monsacré's more striking explications. Through these closely-argued investigations of the text, she has demonstrated the basic correctness of the work begun by Parry and its essential utility for literary interpretation of Homer.

One necessary final note on this approach, and one resultant question. In his 1928 dissertation, Parry had proven the traditional nature of Homeric diction but had not yet formulated the idea with which popular accounts usually credit him, the discovery that Homeric poetry must have been the product of oral composition-in-performance. It was only in a second phase that he discovered through fieldwork, while making live recordings in the Bosnian-Muslim region of Novi Pazar in the early 1930s, that similar extensive and convenient dictional systems were employed by demonstrably illiterate performers of traditional South Slavic heroic poetry. Albert Lord, who had accompanied him on his second expedition, continued after the tragic early death of Parry in 1935 to work along similar lines in the Balkans, eventually publishing in 1960 the landmark presentation of their work, in his Harvard dissertation-book, *The Singer of Tales*. That volume makes the first sustained case for the proposition that Homeric poetry was oral poetry, composed anew every time that a singer performed, through the creative use of formulas at the level of verse as well as larger passages and episodes. Thousands of books and articles inspired by the work of Parry and Lord have now expanded the impact of their fieldwork-based demonstration, applying it to hundreds of oral poetic traditions in scores of languages.

It is interesting to see, from a century's distance, how these two important streams in Monsacré's intellectual history—Parry's study of Homeric diction and the Paris School version of structuralism—flow, ultimately, from the work of Ferdinand de Saussure, the brilliant linguist whose lectures in Geneva were posthumously reconstructed from student notes and published in 1916. As noted above, it was from Saussure that Roman Jakobson and the Prague school drew key concepts for linguistics, which then spread widely to other fields. Saussure was also the most influential teacher of Antoine Meillet, who had taken courses from him in Paris during the period 1885–1889. From him, Meillet clearly learned the value of studying the living, synchronic state of a language. When Parry defended his Sorbonne theses, it was Meillet, as chairman of the jury, who invited to the *soutenance* of May 31, 1928 Matija Murko (1861–1952), a linguistics professor at the University of Prague, then visiting Paris to deliver a series of lectures on his specialty, the folk poetry of Yugoslavia. With Meillet's urging, Parry later absorbed Murko's works, and soon decided to carry out his own fieldwork, during leave from his position in the Harvard Department of Classics. (In another pleasing coincidence, the ubiquitous Roman Jakobson, who had come to know Murko in Prague in the 1920s and made use of his early field recordings, served on the committee for Lord's Harvard dissertation defense in 1949.)

The key role that we now know *performance* plays in the creation of oral-traditional heroic song raises one question for Monsacré's study that goes beyond her assiduous investigation of the relevant formulaic diction. What sorts of living interactions do we imagine between poets who compose in performance, and their audiences, and—even more to the point—how might these have affected Homeric audiences hearing such emotional moments as those that this book explicates? To judge by the account of Ion, in the Platonic dialogue named for him, the professional reciter of Homeric poetry (*rhapsōidos*) regularly plunged into emotional involvement with the characters whose stories he recounted. As Ion tells Socrates (*Ion* 535c), "when I relate a tale of woe, my eyes are filled with tears; and when it is of fear or awe, my hair stands on end with terror, and my heart leaps." He proceeds to agree with Socrates that similar effects are transmitted by the Homeric reciter to a crowd of spectators (here perhaps exaggerated at 20,000 people), "for I look down upon them from the platform and see them at such moments crying and turning awestruck eyes upon me and yielding to the amazement of my tale. For I have to pay the closest attention to them; since, if I set them crying, I shall laugh myself because of the money I take, but if they laugh, I myself shall cry because of the money I lose" (*Ion* 535e, trans. W. R. M. Lamb). Conditions for the dramatic, competitive recitation of Homer in Athens during the late fifth century BCE may not have matched oral-poetic performances of a century before. Did the poet weep, along with the audience and his fictional figures? Was the emotional outpouring framed by actual practices of lament, linked to rituals within the city-state? Were such practices in fact at the root of the creation and spread of oral-traditional heroic poetry in Greek lands, starting perhaps in the second millennium BCE? While such questions remain outside Monsacré's purview, her clear appreciation of the findings of Parry, Lord, and others in the area of poetic diction might logically push the exploration even further, into an account of emotions-in-performance.

Rather than a re-orientation of the book's path, however, a conclusion demands at least the briefest mention of how it fit into the landscape of

Homeric studies when first published in 1984, and where it might stand now. Thirty years ago, feminist studies of the Classics were in their initial phase, inspired to a large extent by the new French feminism of Cixous, Irigaray, and Kristeva. In the United States, the work of Marylin Arthur, Ann Bergren, Laura Slatkin, Charles Segal, and Froma Zeitlin was *au courant* with the latest structuralist interpretations emanating from Paris as well. Still, of the 178 items listed in *L'année philologique* as having been published on Homer in 1984, covering archaeology, studies of individual figures, similes, the formula, narrative technique, social structure, and themes like recognition and supplication, only one, besides Monsacré's, could be identified as feminist in orientation (Anna Di Lello-Finuoli, "Donne e matrimonio nella Grecia arcaica," *SMEA* 25:275–302). Nor, apart from Nagy's 1979 work *The Best of the Achaeans*, were there books at the time that attempted to provide an overarching study of the *Iliad* and *Odyssey* in relation to specific cultural categories. James Redfield's work with a structuralist title invoking "nature and culture" was actually more of a close reading of the figure of Hector, and confined itself to the *Iliad*, as did Seth Schein's *The Mortal Hero*, while *The Wrath of Athena* by J. S. Clay was centered more on theodicy than gender, and mainly on the *Odyssey*. (All three are cited by Monsacré.) Given the great amount of intensive work on Homeric epic subsequent to 1984, especially on gender, intertextuality, reception, and cultural institutions, it is worth recalling how Monsacré brought a unique voice and point-of-view to the center. Despite the wave of more recent work, it must be said that *Les larmes d'Achille* remains unsurpassed in the treatment of its fascinating and crucially important subject. This new translation will bring her much needed perspective on the poetics of gender and emotion to a new generation of readers and scholars.

References and Further Reading

These notes are intended to fill out the above introduction with bibliographic details, following the order in which topics are mentioned, while providing pointers toward related studies. They make no claim to be exhaustive.

On Homeric themes and the poetry of Sappho, see Rissman 1983; on the sympotic transmission of Sapphic poetry: Nagy 2004. On "veiled sentiments" in women's song traditions, see Abu-Lughod 1999 and on Diotima: Halperin 1990, with further bibliography.

For formulaic analysis of the notion of *krêdemnon*, relating women to cities: Nagler 1975; on erotics and martial encounters: Maronitis 2004; on *la belle mort* in Greek epic: Vernant 1979 and 1982. Monographs on Helen by Clader 1976 and on Aphrodite by Boedeker 1974 remain valuable in particular for their dictional analysis.

Regarding women's speech in epic, see Beck 2012; on Helen's speech habits: Martin 2003 (reprinted in Suter 2008), Pantelia 2002. On the *Odyssey* scenes mentioned by Monsacré, see now Vlahos 2011, Murnaghan 2011, Peradotto 1990, and Levaniouk 2011. On weeping by Odysseus, see Peponi 2012.

On women's lament, see especially Loraux 1998, Alexiou 2002, Derderian 2001, Dué 2002, Tsagalis 2004, and the essays in Suter (ed.) 2008.

On the name of Achilles: Nagy 1994, and the original formulation in Nagy 1999 [1979]. On Achilles, Priam and the denouement of the *Iliad*: Mackie 1996, Crotty 1994. For groundbreaking re-analysis of the origins and poetics of the Homeric poems, see Frame 2009.

Among the many introductions to structuralism, Leach 1989 and Culler 2002 stand out as reliable guides to the anthropological and literary applications, respectively. For views on the Paris School and samples of their work, from different perspectives and eras, see Pucci 1971, Gordon (ed.) 1981, Zeitlin's introduction to Vernant 1991, Loraux et al. 2001, and Slatkin 2011 (especially Chapter 7). Central to the study of gender in relation to Greek myth and culture is Loraux 1995.

Most important for the understanding of Milman Parry's work are his collected papers (Parry, ed., 1971), to be read in conjunction with a necessary corrective to its prefatory material by de Lamberterie 1997; and Lord 2000. Foley 1988 provides a broader overview. On Parry's anthropological interests: Garcia 2001; on Murko's relation to Jakobson: Fischerová 2014; on the role of performance in oral-traditional song-culture: Nagy 1996 and 2002; Martin 1989; on rhapsodic art: González 2015. On lament and epic performance, see Seaford 1995 and Bertolín Cebrián 2006. For the stylized expression of emotion within Greek verbal art, see Visvardi 2015.

Among the books on Homer that intersect with Monsacré's concerns or build on her insights, special mention should be made of Felson-Rubin 1994, Doherty 1995, Katz 1991, Clayton 2004, Tatum 2004, and Papadopoulou-Belmehdi 1994.

Bibliography

Abu-Lughod, L. 1999. *Veiled Sentiments: Honor and Poetry in a Bedouin Society*. Berkeley.

Alexiou, M. 2002. *The Ritual Lament in Greek Tradition*. 2nd ed. Ed. D. Yatromanolakis and P. Roilos. Lanham, MD.

Beck, D. 2012. *Speech Presentation in Homeric Epic*. Austin.

Bertolin Cebrian, R. 2006. *Singing the Dead. A Model for Epic Evolution*. Frankfurt.

Boedeker, D. D. 1974. *Aphrodite's Entry into Greek Epic*. Leiden.

Bouvier, D. 1985. "H. Monsacré. *Les larmes d'Achille. Le héros, la femme et la souffrance dans la poésie d'Homère*, préface de P. Vidal-Naquet." In *Revue de l'histoire des religions* 202:439–440.

Clader, L. L. 1976. *Helen: The Evolution from Divine to Heroic in Greek Epic Tradition.* Leiden.

Clay, J. S. 1983. *The Wrath of Athena: Gods and Men in the Odyssey.* Princeton.

Clayton, B. 2004. *A Penelopean Poetics: Reweaving the Feminine in Homers Odyssey.* Lanham, MD.

Crotty, K. 1994. *The Poetics of Supplication: Homer's Iliad and Odyssey.* Ithaca, NY.

Culler, J. D. 2002. *Structuralist Poetics: Structuralism, Linguistics and the Study of Literature.* New York.

de Lamberterie, C. 1997. "Milman Parry et Antoine Meillet." In Létoublon 1997:9–22.

Derderian, K. 2001. *Leaving Words to Remember: Greek Mourning and the Advent of Literacy.* Leiden.

Doherty, L. E. 1995. *Siren Songs: Gender, Audiences, and Narrators in the Odyssey.* Ann Arbor.

Dué, C. 2002. *Homeric Variations on a Lament by Briseis.* Lanham, MD.

Edwards, M. W.1986. "Homer and Oral Tradition: The Formula, Part I." *Oral Tradition* 1:171–230.

———. 1988. "Homer and Oral Tradition: The Formula, Part II." *Oral Tradition* 3:11–60.

Felson-Rubin, N. 1994. *Regarding Penelope: From Character to Poetics.* Princeton.

Fischerová, S. 2014."*Habent sua fata inventiones*: The Role of Czechoslovakian Slavistics in the Forming of the Parry-Lord Oral-Formulaic Theory." In *Roman O. Jakobson: A Work in Progress*, eds. T. Kubíček and A. Lass, 77–102. Olomouc.

Foley, J. M. 1988. *The Theory of Oral Composition: History and Methodology.* Bloomington.

Frame, D. 2009. *Hippota Nestor.* Hellenic Studies 37. Washington, DC.

García, J. F. 2001. "Milman Parry and A. F. Kroeber: Americanist Anthropology and the Oral Homer." *Oral Tradition* 16:58–84.

González, J. M. 2015. *The Epic Rhapsode and his Craft: Homeric Performance in a Diachronic Perspective.* Hellenic Studies 47. Washington, DC.

Gordon, R. L., ed. 1981. *Myth, Religion, and Society: Structuralist Essays.* Cambridge.

Hainsworth, J. B. 1968. *The Flexibility of the Homeric Formula.* Oxford.

Halperin, D. M. 1990. "Why is Diotima a Woman?" In *One Hundred Years of Homosexuality and Other Essays on Greek Love*, 113–151. New York.

Hoekstra, A. 1965. *Homeric Modifications of Formulaic Prototypes: Studies in the Development of Greek Epic Diction.* Amsterdam.

Katz, M. A. 1991. *Penelope's Renown: Meaning and Indeterminacy in Homer's Odyssey.* Princeton.

Leach, E. 1989. *Claude Lévi-Strauss.* Chicago.

Létoublon, F., ed. 1997. *Hommage à Milman Parry. Le style formulaire de l'épopée homérique et la théorie de l'oralité poétique.* Amsterdam.

Levaniouk, O. 2011. *Eve of the Festival: Making Myth in Odyssey 19.* Hellenic Studies 46. Washington, DC.

Loraux, N. 1995. *The Experiences of Tiresias: The Feminine and the Greek Man.* Trans. P. Wissing. Princeton.

———. 1998. *Mothers in Mourning.* Trans. C. Pache. Ithaca, NY.

Loraux, N., G. Nagy, and L. Slatkin, eds. 2001. *Antiquities.* Vol. 3, *Postwar French Thought.* Ed. R. Naddaff. New York.

Lord, A. B. 2000. *The Singer of Tales.* 2nd ed. Ed. S. A Mitchell and G. Nagy. Cambridge, MA.

Mackie, H. S. 1996. *Talking Trojan: Speech and Community in the Iliad.* Lanham, MD.

Maronitis, D. N. 2004. *Homeric Megathemes: War-Homilia-Homecoming.* Trans. D. Connolly. Lanham, MD.

Martin, R. P. 1989. *The Language of Heroes: Speech and Performance in the Iliad.* Ithaca, NY.

———. 2003. "Keens from the Absent Chorus: Troy to Ulster." *Western Folklore* 62:119–142.

Murko, M. 1929. *La poésie populaire épique en Yougoslavie au début du XXe siecle.* Paris.

Murnaghan, S. 2011. *Disguise and Recognition in the Odyssey.* 2nd ed. Lanham, MD.

Nagler, M. N. 1975. *Spontaneity and Tradition: A Study in the Oral Art of Homer.* Berkeley.

Nagy, G. 1994. "The Name of Achilles: Questions of Etymology and 'Folk-Etymology'." *Illinois Classical Studies* 19:3–9.

———. 1996. *Poetry as Performance: Homer and Beyond.* Cambridge.

———. 1999. *The Best of the Achaeans. Concepts of the Hero in Archaic Greek poetry.* Rev. ed. Baltimore. Orig. pub. 1979.

———. 2002. *Plato's Rhapsody and Homer's Music: The Poetics of the Panathenaic Festival in Classical Athens.* Hellenic Studies 1. Washington, DC.

———. 2004. "Transmission of Archaic Greek Sympotic Songs: From Lesbos to Alexandria." *Critical Inquiry* 31:26–48.

Pantelia, M. C. 2002. "Helen and the Last Song for Hector." *Transactions of the American Philological Association* 132:21–27.

Papadopoulou-Belmehdi, I. 1994. *Le chant de Pénélope: poétique du tissage féminin dans l'Odyssée.* Paris.

Parry, M. 1971. *The Making of Homeric Verse: The Collected Papers of Milman Parry.* Ed. A. Parry. Oxford.

Peponi, A.-E. 2012. *Frontiers of Pleasure: Models of Aesthetic Response in Archaic and Classical Greek Thought.* Oxford.

Peradotto, J. 1990. *Man in the Middle Voice: Name and Narration in the Odyssey.* Princeton.

Pucci, P. 1971. "Levi-Strauss and Classical Culture." *Arethusa* 4:103–117.

Redfield, J. 1975. *Nature and Culture in the Iliad: The Tragedy of Hector.* Chicago.

Rissman, L. 1983. *Love as War: Homeric Allusion in the Poetry of Sappho.* Königstein.

Schein, S. L. 1985. *The Mortal Hero: An Introduction to Homer's Iliad.* Berkeley.

Seaford, R. 1995. *Reciprocity and Ritual: Homer and Tragedy in the Developing City-State.* Oxford.

Slatkin, L. 2011. *The Power of Thetis and Selected Essays.* Hellenic Studies 16. Washington, DC.

Suter, A., ed. 2008. *Lament: Studies in the Ancient Mediterranean and Beyond.* Oxford.

Tatum, J. 2004. *The Mourner's Song: War and Remembrance from the Iliad to Vietnam.* Chicago.

Tsagalis, C. 2004. *Epic Grief: Personal Laments in Homer's Iliad.* Berlin.

Vernant, J. P. 1979. "Panta Kala d'Homère à Simonide." *Annali della Scuola Normale Superiore di Pisa. Classe di Lettere e Filosofia* 9:1365–1374. Translation in Vernant 1991:84–92.

———. 1982. "La belle mort et le cadavre outragé." In *La mort, les morts dans les sociétés anciennes,* ed. G. Gnoli and J.-P. Vernant, 45–76. Cambridge. Translation in Vernant 1991:50–74.

———. 1991. *Mortals and Immortals: Collected Essays.* Ed. F. Zeitlin. Princeton.

Visvardi, E. 2015. *Emotion in Action: Thucydides and the Tragic Chorus.* Leiden.

Vlahos, J. B. 2011. "Homer's *Odyssey:* Penelope and the Case for Early Recognition." *College Literature* 38:1–75.

Translator's Note
Truchement ≈ Caretaker

Nicholas J. Snead

I learned the term *truchement* as a first-year M.A. student studying French language and literature at the University of Virginia, where I had the wonderful good fortune to take a Balzac seminar with Peter Brooks, a visiting professor there that year. *Truchement* is an archaic French word meaning 'translator' or 'interpreter.' If you traveled to France today, it is highly unlikely you would ever hear anyone use it.

While *truchement* is no longer a part of contemporary spoken French, it has taken on new life as a useful literary and cultural concept. Brooks has applied the idea to nineteenth-century French fiction, specifically to Balzac's treatment of the 1830 revolution that brought down the government of Charles X:[1]

> A *truchement*, as a go-between, an interpreter offers the possibility of penetrating the unknown, of gaining knowledge ordinarily closed to one dealing with a foreign language ... [It] is the vehicle, or metaphor—figure of a *translatio*—of knowledge both sacred and profane ...[2]

The *truchement* creates the possibility of "penetrating the unknown." This is the case for a metaphorical interpreter that facilitates discourse between humans and God, just as it is for the literal translator who converts words from one language into another.

I consider my role to be that of the *truchement* 'caretaker' of Hélène Monsacré's writing. I have undertaken this project feeling grateful and honored—but also with a deep sense of responsibility. Having spent so much of the last few months immersed in her vision of the *Iliad* and the *Odyssey*, I think I can safely say that writing such a clear analysis of epic tears was a massive

---

[1]   "Balzac: Epistemophilia and the Collapse of the Restoration." *Yale French Studies* (*Fragments of Revolution*) 101:119–131.
[2]   Brooks 126.

undertaking that required great effort and patience. I hope to have done right by the text and by its author.

For *The Tears of Achilles*, the pitfalls of translation were relatively rare. This was due in large part, I think, to the highly polished language of the original. There were, however, several consistent challenges of which readers of the translated version should be aware. The most frequent challenge was handling passages from Homer and other Greek poets cited in *Les Larmes d'Achille*. Monsacré usually gives these citations in French translation. For the passages of Homer in English, I have used the editions of Samuel Butler, revised by Gregory Nagy et al., as the basis for providing English citations.[3] In instances where Professor Monsacré's French translations of the Greek do not accord with the translations of Butler, I have modified the English translation so as to better reflect both Monsacré's argument and the Greek itself.

Another of the specific challenges for this translation was rendering a group of French words that relate in some way to light. Monsacré weaves a series of nouns like *lumière*, *éclat*, *lueur*, *ardeur* and verbs like *briller*, *illuminer*, *scintiller*, *irradier*, *étinceler*, *resplendir* into her discussion of the sparkling, shining radiance of Homeric heroes and the major women of epic. I have found French to be far richer for these types of terms, which connect physical beauty to differently nuanced conceptions of light.

The French verb *pleurer* ('to cry' or 'to weep') also required considerable energy and attention. Of course, there is almost always more than one choice to translate any given word or phrase. In a book about tears, the English words 'cry' and 'weep' are two very similar options, though they are certainly not identical. In my translation, I have not attempted to develop any cohesive semantic approach to distinguish between them. I have relied instead on my ear for style to judge which term sounds better in the surrounding English context. I realize that this approach does create the risk of errors in judgment.

The final challenge I need to mention is the level, stylistic rhythm that makes *Les Larmes d'Achille* such a powerful text. The original is stylistically clean, smooth, even. It makes for a deceptively effortless read. I say deceptive because, while it is easy for a reader of French to get through, it is not at all easy to hone these complex ideas into such sharp and clear focus. Trying to replicate that style in English has proven to be the most difficult piece of the present volume. But it has also been the piece I have enjoyed working on the most.

As with any book-length translation, this one would not have been possible without the support, encouragement, guidance, and trust of a number of wonderful people. I would like to thank Noel Spencer, who first contacted me

---

[3] These translations are available online in the Publications section at www.chs.harvard.edu.

about the project and who has always believed me capable of taking on something of this magnitude, even through a weepy season of my own. Friends Erik Bobilin, Cason and Emily Elam, Sarah Beth and Tom Gehl, R. D. Perry, and Ethan Spencer supported me during that same difficult period. Dr. Kate Lakin-Schultz helped me formulate my thoughts about the concept of *truchement*. Robert and Linda Snead (aka Mom and Dad) and my brother Eric have supported me as a translator for as long as I can remember.

I would like to thank Ioanna Papadopoulou and Leonard Muellner at the Center for Hellenic Studies, who agreed to bring me on board and who helped address the difficulties involved in reconciling French and English citations of Homer. I would also like to thank my teachers and role models from my time as a French graduate student at UVA. I have to recognize two by name: Mary McKinley and Jean-Yves Pouilloux. If I have succeeded in my role as Monsacré's *truchement*, it is largely thanks to them and everything they taught me about interpretation. My understanding of the role of a translator is rooted deep in their conscientious instruction. From them, I learned to tend carefully to a text, both through their direct classroom instruction on how to be a good reader and, perhaps more importantly, by watching, reading, and listening to the solid foundational model of interpretation they provide when they speak and write about Montaigne and Proust.

Finally, I want to express my gratitude to the author herself. Advancing towards the end of the final chapter, enthralled by the discussion of how Achilles merges temporarily with the body of his departed friend Patroclus, I glanced at my copy of the original *Les Larmes d'Achille*. There was hardly anything left to do. Seeing that I was so near the end brought on a momentary tinge of sadness, that same seeping disappointment that creeps in when you are coming to the end of book you have loved and realize that the pages on the right have shrunk down to almost nothing. I wanted there to be more. I have come to know Achilles and the meaning of his tears far better than before. Hopefully, this new version of Monsacré's work will now bring that same epic knowledge to a great many students and scholars.

Preface to the English Edition

Hélène Monsacré

When I wrote this book on Homer, thirty years ago,[1] I tried to grasp the ambiguities of a heroic character: brave, courageous, and yet sensitive.

The greatest hero of all time, Achilles, has supernatural powers and fights with divine weapons, but he cries like a human. His tears do not, however, diminish his virility, but rather enhance and confirm his manhood. The sobs of his female counterparts are trapped in a stereotypical feminine passivity, while Achilles' tears on the battlefield are powerful and effective. The warrior of the *Iliad*, crying the way he cries, conveys that suffering is the condition of his heroism.

The Tears of Achilles was written long before a reevaluation of the role of women and femininity in the Homeric epic under the influence of gender studies; my research is nonetheless the reflection of a turning point in the history of Homeric studies, and I am indebted to the innovative school of thought founded by Jean-Pierre Vernant (1914–2007), Pierre Vidal-Naquet (1930–2006), and Nicole Loraux (1943–2003). It is with emotion and gratitude that I remember these great scholars who are no longer among us. They introduced me to research, and I consider myself fortunate to have been taught by them. Our common interests inaugurated a long-lasting friendship based on mutual trust. It was an honor to maintain a close relationship to the very end with an exceptional scholar like Nicole Loraux; her premature death has been a great loss for classical studies.

The significant role played by tears in the epic occurred to me while I was tracking the values attached to men and women in the world of Homer. In a seminar on "Masculine and Feminine," Nicole Loraux had, in the early 1980s, inspired a new area of research when she turned to topics previously

---

[1] *Les larmes d'Achille. Le héros, la femme et la souffrance dans la poésie d'Homère*, published in the series "L'aventure humaine" (Paris: Albin Michel, 1984), with a foreword by Pierre Vidal-Naquet; also reprinted in paperback by Editions du Félin (Paris, 2010).

unexplored. Her own works, in particular *Les Enfants d'Athéna* (Paris, 1980)[2] and *Les Expériences de Tirésias* (Paris, 1990)[3], are heuristic enquiries about gender divisions through modes of representation and imagination in the ancient world; they enabled her to forcefully establish the absence of female political subjects in democratic Athens, while showing the ambiguities of the Greek male who holds a share of femininity. My study on the role of suffering in Homer has been influenced by her writings.

This book was written quite a while ago, and some youthful naiveté may still show; but if it remains relevant today, it is because my research has helped bring the study of emotions to the fields of history and anthropology. It is with a certain tenderness that I recall Jean Pierre Vernant's astonishment and perplexity when I first told him I would work on the expression of emotions, and on tears in particular. Reading the *Iliad*, I had discovered that when Achilles does not fight, he cries. Initially, Vernant was skeptical: "The great Achilles, the paradigm of virility, displays strength through his tears? That demands a closer examination..."

At the time I wrote this book, readings of the Homeric epic were dominated by a prevailing bias, which opposed virility to sensitivity. Hence, a close reading of the *Iliad* was necessary in order to understand the gendered division of labor and the role of Achilles' heroic tears. Pierre Vidal-Naquet acknowledged the importance of my project when he insisted, in his generous foreword to *Les Larmes d'Achille*, on the necessity of going back to the original text: the anthropology of Homer is, above all, an anthropology of the text itself.

₪

I would like to thank all those who have made the publication of this book possible, as well as those who made sure it would not be forgotten. Among the former is Francis Esménard, President and CEO of Albin Michel publishers, whom Claude Mossé, another great French figure of classical studies, had convinced to publish it. Among the latter is Paul Veyne, who wrote a warm review of the paperback edition, and who has been, for more than twenty years, a steadfast—and witty—friend. Who else but Paul Veyne could describe in such Homeric terms the furor that seized him during an encounter with a pack of wild boars on his estate in Provence? "I was like Achilles, 'a brutal rage had taken hold of me,' and I rushed for my rifle..."

---

[2]   Also published as *The Children of Athena. Athenian Ideas about Citizenship and the Division between the Sexes* (Princeton, 1993).
[3]   Also published as *The Experiences of Tiresias* (Princeton, 1995; reprinted 2014).

Eva Cantarella and Pierre Judet de La Combe have, beyond the bonds of friendship, allowed me to remain in contact with Homer and the ancient world. And even though I have left academia, the ancient Greeks are still at the heart of my profession as an editor in Paris—in particular at Les Belles Lettres, with its emphasis on classical texts.

It is my great pleasure to thank the Center for Hellenic Studies for giving my book new life by including it among its prestigious catalogue. I owe a special debt to Gregory Nagy, whom I had the opportunity to meet in Paris in the early 1980s, when he came blowing a fresh wind, swirling and irresistible, among the students working with Jean-Pierre Vernant and Nicole Loraux on the Rue Monsieur-le-Prince,[4] challenging their certitudes with his deep knowledge of Homer and his impressive grasp of archaic poetry.

I am also deeply grateful for Richard P. Martin's beautiful and generous Foreword. He deftly connects the book to contemporary issues by identifying my work as part of the history of structuralism, while at the same time highlighting the timeliness of the topics of emotion and gender, which were barely emerging at the time the book was first published.

I sincerely thank the talented Nicolas J. Snead, who has succeeded in converting my literary—rather than academic—style into beautiful English, and in subtly conveying the spirit of my essay.

My gratitude also goes to Jill Curry Robbins, whose patience and efficiency through the production process has been both enduring and reassuring; and to Noel Spencer, who will shepherd the electronic version of the book.

The American journey of *The Tears of Achilles* has benefited from the efficient and invaluable help of my friends Susan Rubin Suleiman, professor of French literature and comparative literature at Harvard University, and Astrid von Busekist, professor of political theory at Sciences Po Paris.

Finally, my affectionate thoughts go to a loyal friend and fellow student of Nicole Loraux, Ioanna Papadopoulou, who has put her exceptional weaving skills into motion, patiently creating a bond between my book and the Center for Hellenic Studies.

In 1984, I dedicated *Les Larmes d'Achille* to my parents. Today, thanks to the new life provided by the Center for Hellenic Studies, I am happy to offer *The Tears of Achilles* to Christophe, my husband, and our two children, Noémie and Emmanuel. They are "my sweet light."

Paris, March 2017

---

[4] The address of the Center for Comparative Research on Ancient Societies (Centre de recherches comparées sur les sociétés anciennes, CNRS/EHESS).

Introduction

"Since when is it that men (and not women) no longer cry? Why was 'sensibility,' at a certain moment, transformed into 'sentimentality'?"[1]

Initially this line of questioning from Roland Barthes referred to the romantic hero. But we can go further still: on the threshold of history and Western literature, an immense poem, the *Iliad,* recounts both the accomplishments and the weeping of the heroes of the Trojan War; within this poem, an immense hero, Achilles, displays both his strength and his tears. Could we today imagine even the idea of a heroic sensitivity? We who forbid the tears of young boys and who see in a sobbing man the negation of masculine values, having inherited these ideas from the Greeks of the time of Pericles, who reserved crying for women, an activity on par with weaving wool ...

The clearest difference between the system of values in Classical Greece (fifth century BCE)—which forbids men's tears—and a Homeric ethic—which demands that the heroes of the *Iliad* express their pain with a violence similar to that which drives them on the battlefield—raises questions about a codified form of expressing emotion and heroic suffering in the *Iliad.*

This difference in values is not, however, at the origin of this work. Originally, I intended to map out the system of distribution of masculine and feminine values in Homeric epic, and more specifically in the *Iliad.*[2] Of course, it might seem paradoxical to attempt to comprehend femininity in the Homeric poem most focused on war, but it was specifically the minor and restricted role of femininity in the poem that made it an interesting scholarly pursuit.

To discover how roles were distributed, how the masculine and feminine domains were drawn up (first in themselves and then in relationship to one another), and to verify the existence of a "code" of femininity—a network of

---

[1] Barthes 1978:180–181.
[2] This book began as a doctoral thesis defended at the École des Hautes Études en Sciences Sociales in May of 1983. The jury was composed of Cl. Mossé (president), J.-P. Vernant, and P. Vidal-Naquet.

terms that together defined a system other than the official code of masculinity: this was my project.

Of course, the danger of anachronism is great. What, in fact, is the role of our modern sensibility in this analysis? Is it relevant to propose, to presuppose rather, an opposition as simple as that of masculine and feminine in the epic universe of the *Iliad*? To all these questions, I had no preconceived theoretical response.

By studying the ambiguities of each pole and by bringing to light an interplay of interferences, oscillations, transgressions, and inversions at the heart of the global system, which tends to place the masculine on one side and the feminine on the other, I attempted to determine the positive and negative aspects of each term of the pair. Following this initial examination, I asked if it were possible—and, if so, at what point—to establish a gendered code of epic values? The answer is both yes and no.

Yes, in the sense that a certain number of characteristics belonging to each sphere were easily classified; and no, in the sense that I unfailingly encountered one motif that blurred the distribution of masculine and feminine values: tears. In fact, tears belong as much to men as to women in the epic. How are we to make sense of this?

The weight of modern ideas about the distribution of men's and women's roles had led me to simply ignore the question of crying in the heroic male figure that I was trying to define. On the map of masculine and feminine, the continents were poorly placed. I therefore began anew—working now from the opposite direction—by placing the status of heroic suffering at the center of my research.

Roland Barthes's questions only became essential for me in hindsight. This book deliberately retains a record of these two approaches, neither of which would work without the other.

In the end, the very nature of my conclusions remains to be examined: does the system of values that was outlined over the course of this inquiry only apply to one literary work, or does it represent a real society? The old problem of the relationship between a literary work and society, between literature and history (a question that I do not wish to address in depth here), takes on different forms with the *Iliad* than with, for example, *The Princess of Clèves*—forms that are related to the specific place of the Homeric poems in Greek literature and history.

I do not wish to offer an introduction to Homer here, nor do I wish to present the countless problems—some of which remain unsolvable—that Homeric specialists have been studying for the last three millennia. I will limit myself here to offering several main points that will serve as a basic frame of reference.[3]

The *Iliad* was composed in the second half of the eighth century BCE. Ancients attributed it, as well as the *Odyssey*, to a poet about whom we know nothing more than a name. Before being written down, the poems were recited by professional singers called bards. To stitch together legendary themes, to sing and to improvise, these singers relied on a highly trained memory and a stock of preformed verses, or half-verses, the famous "formulas" and Homeric epithets.[4] The *Iliad* and the *Odyssey* are the remains of a great shipwreck that destroyed the many epics created by an essentially oral culture.

The society described in the poems is not Mycenaean society prior to 1200 BCE, as was long maintained and as some still maintain; nor is it the society of the eighth century, contemporary to the recording of the poem, which witnessed the rise of political organization around the city-state. Nor again is it a fantasized society without any anchor in history. The work of the historian Moses I. Finley allows us to recognize enough coherence in the *institutions* that appear in the poem, and also enough similarity with better-known traditional societies, that we can be sure that, even if the stories told by Homer never took place, Homeric society, on the other hand, did indeed exist during the period we call the "Dark Ages," which run from the end of the Mycenaean era to Homer.[5]

There is, then, a distance between the time when the narrative is elaborated and the indefinite past to which it refers. But how can one speak of the double relationship that the work maintains, first with the society that produced it and then with the society that it represents, when we know little more about either than what the work tells us?

Imagine that we would like to consider the relationship of *The Princess of Clèves* to the seventeenth-century society of the time of its composition, as well as to the society of Henry II, the fictitious setting of the novel. Imagine that we have no other documentation for these two periods than *The Princess of Clèves*. Historians of customs and institutions would certainly find things to draw upon, though they would have trouble separating out the two eras; so, too, the historian working on Homer. But when attempting to locate a system of values, how does one tease out what belongs to Madame de La Fayette herself, what to the literary genre in which she chose to express herself, what to her own narrow,

---

[3] For an introduction to the subject, see for instance Vidal-Naquet 1975 or, more recently, Schein 1984.

[4] See esp. Parry 1928a and 1928b; see also the contributions assembled in Kirk 1969 as well as Russo 1963 and Hainsworth 1968.

[5] See especially Finley 1983, Finley 1973a, and Finley 1973b. For a more recent treatment, see Mossé 1980:7–19.

aristocratic circle, and what, finally, to the common base of seventeenth-century French society? The probability of error is high if one draws conclusions carelessly about the society on the basis of the work. One must remain even more cautious with the *Iliad* when studying the expression of emotion, the theme that—among other difficulties that I will return to—is most susceptible to highly literary stylization.

Of course, the Homeric scholar is in a slightly better position than our hypothetical scholar of *The Princess of Clèves*, because the epic, without a doubt, held a more central place in its society than did the *précieux* novel in seventeenth-century France, at least if we judge by the poems themselves and the status of the bards, their audience, and their social role.

A still more important matter remains. There is indeed a relationship between *The Princess of Clèves* and seventeenth-century society, and the historian studying the history of the system of values during the time of Louis XIV would not be able to ignore this novel. The historian of antiquity, on the contrary, has no choice: other than Homer, there is no access to the society of the "Dark Ages." Thus this work is not just a literary study; it is also an exploration of the mentality of a historic society.

It is a limited exploration, however, when we are dealing with emotion. In an epic text, how were poets able to represent emotion? How can we understand today their way of speaking? Did Achilles "copy" the behavior of warriors from those distant times? Or might it be the reverse: did the epic influence certain real behaviors? We are missing a *Don Quixote* to measure the distance; we will never know.

What is crucial to me is that in Homer's *Iliad*, one of the foundational texts of Western culture, men—because they are heroes—are arrayed with all capabilities. And among these is the ability to externalize pain through tears without at all weakening the preeminence of men over women. Values are not fixed, and the behaviors they require are even less so. Sensitivity in Homer is not sentimentality, and, in this idealized world of heroes, masculine strength is *also* expressed in tears. Images of masculinity are constantly shifting.

Part I

The Borders of Heroism

1

Proper Relations to Aphrodite
A Criterion in the Definition of Heroic Conduct

It might seem paradoxical to approach the question of heroism in the *Iliad* by way of Aphrodite, thus giving sustained attention to episodes where the majority of the action occurs within the walls of Troy. Yet it is also a way to examine fundamental values of the Homeric universe. By initially abandoning the battlefields for the city of Troy it is possible to grasp a "problematic" rather than a "superhuman" heroism. But there is a correlation between warlike rage and separation from Aphrodite, and it is accompanied by cowardice and defined by an excessive proximity to the goddess or even an immersion into her world.

The fame of Paris has nothing to do with great deeds on the plains of Troy and everything to do with being favored by Aphrodite. This fact will serve as our starting point: heroic conduct is defined as much by what it is not as by what it must be. In this context, being close to or far from the "world" of Aphrodite during the siege of a city is one of the defining characteristics of the quality of a warrior.

Hector: The Paradigm of the Warrior

For the heroes of the *Iliad* "everything pivoted on a single element of honor and virtue: strength, bravery, physical courage, prowess. Conversely, there was no weakness, no unheroic trait, but one, and that was cowardice and the consequent failure to pursue heroic goals."[1] Hector is a hero without fault; his brother Paris, on the other hand, is a coward. Hector represents the model of warlike masculinity, Paris the opposite, both on the battlefield and inside the walls of the city of Troy.

---

[1] Finley 1978b:31.

Hector's name speaks of his valor: "he who holds"[2] the ramparts of the city. He is also the main Trojan aggressor, the commander who is constantly inciting his companions and his troops to take on the Greeks. What matters for the hero is to be "far in front, foremost," to "never remain with the body of his men" (*Iliad* 22.458).[3] This rule defines the position of the warrior on the battlefield as much as the wounds he inflicts or receives; the noble wound, which attests as much to the character of the one who inflicts it as to the one who receives it, is the blow that strikes "head on," as Idomeneus says to Meriones (*Iliad* 13.288–289):

> If you were struck by a dart or smitten in close combat, it would not be from behind, in your neck nor back, but the weapon would hit you in the chest or belly.

Hector asserts on multiple occasions his desire to fight head on and to battle "openly," "face to face."[4] Thus, catching Periphetes, who had just fallen "as he was turning back" (*Iliad* 15.645), "[Hector] then thrust a spear into his chest" and killed him (15.650); or later on, in response to Euphorbus' wounding of Patroclus in the back, Hector finishes him off by striking him "in the lower part of the belly" (16.821). For the hero, it is a matter of exposing himself fully to the risks of combat as a man, unlike the coward, who resembles a woman or an infant (7.235–236).

Paris: A Representation of Cowardice

Hector's candid, loyal, and efficient attitude corresponds inversely with that of Paris. Even in battle, his exploits are recounted briefly by the poet, as if his true function is not related to the war. He kills two adversaries with his spear

---

[2]   Chantraine 1963:18–19: "... Ce ne peut être un hasard que les aèdes aient donné au principal héros troyen le nom d'*Hectōr*, lequel signifie en grec 'celui qui tient bon' (de *echō* avec le suffixe *tōr*) et l'on sait que les vers 402–403 du chant 2 expliquent le nom *Astuanax* par le fait que le père de la ville était 'le protecteur de la ville'" ["... it can not be by accident that the bards gave the principal Trojan hero the name *Hectōr*, which in Greek means 'he who holds true' (from *echō* with the suffix *tōr*) and we know that verses 402–403 of Book II explain the name *Astuanax* by stating that the father of the city was 'chief guardian of Ilion.'"]

[3]   Translator's note: English citations of the *Iliad* and the *Odyssey* are from Samuel Butler's translations, revised and edited by Gregory Nagy et al. These translations are available online in the Publications section of the Harvard Center for Hellenic Studies website (chs.harvard.edu). In some places, Butler's text has been altered to coincide with the details Prof. Monsacré emphasizes in her arguments. For more on citations of the *Iliad* and the *Odyssey*, see the Translator's Preface, p. xxvi.

[4]   For example, against Ajax at *Iliad* 7.242–243; or against Achilles at *Iliad* 18.307–308 ("I shall not shun him, but will fight him face to face") and 20.71–372.

(goaded on in one case by Hector).[5] He kills one other Greek with his bow,[6] as well as one of Nestor's horses.[7] All the rest of his arrows only cause injury.[8] When he tries his hand at single combat, he advances to the front lines only to be first to retreat. During the first confrontation of the two armies, confident in the strength of the Trojans around him, he dares to advance beyond the lines (*promachiken; Iliad* 3.16). He appears here to be particularly bold since, armed with two spears, a sword, and a bow,[9] he can take on the Greeks with any weapon. However, his armor is incomplete: just before the confrontation, he has to barter his panther skin for his brother Lycaon's cuirass (3.322–323). His arrogance lasts only for the moment of the initial challenge: at the sight of Menelaus advancing, he "quailed ... and shrank in fear of his life under cover of his men" (3.31–32).[10] His challenge would have ended there if Hector had not goaded him with insults to confront his adversary. The rest is well known. Aphrodite intervenes to bring her protégé to shelter inside the walls of his bedchamber, while a raging Menelaus continues to search for him on the battlefield. Commentators have always recognized a comic tone in this confrontation. Paris is decidedly not a noble warrior. While he may happen to kill and inflict injury, he does not first openly confront his enemies. For example, when he hits Diomedes with one of his arrows, he is hidden behind a pillar, which was erected in honor of Ilos, eponymous hero of Troy, and which, in a subtle way, recalls the walls of the city that Paris stays behind most of the time (*Iliad* 11.371–372). With Diomedes wounded, Paris "sprang forward from his hiding-place" (11.379) to triumph over him, but Diomedes dismisses the importance of this wound (11.386–391):

> If you were to be tried in single combat fighting in full armor, your bow and your arrows would serve you in little stead. Vain is your boast in that you have scratched the sole of my foot. I care no more than if a

---

[5] With Hector: *Iliad* 7.9–11; and alone: *Iliad* 15.342.

[6] Euchenor: *Iliad* 13.662.

[7] *Iliad* 8.83–85. I would point out that as soon has Paris has killed the horse it is Hector who rushes toward Nestor for the actual combat. Paris has already disappeared, and the duel that follows is between Hector and Diomedes.

[8] Diomedes: *Iliad* 11.376–377; Machaon: 11.507; Eurypylos: 11.582–584.

[9] Mazon 1967:157: "Rien de plaisant comme ce Pâris attifé en matamore, qui prétend défier tous les Grecs, puis replonge dans la masse, aussitôt qu'il voit Ménélas" ("Nothing is quite so amusing as this Paris decked out and blustering, who proclaims himself ready to challenge all the Greeks and who then dives back into the crowd as soon as he sees Menelaus").

[10] The same idea is reinforced at *Iliad* 3.36–37. The contrast, throughout this scene, is striking between the excess of Paris and the poise of Menelaus. For Paris, there is an excess of "sophistication" and, as well, of fear. Conversely, Menelaus is delighted when spots his personal enemy among the Trojans.

girl or some inept boy had hit me. A worthless coward can inflict but a light wound.

In the world of the *Iliad*, where the model of combat is an open confrontation using identical weapons, Paris is not a true adversary. He is an archer, yet the bow is specifically excluded as the weapon of great warriors.[11] Archers, in fact, are duplicitous (Pandaros, Dolon) or considered bastards (Teucer) and cowards (the Locrians, whose weakness is stated explicitly at *Iliad* 12.712–716). Like the arrows that he fires while hidden, Paris always appears and disappears very quickly from the scene of battle, as if his function in the poem were not to be at the front with the other Trojans, but inside the walls of the besieged city, with the women and old men of Troy. It is possible, I think, to make sense of this set of polar opposites—Hector, best of the Trojan warriors, battling constantly on the plains of Troy, and Paris, paltry fighter, more at home inside the city walls—by considering the relation of the two brothers with the world of Aphrodite, and consequently with the feminine sphere.

The Stability of Hector

In *Iliad* 6, when Hector returns to Troy and asks Hecuba to go with the Trojan women to plead for the aid of Athena, he does not attempt to linger in the city. He is on a mission, a "messenger" who has temporarily left the world of battle.[12] And it is perhaps here, far from combat, that his heroism reaches its greatest heights. Three types of temptation put him to the test inside the city of Troy; three women threaten his ardor.

Hector is able to remain steadfast before Hecuba. Despite the maternal tenderness she expresses in her affectionate gestures (*Iliad* 6.252), he resists the wine and rest she offers him for fear of letting these things cut into his courage: "Honored mother, bring no wine, lest you unman me and I forget my strength" (6.264–265).

Still in his armor, he enters into Paris' home, only to find him in his bedroom. He refuses to sit when Helen offers him a seat (*Iliad* 6.354 and 6.360); battle, he says, is calling him: "I am in haste to help the Trojans" (6.361–362).

Finally, obviously the greatest temptation, he sees Andromache on the ramparts. Here again, he refuses to linger within the city walls, which would be cowardice: "But with what face should I look upon the Trojans, men or women, if I shirked battle like a coward?" (*Iliad* 6.441–443).

---

[11] On the bow as a non-noble weapon in the context of war, see Le Goff and Vidal-Naquet 1979:274.
[12] See Redfield 1975:121. As soon as he enters the city, the women question him about the fates of their husbands and brothers (*Iliad* 6.238–240).

The entire episode is situated under the signs of haste and shame.[13] Hector worries about allowing himself to become contaminated by the tenderness of these three women. He also fears that he will be taken for a coward for appearing within the city. As if struggling with a gnashing guilt, Hector constantly feels the need to return to his proper place, outside, with the men in battle. Indeed, other than Paris, Hector only encounters women: the women of Troy gathered together, his mother, his sister-in-law, his female servants, and finally his wife.[14] This is not the typical condition of a warrior, who usually speaks only with his comrades and his enemies. Moreover, it is telling that the order from the Trojan seer Helenus instructs Hector to address only Hecuba and the "matrons" (*Iliad* 6.87), whereas Hector presents his mission to the army in terms of "the old men of our council and our wives" (6.113–114). Any reference whatsoever to feminine intervention at the heart of the activity of war, even when advised by a seer, requires masculine backing.

The Weakness of Paris

Things go quite differently for Paris. In two rather long passages, Homer presents him in his bedchamber in the company of Helen (*Iliad* 3.382–448 and 6.321–366). He leaves the dust of the battlefield, with the help of Aphrodite, for his "his own perfumed bedchamber," "his bed in his own room" that is "engraved" (3.382, 391, 448).[15] He is the only hero removed from the area of combat and placed in his *thalamos* 'bedchamber'. At one point he makes love to Helen there while the battle is raging (3.447–448), and at another point he prepares his armor there (6.321). In both instances, his attitude is paradoxical: the *thalamos* is not the place for a man, especially during times of war, and especially in the middle of the day. Nor is it the place for a warrior to polish and look after his arms, surrounded by his wife and his female servants.[16]

The strange thing about Paris is that his character embodies a certain number of masculine values that are subverted by the fact that they are inconstant; when following Paris, we are always coming away from the battlefield back into the interior of the palace. If his abilities as a warrior are sometimes

---

[13] Concerning "shame culture" and the notion of *aidôs*, see Dodds 1965:29–30 and Redfield 1975:115–119.

[14] See the remarks of Redfield 1975:121. Lastly, I'd point out that Hector encounters, besides Paris, one other male, his own son Astyanax. The interplay of these encounters suggests that in this episode Paris occupies the place of a woman, or even of a young child; see again the words of Diomedes at *Iliad* 11.386–391, cited above, pp. 9–10.

[15] When Hector is presented resting on a bed, he is no longer alive; his bedchamber only exists as a mortuary setting (*Iliad* 24.720).

[16] A paradox pointed out by the scholia to *Iliad* 6.319 and 321, and analyzed by Griffin 1980:7–9.

asserted (*Iliad* 6.522), they are never convincing. When he lays down a challenge before an adversary, he needs the authority of Hector to follow through in his efforts, which, incidentally, are unsuccessful.

Heroes shine, heroes are beautiful, but their luster shines on the battlefield. Paris is beautiful too, but in his bed. While elsewhere beauty is a visible sign of courage, Paris belies this sign. And the brilliance of Hector as he enters his home, the glow of his enormous spear and his sparkling helmet,[17] references the flickering beauty and clothing of Paris stretched out on his bed (*Iliad* 3.392). The grace that illuminates Paris' body and his clothing calls to mind another ambiguous figure of the Greek imagination: Pandora, the first mortal woman, made by the gods. In a certain way, and on another level, Paris is also defined by his double nature: an exterior of beauty and seduction, a deceptive appearance that hides a nefarious and devious interior.[18] Hector evokes this duality when he is berating Helen's spouse (*Iliad* 3.43–45):

> Will not the flowing-haired Achaeans mock at us and say that we have sent one to champion us who is fair to look at but has neither might in his heart nor any strength?

Hector: The Model of Virility

Because Paris is entirely under the control of Aphrodite, because he is like a manifestation of the goddess, he is poorly suited for war, which is the ultimate masculine activity and which assures everlasting glory through the achievements it calls forth. The actions of war do not fall within the realm of Aphrodite, as Zeus makes clear when Aphrodite, in a pitiful condition, comes to him seeking solace for her wounds: "My child ... it has not been given you to be a warrior" (*Iliad* 5.429). In addition, one might push the Pandora-Paris comparison further, or, to state it another way, one might specify more closely Paris' feminine side. He is the *object* of Helen's desire; Aphrodite praises his allure, and he demands the presence of his wife in his bedchamber (*Iliad* 3.390), where he waits having been brought by Aphrodite. In this episode, the reversal of gender roles appears clearly. He distinguishes himself from the other heroes, and especially from Hector, his exact opposite, as the "attendant" of Aphrodite and not Ares.[19] Even when meeting Andromache, Hector knows where his true place is. Challenged by three types of feminine temptation—maternal love, Helen's

---

[17] *Iliad* 6.319–20, 342, 359, 369, 440, 469–470, 473, 694–695.

[18] See Vernant 1979a:187–194 and Loraux 1978:49 (reprinted in Loraux 1981c:85–86).

[19] *Therapontes Areos* is a common epithet for warriors; see, for example, *Iliad* 2.110; 21.540, 663, 704, 842, etc.

seductive softness,[20] and his wife's affection—he nevertheless keeps his distance from the powers of Aphrodite.

For Hector, his roles as spouse and father only emphasize his duty: to fully belong to the sphere of men, which subordinates the network of private relationships (or those of the city) to practice war in pursuit of *kleos* 'glory'. At a fundamental level in the epic, the sphere of Aphrodite's influence is in thinking from the perspective of the world of women. The code of heroic conduct demands that warriors protect themselves from this influence, as Hector does, because the powers of Aphrodite dissolve the warrior's energy. For Paris, the feminine part of the man conquers his masculine qualities. More of an amorous partner than a warrior, he is more often the "husband of lovely-haired Helen" than the "son of Priam."[21]

But this binary opposition alone is insufficient for the *Iliad*. For "mighty" Diomedes, only his warlike qualities are emphasized. The son of Tydeus,[22] fully aligned with manly pugnacity, is "the only one who is a warrior and nothing else, the entirely successful warrior,"[23] the same one who wounds Aphrodite and drives her from the battlefield. There is a great distance[24] between these two extremes—the femininity of Paris and the hyper-masculinity of Diomedes. It is difficult not to stumble over this major contradiction: the male model of war, which one might expect to find neatly laid out in the *Iliad*, is anything but a clearly formulated idea in the epic.

It is difficult to ignore the fact that figures as prominent as Paris and Diomedes, who are obviously opposites,[25] are also, and above all, fundamentally ambiguous. The former, through his complete subordination to the feminine world, finds himself below the heroic norm; the latter is so perfectly warlike that he oscillates between civilization and savagery.[26] In relation to these two types of extreme, the character of Hector is exemplary: he is as much the commander

---

[20] On the sexual connotations of Helen inviting Hector to sit down in her *thalamos*, see Arthur 1981:31n24, 44; Griffin 1980:6–7; and Schmitz 1963:133.

[21] A clear way for the poet to underline his equivocal character, "husband of lovely-haired Helen": *Iliad* 3.329; 7.355; 8.82, 355; 11.369, 505; 13.766; "son of Priam": 3.356; 6.512.

[22] The prestigious lineage of Diomedes is underlined more often than that of any other hero in the poem; on this point and on Diomedes in general, see Schnapp-Gourbeillon 1981:95–131.

[23] Vidal-Naquet 1975:31: "le seul qui ne soit que guerrier, le guerrier de la réussite totale."

[24] This is, broadly speaking, the argument of Arthur 1981:24–25. In the same study, Arthur convincingly shows that *Iliad* 6, in its narrative structure, temporarily muddles the opposition between the masculine and feminine world. Hector and Andromache, together one last time on the ramparts, leave their respective spheres for a brief moment to participate in the other's; or to put it another way, the border between the worlds of men and women is blurred for about 100 verses (392–502).

[25] On Diomedes' outright disadvantage in the encounter with Paris, see pp. 9–10 above.

[26] On the duality of the character, I draw here on the conclusions in Schnapp-Gourbeillon 1981:124–131, concerning the "peculiar ambiguity" of Diomedes; see also Daraki 1980:16–23.

of the Trojan army as he is the prince of the city of Troy—that is, of a *city* where society is fully represented. Just as much as Hector's accomplishments in battle, his progressive isolation from the familial community over the course of the *Iliad*'s plot establishes his heroism. While embodying the virtues of the son, the husband, and the father, he can be the adversary of Achilles and the symbol of Trojan *andreia* 'manliness' because he chooses to be, and to remain for posterity, a warrior who accepts death.

The Aphrodite of the *Iliad*, far from being completely removed from the field of warlike values, allows us to outline in counter-relief the territories of cowardice, excessive fervor, and proper courage. Even in the universe of the *Iliad*, one regularly encounters Aphrodite: in order to define heroism, one must pass through the world of women and at the same time radically distinguish oneself from it.

2

Physical Evidence of the Hero

To specify certain masculine values, I will endeavor in this chapter to provide an account of the bodily information that the poet provides about his heroes. This examination will not be a question of prescribing "Homeric medicine," but of the image of the warrior's body as it is represented in the *Iliad*. This approach is somewhat complex; in fact, to speak of the warrior's body—and herein lies the problem—is above all to consider the aesthetic criteria of Homeric thought. By staying close to the text, we will perhaps prevent the temptation to interpret Homeric aesthetics and poetry in an arbitrary fashion.

Without adding to the already lengthy list of works focused on "Homeric psychology," an extremely complex scholarly question,[1] I will simply remark upon the predominance of concrete images in the epic whenever translation of what we call emotions is required. Through a tight interweaving of physical and moral phenomena, with Homeric vocabulary generally tending toward the concrete rather than the abstract, physical and psychological experiences are often merged together. The absence of any rigid compartmentalization of physical and mental activities is a typical characteristic of the epic: the words *thumos*, *ētor, kēr, kradiē*—and, to a lesser degree, *phrēn*, which often refers to intellectual life—at times mean the organ, and at times the function of that organ.[2]

Fear, warlike rage, suffering, joy, erotic desire, and so many emotions in Homer are inseparable from their physical manifestation—are, one might say, constituted by those physical manifestations. With this phenomenon as the point of departure, we will consider the question of heroism from the perspective of the warrior's "body language," and in so doing will make an attempt to extract from this corporeal screen an understanding of epic values.

---

[1] From the immense bibliography on the question, I have consulted: Magnien 1927, Böhme 1929, Larock 1930, Snell 1948 (English translation 1953), Onians 1954, Dodds 1965 (especially Chap. 1), Russo and Simon 1968 (reprinted in Wright 1978). More recent studies include Ireland and Steel 1975 and Redfield 1975:171–182.

[2] Russo and Simon 1978:42

In the Homeric world, all qualities are thought of in concrete terms; for reasons inextricably tied to the epic genre and the archaic phase of thought from which it grew, Homeric poetry brings to life the strength and deeds of its heroes through the use of images. The concrete reality of the warriors who confront each other outside of Troy is evoked at length throughout the poem. Attempting to read the "physical text" is a means of exploring the question of masculinity in the epic, as the hero's body is without a doubt "the place" where the primary signifiers of epic thought are condensed.

Beauty and the Skills of the Warrior

Achilles, the most prestigious of the heroes in the *Iliad*, is described over and over as the most beautiful.[3] From this common point—strength is beautiful in the *Iliad*, and the warrior's valor shines in his countenance—the hero can be recognized as much by the flash of his beauty as by the feats he accomplishes.[4] The two aspects are inseparable from each other. Thus, if Thersites is the epitome of the anti-hero,[5] which has long been recognized, this is related as much to his cowardice as to his ugliness. The aristocratic ideology of the *Iliad* short-circuits the question of social hierarchy by removing the people's spokesman among the soldiers, Thersites, from the discussion; in order to exist, heroic virtues must be attested and confirmed by the physical beauty of those who practice them. The inadequacy of a character like Thersites in the world of heroes is represented in and by his ugliness.[6] His physical defects lead to his cowardice: practically handicapped, slouching, nearly bald (*Iliad* 2.217–220); compared to the Homeric canons of virile beauty, he is the exact opposite of the accomplished warrior. The ugliest (*aischistos*, 2.216) and, at the same time, the weakest (*chereioteron*, 2.248) of the Greeks, he is in every respect the opposite, as well as the caricature, of Achilles.

It is evident that the arms, legs, and chest define the warrior in the *Iliad*. Height and shoulder width are also signs of merit.[7] When, on the ramparts, Priam asks Helen for details about the Achaean commanders, the imposing and

---

[3] Explicitly at *Iliad* 2.673–674 (*kallistos*), 21.108, 24.629–630.

[4] We saw above how Paris subverted the norm, pp. 8–10.

[5] *Iliad* 2.212–277; cf. von der Mühll 1952:42, and see also Finley 1983:136–139; Chantraine 1963:passim; Dumézil 1982:197–200, and especially Nagy 1979:259–264 ("The Worst of the Achaeans").

[6] Chantraine 1963:21–22 shows that Homer is playing on the name Thersites—'the audacious, the brave'—to define his character negatively in relation to Achilles and Odysseus: "Thersite l'intrépide: oui, mais en paroles seulement" ("Thersites the intrepid: yes, but only in words").

[7] On height, cf. for example: Achilles (*Iliad* 21.108; 24.629–630), Ajax (3.226–227; 9.169), Hector (6.263, 440; 7.233, 287). On width of shoulders: Patroclus (16.791), Hector (16.360).

brilliant presence of Agamemnon, the breadth of Odysseus' chest and shoulders, and the great height of Ajax all catch his attention (*Iliad* 3.166–227).[8]

More than expertise in combat, what counts is the power of the limbs, and most of all the power in the arms. The *telos* 'end, goal' of battle is in the arms of the warrior. Patroclus states this clearly to Meriones: "the outcome [*telos*] of battle is in the force of hands" (*Iliad* 16.630).[9] The important thing for the hero is to be "confident in his hands" (*chersi pepoithōs*, 16.624), to have hands that are formidable because of the likelihood they will enter into a fury (*cheires aaptoi/ mainonth'*, 16.244–245).

It is not surprising then that, from the beginning of the poem, the preeminence of Achilles is asserted in this manner: "it is my hands that do the better part of the fighting" (*Iliad* 1.165–166).

Complementing the arms, where offensive power resides, are the legs that run charging into battle and then hold firm before the enemy. There are many different ways in Homer to describe strength and efficiency: walking with long strides,[10] running quickly,[11] remaining solidly on one's feet as opposed to the coward who "keeps shifting his weight first on one knee and then on the other,"[12] planting on one's legs to confront the enemy.[13] Flexibility and resistance equally define the legs of the warrior.[14] Without engaging here in a developed discussion on the symbolism of the knee in Homer,[15] the importance of this key part of the hero's body is nevertheless evident. As the site of vital power and the joint that expresses bravery, the knee, depending on whether it is stiff or supple, robust or weak, determines the success of ventures on the battlefield. The career of the hero depends foremost, then, on the proper functioning and quality of the muscles and joints in his limbs.[16] The heroic ideal of beauty and youth finds

---

[8]   In the *Odyssey* also, the width of Odysseus' shoulders is explicitly evoked, notably at the moment of his combat with Irus: throwing of his rags, he uncovers the beauty and power of his thighs, the width of his torso, and the muscles in his upper arms, *Odyssey* 18.67–69.

[9]   The poet also evokes the palm of the right hand that grips the sword, the "strong" hand, and the "brawny" hand: *Iliad* 3.376; 7.264, etc.

[10]   For example, Ajax: *Iliad* 7.212–213; Hector: 15.306–307.

[11]   Proverbial speed of Achilles—for example, *Iliad* 13.325—whom we see "speeding right onwards," at 21.302.

[12]   *Iliad* 13.281.

[13]   "Hector, standing firm with his legs apart," *Iliad* 12.458.

[14]   Flexibility and speed: see, for example, Hector who skillfully moves his feet and knees: "Hector rapidly moving his feet and calves," *Iliad* 15.269, or Odysseus who wins the foot-race, after having his hands and feet made light by Athena (23.772); see Snell 1948:6–9; Vivante 1955:40–41; Daraki 1980:15–16.

[15]   Knee and vital fluid, creation: see Deonna 1939:228–231 and Onians 1954:174–186.

[16]   See Snell 1948:6–9. To the extent that we are trying here to read the body of the warrior ("lire le corps du guerrier"), by proposing as a postulate that the poet projects a certain number of the values of the heroic universe *in* him and *on* him, we can not adopt Snell's overly reductive point

confirmation in stature, agility, stride, posture, and strength, which are linked solidly together in this characterization of the body.

The state of the body bears a double significance as both a sign of life and of individual bravery. In Homer, being alive is synonymous with having functioning knees;[17] the vital breath goes conjointly with the movement of the legs, as Achilles states to Phoenix: "while I have breath in my body, and my limbs are strong" (*Iliad* 9. 609–610). Conversely, the man about to die feels his life, his force, leaving his limbs, and killing an enemy is described with the phrase *gounata luein* 'loosen his knees'.[18]

The same relation of opposites characterizes physical states like vigor and fatigue: flexibility and lightness on one side, stiffness and heaviness on the other. Once again, the power of concrete images in the epic can be seen: fatigue and exhaustion strike down on the warrior and his limbs "weary" (*Iliad* 4.230). Fatigue acts through "repeated assaults" (5.811) and drives[19] into the body—hands, arms, shoulders, knees[20]—which it wears out and weighs down.[21]

It is youth then, with its strength still intact, that is the primary ally of the warrior; and it is his youthful beauty that will, in feats and in glorious death, permanently establish him in the heroic sphere.[22] This explains, even outside of poetic conventions, the surprising "maximization" in the *Iliad* of the warrior's body, a body that is both medium and mirror of the merits of masculine *aretē* 'value, virtue'.

At first glance, the warrior can gauge his opponent; he can estimate the value of his brilliance, his size, or the shape of his physical appearance, even before seeing him in action. This is because, at the moment of confrontation, the warrior's body radiates power, as if having undergone a metamorphosis.

---

of view that basically sees nothing more in the Homeric hero than a sort of puppet manipulated by the gods and characterized by the plurality of his articulated limbs.

[17] For example, *Odyssey* 18.133: "As long as the gods grant him excellence and his knees are steady" (= he is still alive).

[18] Equivalence: having your limbs and knees split (e.g., *Iliad* 4.469; 7.12, 16; 11.579; 21.114, etc.) or your *menos* broken (5.296; 6.27; 8.123, etc.).

[19] *Iliad* 5.811. Pain (*achos*, *Odyssey* 18.348), anger (*cholos*, *Iliad* 9.553), and rage (*lussa*) sink into and penetrate the warrior in like fashion (the verb is *duō*). The same idea is present when Odysseus tells of how Circe literally took "the tiredness and stiffness out of my limbs" (*Odyssey* 10.363).

[20] See, in particular, *Iliad* 2.839; 4.230; 5.797; 7.6; 13.711; 16.106; 19.166; 21.32, 270.

[21] Literal meaning of the verb *teirō*; see *Iliad* 5.796–797; 17.745; 19.51–52. In these three examples dealing with three of the greatest heroes—Diomedes, Ajax, Achilles—sweat and fatigue are paired together to exhaust the warrior; see Onians 1954:191–193. On the heaviness brought on by fatigue, cf. 19.165–166: "... and his limbs will grow heavy under him."

[22] For all things related to the esthetic conception of heroism, I refer here to the courses (*Collège de France* 1976–1977) and writings of Jean-Pierre Vernant, which have provided so much inspiration for my work: Vernant 1979b, 1980 (reprinted in Gnoli and Vernant 1982), and 1981b.

The Body Transformed by Courage

Before any collective confrontation or, *a fortiori*, any single combat, Homer presents the warriors in the grips of a peculiar physical condition: courage, which fervor imprints on the hero's body. The biology of the representation of courage occurs in three major phases: penetration of strength into the hero, respiratory and muscular changes, and finally the outward expression of this energy by the arms and legs. *Menos*, this primary energy, both mental and physical, moves the hero.[23] This energy is most often communicated or reactivated by a divinity; a certain god will "set" *menos* in the "heart" (*Iliad* 5.125; 16.529) of a protégé, or "breathe" it into him (10.482; 15.60; 19.159, etc.). Driven by *menos*, warriors pant, they advance "exhaling their *menos*" (2.536; 3.8). Strength literally takes *possession* of the body: "He rages like a madman" (9.239), Odysseus says when referencing Hector's prowess. Later, when Hector is putting on Patroclus' armor, his fervor is presented in the following terms: "he was entered by Ares the terrifying, the Enyalios. And his limbs were all filled inside with force and strength."[24]

The mind and body of the warrior are modified by this warlike fervor, which penetrates him in a literal sense. In Book 13, the Achaeans are rescued from a bad position by Poseidon, and the god revives the courage of the two Ajaxes: "[he] filled their hearts with daring. He made their legs light and active, as also their hands and their feet" (*Iliad* 13.60–61). The effects are seen right away, and the two warriors discuss their impressions of the physical sensations they are now feeling (13.73–80):

> "Moreover I feel the lust of battle burn more fiercely within me, while my hands and my feet under me are more eager for the fray."

And Ajax son of Telamon answered,

> "I too feel my hands grasp my spear more firmly; my strength is greater, and my feet more nimble; I long, moreover, to meet furious Hector son of Priam, even in single combat."

Under the sway of his fervor, the warrior is struck by a general trembling of the muscles. His strength increases, and his heart swells with lust for battle (13.74);[25]

---

[23] On *menos* as a vital impulse, warlike ardor, and spiritual energy, see Böhme 1929:22, as well as Dodds 1965:20–22; Redfield 1975:171–174; Daraki 1980; and especially Dumézil 1983:184–190.

[24] *Iliad* 17.210–212. I would point out the force of this image. The warlike spirit sinks deep into the warrior, just as *lussa*, another synonym for Ares, does. This spirit fills his limbs from the inside.

[25] See also *Iliad* 21.571–572, for Agenor whose heart races and bounds at the thought of fighting Achilles; at 23.370–371, during the chariot race, the drivers' hearts pound.

Menos makes him more agile (78). His limbs twitch; flooded by the desire to fight (75, 78),[26] his feet carry him forward (79). Sometimes, at the height of his rage, his teeth gnash,[27] and he foams at the mouth.[28] In all cases, the overflow of strength is clearly inscribed on the body and the face of the hero who is under its influence.

And finally, the ultimate and decisive specification of the text, the hero, at the height of his fervor, shines with the fire of his bravery. Menacing warriors are literally "clothed in valor as with a garment."[29] They shine and flash; from their eyes[30] and from their armor especially[31] a terrible glow escapes that lights up the distance.[32]

The Body Transformed by Fear

Just as strength alternates back and forth between the two camps, terror regularly changes sides. "There is no hero who will not tremble one day,"[33] Nicole Loraux has written in a recent study that shows how fear in the *Iliad* is the logical counterpart of courage. Knowing fear is effectively the other obligatory moment in the activity of war. It is "the power of death that emanates from the body of the combatant covered by his arms and ready to display the extraordinary vigor of combat, the strength (*alkē*) that inhabits him."[34] This power makes the hero, like Gorgo whom he resembles, absolutely terrifying. None of the warriors escape it, and each is alternately terrifying and terrified. In the

---

[26] Occurrences of *maimaō* 'spring with desire' are frequent: *Iliad* 15.604, 742; 20.284, 468; 22.243, etc.; see Onians 1954:21–22.

[27] Achilles who "gnashed his teeth," *Iliad* 19.365; see on this point Vernant 1981a:142–144.

[28] Hector furious: "he foamed at the mouth," *Iliad* 15. 607.

[29] *Iliad* 7.164; 8.262. Valor is like an article of clothing that covers the body of the warrior (*epiennumi*); a metaphor that, by itself, could support my argument. A similar image at 20.381, where Achilles "clothed in valor as with a garment," springs upon the Trojans, and at 9.231 during the embassy scene, Odysseus, using the verb *duō*, asks Achilles to "clothe himself in bravery." Inversely, Agamemnon, in certain passages, wears his insolence on his face: *Iliad* 1.149; 9.372.

[30] Fire in Hector's eyes: *Iliad* 12.466; in Achilles eyes 19.16–17, 365–366, etc. On eyes containing and projecting fire, see Mugler 1960:60–62; and, in general, on the light associated with force, see Vernant and Gnoli 1982:59–60 and Vernant 1981a:142–143 (on the demonic power of the warrior's gaze).

[31] For example, Hector: *Iliad* 12.463–464; Achilles: 19.379–381; 20.46, etc.

[32] Hector entering the house of Paris is preceded by the glow of his spear: *Iliad* 6.319–320; the glow of Achilles' shield rising into the sky: 19.375–376.

[33] Loraux 1982a:119: "Il n'est pas de héros qui un jour ne frissonne"; see also, from a more philological perspective, Harkemanne 1967.

[34] Vernant 1981a:143: "la puissance de mort qui irradie de la personne du combattant recouvert de ses armes et prêt à manifester l'extraordinaire vigueur au combat, la fortitude (*alkē*), dont il est habité."

expression of terror, then, the same physical transformations that operate in moments of bravery can be found, but in negative, inverted forms.

The expressive capacity of the warrior's body allows for the observation of a certain number of clinical signs in the register of fear, similar to those in the register of courage. Terror, often expressed in Homer by an immediate trembling,[35] enters into the warrior and takes over his limbs (*Iliad* 3.34; 8.452; 14.506, etc.; 7.215; 20.44). A god can raise it inside the body: "Then father Zeus from his high throne struck fear into the heart of Ajax,"[36] and gods can also remove it from the body: "Athena ... took away all fear from her."[37]

Similar to the spasm of courage, a contraction or brutal palpitation characterizes the heart of the terrified hero.[38] A generalized trembling seizes his body: his knees falter, his legs are paralyzed and no longer stand firm (*Iliad* 10.374; 11.547; 13.281). His complexion turns pale and green (*Iliad* 3.35; 10.376: 13.279, etc.); the hairs on his skin stand up (*Iliad* 24.359); his teeth gnash (*Iliad* 10.375; 13.283);[39] his eyes cast a panicked gaze (*Iliad* 11.546). In short, the mechanism of fear inhibits, term for term, the qualities that were optimized by courage.

Armor: An Extension of the Body

For a more precise investigation of the hero's body, it will be helpful to make a detour by way of his armor. If the presence of arms is, in effect, obvious in the *Iliad*, spending some time on the symbolic power that arms possess in the epic will not be insignificant.[40] Armor is at the same time a protection, an intermediary, a complement, and, for our purposes especially, an extension of the body. For the activities of war, the body and the armor share a series of identical properties.

To describe warriors who are putting on their armor, Homer uses, among others,[41] the verbs *ennumi* 'to put on' and *duō* 'to get into, enter';[42] Greeks and Trojans leave for combat "their bodies dressed in rigid bronze" (*Iliad* 19.233),

---

[35] On the names of fear in the *Iliad*, *deos* 'logical fear' and *phobos* 'sudden terror, panic'—see Loraux 1982a:passim. *Tromos*, generic expression of fear: *Iliad* 3.34; 7.215; 8.452; 10.90, etc.

[36] *Iliad* 11.544. Note the use of the verb *ornumi* that also characterizes *menos*.

[37] *Odyssey* 6.140 (Nausicaa, frightened by the sight Odysseus); see p. 18, n. 19 above.

[38] The heart "beat quickly": *Iliad* 7.216; 13.282; it is as if courage is "sucked out" of the warrior by the effect of fear: the Greeks, facing Hector, were frightened and "their hearts fell down into their feet," 15.280.

[39] See Harkemanne 1967:77.

[40] Cf. Vernant 1974, particularly 25–26.

[41] Principal verbs used for the preparation of arms, in the general sense, according to Trümpy 1950:74–89: *thōrēssō* (*Iliad* 8.530; 19.352: 22.369), *hoplizō* (8.55), *korussō* (2.273; 4.274; 7.206; 19.397), etc.

[42] *Iliad* 14. 383; 19.233; 6.340; 11.16; 16.64.

they conceal themselves, "dress themselves" with their large shields (14.371–372). Like a second skin, armor is adapted, adjusted, and fitted as precisely as possible onto the parts of the body it protects. On the skin,[43] "close fitting" cuirasses, belts, greaves, and ankle plates join together and cover the forms of the hero.[44] After having put on his new armor, Achilles verifies that it fits him properly: "Then radiant Achilles made trial of himself in his armor to see whether it fitted him, so that his limbs could play freely under it" (19.385).

This tight correspondence—body of the warrior/armor—besides being the primary condition for effective combat, further emphasizes the physical qualities attributed to the warrior. Well-fitted, radiant like the fire of his eyes, imposing like his strength, armor is the double of the hero. It is not irrelevant to point out that when Patroclus puts on Achilles' armor, it fits him "naturally": "he donned the cuirass of the swift-footed descendant of Aeacus, richly inlaid and studded ... He grasped two redoubtable spears that suited his hands."[45] On the other hand, however, when Hector, after having killed Patroclus, wants to put on the armor, the intervention of Zeus who "fitted the armor to Hector's skin,"[46] is required. Homer is not responding to a need for realistic detail when he introduces this nuance; the morphology of Patroclus, like that of Hector, is not in question here. Rather, it is the symbolic identity of Achilles and Patroclus that is underlined. As Cedric Whitman has pointed out, if Achilles' armor is ill-suited for Hector, it is because "Hector cannot play the role of Achilles, whereas Patroclus could."[47]

In a certain way, the armor is effectively the hero himself. Depending on which man is carrying them, weapons are formidable and feared to a greater or lesser degree; to be afraid of a confrontation is to fear the man as much as the spear associated with him. In this way, Diomedes is amazed by the audacity of Glaucus:

---

[43] *Iliad* 12.464; 13.241; 17.210; 22.322; see Trümpy 1950:77–78, who emphasizes the meaning of the word *chrōs* 'skin'. In the same vein, I'd point out the image of "cheek-pierced" (*chalkopareios*) helmets: 12.183; 17.294; 20.397.

[44] *Arariskō: Iliad* 4.134; 11.18; 13.188; 18.611; 19.370; *harmozō*: 3.333; 17.210.

[45] *Iliad* 16.132 and 139. I would point out, by contrast, that in the duel in Book 3, Paris had borrowed his cuirass from Lykaon and had to adjust it to fit his chest (332–333).

[46] *Iliad* 17.210. Note the equivalent image in Hesiod, which is used to describe Pandora's jewels. "Pallas Athena placed on her skin every manner of ornament" (*Works and Days* 76; trans. Nagy).

[47] Whitman 1958:201. In his chapter dedicated to Achilles (181–220), Whitman shows in detail how Achilles and Patroclus form a homologous pair, and more generally, how the hero and his armor do the same. When Patroclus' helmet is knocked off of his head by Apollo and its plumes are covered with blood and dust (16.793–796), it is clear what is to come; the mortal wound will not be long behind. Patroclus, like his helmet, will fall, and the poet, at this same moment, has also foreshadowed the death of Achilles.

Who, my good sir ... are you among men? I have never seen you in battle
until now, but you are daring beyond all others if you abide my onset.

Iliad 6.123–126[48]

On the battlefield, weapons are like living beings; they are granted specifically human qualities. The warrior's desire for destruction passes into his
weapons and occupies them, as indicated by a developed series of metaphors:
weapons gleam maliciously,[49] are "courageous,"[50] furiously desire to strike their
enemy.[51] Their conduct—if this term can be used—is identical to the warrior's:
tired after a long struggle, they sweat,[52] they warm up when plunged into blood
(*Iliad* 20.476). They even have cannibalistic impulses, eager as they are to bite
into and devour the flesh of the enemy.[53]

The boundary between the qualities belonging to the individual hero and
those belonging to his weapons is not clear. Their relationship is complementary:
through a sort of back and forth, the ardent warrior transfers his fearlessness
to his weapons; reciprocally, his weapons engorge his bravery.[54] Furthermore,
there is an interplay in the circulation of force operating in his weapons identical to that in the warrior himself. They are driven, from the interior, by a
destructive instinct and, through their splendor, project their power externally.

The magical power of weapons is to increase tenfold the strength of the
person who wields them and to terrify the person who sees them being wielded.
In a certain way, the weapon, like the hero, carries upon it the recognizable signs
of its own power. For Achilles, the exceptional hero, exceptional weapons terrify
even his companions the Myrmidons (*Iliad* 19.74–75); the reaction of the Trojans
is then expected (20.44–46):

There was not a Trojan but his limbs failed him for fear as he beheld
the fleet son of Peleus all glorious in his armor, and looking like Ares
himself.

Beyond even their extraordinary value (which can be religious or derived from
their constituent precious metals), weapons embody above all the quality of
the hero who carries them: they are "active" like the hero in battle, and the

---

48 See also 5.790 (spear of Achilles).
49 See the remarks in Stanford 1936:138–139; Marg 1942:168–169; and Griffin 1980:34–36.
50 See, for example, the valorous shield: *Iliad* 11.32.
51 *Iliad* 5.661: the "spear ... tore furiously through the flesh"; 4.126; 8.111; 16.74–75; 20.339, etc.
52 "The bands that bear your shields sweat upon your shoulders," 2.388.
53 *Iliad* 11.573–574; 13.830–831; 15.316–317; 21.70, 168; cf. Marg 1942:169
54 As soon as he puts on his armor, Hector is transformed: "he was entered by Ares the terrifying"
    (*Iliad* 17.210–213). The reactions of Achilles are even more violent: fits of rage, flaming eyes,
    gnashing teeth, etc. (*Iliad* 19.16–19, 365–391); cf. Griffin 1980:36–37.

hero's antagonist has to confront them as well to make it through the fight. For a hero, to kill an enemy and seize his weapons is a permanent mark of superiority. When one displays the weapons of the fallen, the latter is physically brought back to life—in his beauty, his size, his strength—demonstrating how the victor has triumphed over him: "And the one indisputable measure of success is a trophy."[55]

If "for Homer, the human body is a marvelous network of connecting parts he can pierce or sever or use for pictorial and emotional effects,"[56] it is because, in a broader perspective, this body *speaks* each phase of the demands of heroism. Determination, strength, and courage are painted in the *Iliad* on the surface of the text, on the surface of the warrior's body.

The body of the hero is both record and reflection of heroic values. If, in the effort of the struggle, a man's body is constantly placed at the forefront, if anatomic details of a surprising precision abound,[57] it is because, in the epic system, the physical representation of the hero completes and authenticates his heroic character. It is because, as Jean-Pierre Vernant has written, "size, beauty, youth, unique form, splendor, and head of hair are aspects of the body where we find incarnated at once the aesthetic, religious, social, and personal values that define the status of a specific individual in the eyes of the group)."[58]

And this body is also, inherently, a desirable body.

---

[55] Finley 1983:147.
[56] Vermeule 1979:97; see also 98–101 and 234n13.
[57] For example: *Iliad* 14.465–468, 496–499; 16.345–350; 17.617–618; 20.478–483.
[58] Vernant and Gnoli 1982:66: "taille, beauté, jeunesse, forme singulière, éclat, chevelure sont des aspects du corps dans lesquels s'incarnent les valeurs à la fois esthétiques, religieuses, sociales, personnelles, qui définissent, aux yeux du groupe, le statut d'un individu singulier."

3
Erotic Images of War

Erotic images of war in the *Iliad* could, by themselves, justify a study of considerable proportion. It is a vast question, this relationship between eroticism and war ... I will attempt in this chapter simply to underline a series of associations found in the vocabularies of both war and love. Examining the main scenes linking eroticism and combat, I will seek to specify the categories of masculine and feminine in the epic.

While the limits of this examination may be arbitrary, I will focus on three aspects of the question: war as an erotic activity, erotic metaphors of combat, and finally the eroticization of death.

Erotic Representation of Combat

There is no need to emphasize the parallel that exists between a duel of two heroes and "erotic combat": both cases deal with an encounter of two bodies. Pierre Guiraud has studied this analogy in depth in works from the medieval and modern eras.[1] "The military metaphor," he writes, "is so coherent, so relevant, that all the modes, means, and phases of combat and all the phrases describing them contain a powerful sexual image."[2] This is also the case in the Homeric epic.

As we have seen,[3] the warrior who charges against the enemy undergoes a physical transformation at the moment of confrontation. He is driven entirely by the desire to meet his opponent, to enter into contact with him. He attacks armed with a spear that he intends to plunge into the flesh of his enemy. His goal is undoubtedly to accomplish the feat that will assure his fame, but, on a

---

[1] Guiraud 1978; particularly chaps. 4 and 5: "Les symboles de la libido" and "La rhétorique de l'érotisme."

[2] Guiraud 1978:120: "La métaphore militaire est si cohérente, si pertinente que tous les modes, moyens et phases du combat et toutes les phrases qui les expriment contiennent, en puissance, une image sexuelle."

[3] See p. 19 and following, above.

more immediate level, it is also to assuage his desire to possess the adversary. For in combat the urge that drives the warrior is similar to the urge of love: Nestor evokes "the desire for war" (*Iliad* 9.64), and Achilles incites the bravery of the Myrmidons by reminding them of their taste for the melee: "The hour is now come for those high feats of arms that you have so long been pining for" (16.207–208). And with Hector absent from the battle, his troops miss him: "the Trojans, who miss [him] greatly [*pothēn*] when [he is] not among them" (6.362).[4] It is as if, during times of war, the only possible interventions by the powers of love are restricted uniquely to the sphere of men.

In fact, the battlefield encounter, in certain regards, resembles a lovers' rendezvous. Emily Vermeule has shown this clearly in her work;[5] here, I will be following her and building on a number of her observations.

During hand-to-hand fighting, certain physical characteristics of femininity are attributed to the warrior. His skin (*chrōs*) is beautiful (*kalos, Iliad* 5.858; 22.321), tender (*terēn, Iliad* 4.237; 13.553; 14.406) like that of a young girl (*parthenikēs ... terena chora*; Hesiod *Works and Days* 519 and 522) or the Heliconian muses (Hesiod *Theogony* 5), or like the flowers in a meadow (*teren' anthea poiēs, Odyssey* 9.449). It is fair and white like a lily (*leirioeis, Iliad* 13.830), luminous like the voices of the Muses (Hesiod *Theogony* 41) or the cicada (*Iliad* 3.152).

The neck is fragile, delicate (*hapalos, Iliad* 3.371; 17.49; 23.327; *Odyssey* 22.16) like the cheeks of Achilles' female captives (23.123) or the fair skin of a "virgin" (*parthenos*, Hesiod *Works and Days* 519).

There are many epithets—*kalos, hapalos, terēn, leirioeis*—that, in underlining the fragility and delicacy of his skin, potentially transform the warrior into a romantic partner. Whiteness of complexion and body is, in fact, a trait typical of women who live inside.[6] For Hector, evoking Ajax's pale skin is, in a certain way, calling him a woman; Hector belittles Ajax's courage by implying he has no more strength than an unarmed woman.[7]

There are other signs in the *Iliad* that indicate that combat-to-death ironically resembles a lovers' rendezvous between a man and a woman. To arouse erotic desire in Zeus, Hera wraps her bosom in the girdle containing all of Aphrodite's charms: into the girdle "had been wrought—love, desire, and ... sweet flattery" (*Iliad* 14.216). In the universe of war—necessarily an exclusively

---

[4] In the same way, the Greeks desire Achilles who has separated himself from them: 14.368. On *pothos*, desire mixed with regret that is focused on someone who is absent, far away, or dead, see Vermeule 1979:154–155, and Vernant 1977:430–441.

[5] Vermeule 1979:99–105.

[6] *Iliad* 3.121; 6.371, 377. To enhance the beauty of Penelope, Athena makes her "whiter than sawn ivory" (*Odyssey* 18.196, etc.).

[7] An idea evoked explicitly by Hector himself when he confronts Achilles: *gumnon eonta / autōs hōs te gunaika, Iliad* 22.124–125. On the force of the insult in such a comparison, see p. 40 below.

masculine universe—it is "pressing forward to a place in the front ranks" or "charg[ing] at the foe" (*promachōn oaristun*),[8] labeled with the same word (*oaristus*), that drives warriors into confrontation.

In combat, bodies blend and mix together ("Our only thought and plan is to fight them [body to body, locking arms in our fury]," *Iliad* 15.509–510; see also 5.143; 13.286; 21.469) as in love (*Iliad* 2.232; 3.445; 6.161; *Theogony* 375, 994). In the two forms of bodily contact, the verb *meignumi* expresses this union. Another similarity should be pointed out: in both cases, one of the partners is dominated by the violence of the other.[9] The woman, in the case of love, is tamed by the man: Thetis, in sharing a bed with Peleus, is made subject to him (*damassen*, *Iliad* 18.432; see also 3.301 and *Odyssey* 3.269); the unfortunate warrior, subjugated by the force of his adversary, is also tamed (*Iliad* 3.436; 5.646, 653; 8.244, 290; 11.309).[10]

The enemy, like the erotic partner, is a possessed object, reduced to the mercy of another. The analogy between the two themes is clear in the *Iliad*: erotic activity serves as a model for war and lends to it a part of its language.[11]

The discourse of war appears in a series of associations where a sexual connotation is evident: the dance of young people contrasted with the dance of Ares, veils of a woman and walls of a city, and marriage both between men and women and in combat.

Erotic Metaphors

The dance of Ares

To incite the ardor of his companions, Ajax reminds them that Hector is "telling [his men] to remember that they are not at a dance but in battle" (*Iliad* 15.508). The reference to the *choros* 'chorus' here serves to ward off any temptation toward sluggishness: war is not entertainment, and the only agile movement allowed is that involved in the blows of battle. To confuse the battlefield with a *choros* is to forget to be a man, to fall into the sphere of Aphrodite's "delightful

---

[8]   *Iliad* 13.291 and 17.228. The same image with the verb *oarizein* is used during the "Achilles-Hector rendezvous," 22.127–128. The other occurrence of this verb is in the exchange between Hector and Andromache, 6.516. For interpretations of these passages, see Segal 1971b:35–36; Vermeule 1979:103, 157, 235n24.

[9]   See Benveniste 1969 1:307.

[10] On the meaning of *damazō*, *damnēmi*, see Vernant and Detienne 1974:85–87.

[11] Vermeule 1979:101–102 cites, among other passages, Hesiod *Theogony* 120–122, "Eros that relaxes the limbs, and in the breasts of all gods and all men, subdues their reason and prudent counsel" (trans. Nagy and Banks). See also J. Svenbro 1984 who, in a symmetric but inverse perspective, shows that Sappho uses the model warrior from the *Iliad* to define the *philotas* 'love' of women.

matrimonial duties" (5.429). In contrast with the world of war, the *choros* in the epic is, in fact, associated with luxury, pleasure, and peace.[12]

On the shield of Achilles, Hephaestus depicts several dance scenes, one of which shows a chorus of young people dancing (*Iliad* 18.590–605). The gentleness of the scene, the beauty of the young girls, and the harmony of the movements at this charming "place of dancing" (18.603; *Odyssey* 18.194) are emphasized; everything indicates that the young men and women in the chorus are under the protection of the presiding goddess, Aphrodite.[13]

By evoking the ballet that two warriors execute, the bodily contact between two partners becomes metaphoric for an unfolding dance "to the death"; the battlefield is the place of uniquely masculine activity, and as a result the only dance possible, a virile dance, is that of Ares. Hector confirms the metaphor to Ajax before attacking him: "in hand to hand fighting I can dance the dance of cruel Ares" (*Iliad* 7.241).[14] The force of the inversion becomes even clearer when we note that it is the scavenging dogs who lead the dance and celebration around the corpses (13.233; 17.255; 18.179), this kind of pleasure being their exclusive privilege.[15]

In the threats and curses that the Trojans and Greeks fling at each other, ironic allusions to the "dance of Ares" and to the "feast of the dogs" figure prominently as forms of encouragement; reciprocally, simply calling one's adversary a dancer carries the weight of an insult (*Iliad* 16.617–618). When Priam laments the loss of Hector, his first words are reproaches aimed at his remaining sons. Those who died with Hector were brave (*aristoi*, 24.255); those who are still alive are "liars, and light of foot, heroes of the dance" (24.261).[16] Among these sons is Paris: siding once again with effeminate men, Paris, after the duel with Menelaus is broken up by Aphrodite, looks more like he is returning from a ball than from the battlefield (3.393–394).

---

[12] Cf. the Phaeacians in the *Odyssey* (warm baths, banquets, dance): *Odyssey* 8.248–249; Paris *Iliad* 3.54–55, etc.

[13] See Boedeker 1974:43–57 on the relationship between dance and Aphrodite.

[14] Note, too, the five-fold repetition of *oida* within five lines (*Iliad* 7.237–241); the poet summarizes through Hector's voice the primary actions a warrior must know how to perform in order to be effective in the field; the repetition of the verb creates a rhythm connecting each enunciation.

[15] On the "dance of the dogs," see Vermeule 1979:103–105, 235n24; on scavenging dogs, see Schnapp-Gourbeillon 1981:165–169.

[16] MacLeod 1982:111 compares this verse to *Iliad* 3.106 where the sons of Priam are called "high-handed and ill to trust" and points out the play on the word *aristoi*: they excel at dance, not combat.

The veils of a city

In an extraordinary image, Homer draws a parallel between the veils of a chaste woman and the unbreached walls of a city. Advising Patroclus to return to camp after the Trojans have been driven back from the ships, Achilles dreams aloud of taking Troy with only his friend: " ... and that not a single man of all the Trojans might be left alive, nor yet of the Argives, but that we two might be alone left to tear aside the sacred veil from the brow of Troy" (*Iliad* 16.99–100). In evoking the sacred veil of Ilion, "Achilles compares Troy, the city unviolated up to this day, to a female captive whose veil he, as the victor, will tear away by force."[17]

In an in-depth study of the use of the word *krēdemnon* 'veil' in Homer, Michael Nagler explicates this analogy and shows how the chastity of women can be likened, symbolically, to the safety of a city.[18] The intact "veil" (either a piece of fabric or a rampart) attests to both female chastity and the safety of a city, and in both cases male warriors act as protectors as well as assailants.[19] Here again, masculine action and power is conveyed in a sexual image: in the poetic context of the *Iliad*, taking a city and destroying its ramparts is like possessing a woman by force and tearing away her garments.

The same image appears in the *Odyssey*, where it recalls the Greek victory over the Trojans. Odysseus remembers the sack of Troy as "the day when we loosed Troy's fair diadem from her brow" (*Odyssey* 13.388). The metaphor that equates the city with a woman is doubly significant if we remember that, in the world of the *Iliad*, pillaging goods and the abduction of women go hand in hand. "Many a bloody battle have I waged by day," says Achilles, "against those who were fighting for their women" (*Iliad* 9.327).

This correspondence is even found on the level of plot: at the fateful moment for Troy, the moment when Hector dies, the two most important women of Troy remove their veils. Hecuba lamented and "flung her veil from her" (*Iliad* 22.406–407) and Andromache

> threw far from her head the splendid adornments that bound her hair, her frontlet, her snood, her plaited headband and, to top it all, the headdress that had been given to her by golden Aphrodite on that day when Hector, the one with the waving plume on his helmet, took her by

---

[17] Mazon 1937–1947, 3:103: "Achille compare Troie, la cité inviolée jusqu'à ce jour, à une captive à qui, vainqueur, il arrachera de force son voile."

[18] Nagler 1974:44–63.

[19] On this notion of intact/pure, see Redfield 1975:161.

the hand and led her out from the palace of Eëtion, and he gave countless courtship presents.

Iliad 22.468–472

The removal of these two veils prefigures and, at the same time, attests to the
fall of Troy; the gesture serves as an illustration of the metaphor.

The allusion to Andromache's wedding further accentuates the dramatic
and symbolic nature of the episode. Contrast creates a striking effect: a black
cloud of sorrow engulfs her (*Iliad* 22.466), replacing the brilliant veil, a gift from
Aphrodite, which slips to the ground. The veil that she throws off had been
the visible sign of her status as a virtuous woman and wife. From this moment
forward, deprived of Hector, she is at the mercy of the attacking Greeks.[20] Her
fallen *krēdemnon* corresponds in the feminine sphere to the dishonor of Hector
dragged through the dust.[21] The system of values operating in the metaphor of
the city-woman is thus also expressed in the actions of "reality."

Marriage in battle

On the battlefield, marriage is mentioned explicitly several times. In each
instance, marriage marks a separation between what is playing out in battle
and what happens between men and women in times of peace. At the precise
moment when warriors are slain, Homer evokes the recent or coming marriage
of two Trojans, thus highlighting the relentless threat that hovers over the
warriors in hand-to-hand fighting.

Iphidamas, expiring from the blows of Agamemnon, is presented as a young
groom. The theme of marriage frames his appearance in the poem: he leaves the
bridal chamber (*Iliad* 11.227) for the plains of Troy, where we find him "sleeping
a sleep as it were of bronze, killed in the defense of his comrades, far from his
wedded wife, of whom he had had no joy" (11.241–243). The connection between
the themes of marriage and war is clearly established here, and the differences
are made all the more significant.

Similarly, Othryoneus is killed by Idomeneus as a result of pursuing a
marriage with one of Priam's daughters. In place of the *hedna* 'gifts offered by a
suitor to the parents of a young woman' that he could not offer for the daughter's hand, he promises great feats that will drive away the Greeks. Idomeneus

---

[20]   Hector himself mentioned this threat during their conversation on the ramparts: violence and
slavery await Andromache if Troy falls: "... some Achaean man, one of those men who wear
khitons of bronze, takes hold of you as you weep and leads you away as his prize, depriving you of
your days of freedom from slavery" (*Iliad* 6.454–455).

[21]   See Nagler 1974:50.

defeats him and proposes his own version of a marriage without the customary gifts (*Iliad* 13.381–382):

> So come along with me, that we may make a covenant at the ships about the marriage, and we will not be hard upon you about gifts of wooing.

Transforming the battlefield and the enemy into a scene of marriage negotiations is again a paradoxical way for the poet to refocus the audience's attention on the relevant space of combat. On the plain of Troy where they confront each other, warriors can obtain glory or death, but not a bride. Homer plays with the mix of two different spheres—combat and marriage—to further emphasize the only type of "exchange" possible during times of war.

A final intersection that I will consider is the inversion on the battlefield that allows women to exchange roles with vultures. Twice, in fact, the poet establishes a parallel between the birds and women:

> [The Trojans] who were lying on the plain, more useful now to vultures than to their wives.

Iliad 11.161–162

and

> [T]here will he rot, reddening the earth with his blood, and vultures, not women, will gather round him.

Iliad 11.394–395

In these two passages, Homer manages a remarkable telescoping of two different symbolic planes, which permits us to tease out multiple levels of feminine signifiers. First of all, the reference to erotic exchange with women is clear. Second, women's social role in the rituals of mourning is mentioned.[22] Finally, women's powers of mortification emerge from this overlapping of images.[23] With the putrefying corpses and the patiently waiting vultures, it is difficult not to draw a link to the Sirens who relentlessly await their masculine prey. Reminiscent as well are the similar powers of the Harpies, the Keres, and the female Sphinx. Commenting on this passage—literally "they will be much dearer to the vultures (that is more loved) than to their wives"—Emily Vermeule sees a harbinger of the fate awaiting the women and children of a fallen city.[24] But the multiple layers

---

[22] A mourning woman will "tear her cheeks for grief" (*Iliad* 11.393).

[23] See Vermeule 1979:169 and Chap. 5, "On the Wings of the Morning: the Pornography of Death"; also Kahn 1980.

[24] Vermeule 1979:103.

of meaning in the text are still denser, because, between vultures and women, between men as "prey" and men as "lovers," there are a number of analogies.[25]

Women and vultures operate in opposite poles, corresponding exactly to the opposition between the feminine world and the world of war. Women care for the bodies of dead warriors, washing them, anointing them, applying perfumes, and dressing them,[26] whereas vultures tear these bodies apart and feed on the decomposing flesh. However, looking beyond the surface opposition of the text between women and vultures, certain similarities align women with the scavenging birds. On a deeper level, women and vultures are united by their love of men. And the vulture's love of feasting on men inevitably evokes a somber aspect of femininity: the woman-devourer, the woman-harpy, or the woman-siren with her fields of rotting corpses.

Examination of this series of images makes clear that the space of battle subverts norms by reversing sexual roles: on the battlefield the only marriage possible is with Thanatos, the personification of death with a female face.[27]

War at the Heart of the Opposition between Eros and Thanatos

At the moment of their confrontation, Achilles says to Hector, "Therefore there can be no love between you and me" (*Iliad* 22.265). The power of Eros does, however, intervene at points in this aggressive encounter. Without delving here into an in-depth examination of the relationship between Eros and Thanatos—an examination that would reach well beyond the scope of my work—I will consider only Hector, whose death is the climax of the poem. Hector is, in fact, never so beautiful or so desirable as he is at the moment of his death.

Achilles carefully observes—and perhaps with a certain admiration (*eisoroōn*, *Iliad* 22.321)[28]—Hector's "fair flesh" before driving his spear "through the fleshy part of the neck" (22.321 and 327).[29] After having killed him, he strips off his armor, and it is then that the beauty of Hector's naked body finds its strongest expression (22.369–371):

---

[25] On vultures, see Detienne 1972:47–57.

[26] See Mylonas 1962:478 and Alexiou 1974:10–11.

[27] My primary reference here, as in this chapter as a whole, is J.-P. Vernant's 1981–1982 seminar at the *Collège de France* (Vernant 1982b).

[28] On the meaning of *eisoraō* 'to look upon with admiration, contemplate', see *Iliad* 12.312. Sarpedon says to Glaucus that the Lycians "look up to us as though we were gods"; similarly for 'to look upon with respect', see Eumaeus to Odysseus at *Odyssey* 20.166: "Stranger, are the suitors treating you with more respect?"

[29] On *hapalos*, see p. 26 above and Plato *Symposium* 195D–196B.

The other Achaeans came running up to view his wondrous strength and beauty.[30]

Hector lying in the dust is, in the manner of an erotic partner, "softer to touch" (*malakōteros amphaphasthai*, 22.373) than ever before.[31] His "dark hair" and his "head once so comely" are the last elements of his beauty that the poet mentions and the place where the poet ends the story of Hector on the battlefield.

Passing from the plain of Troy by way of Achilles' camp to the funeral bed prepared inside the walls of the city, Hector's body is subjected to a wide range of punishment, but neither its beauty nor its integrity is damaged. Achilles relentlessly defiles the body, which he drags daily across the ground, but he is unable to deface or mutilate it. A series of interventions by the gods, which play on the overlapping registers of dissimulation and manipulation (anointment with supernatural substances), effectively preserve the corpse (*Iliad* 23.184–191):

> The dogs came not about the body of Hector, for Zeus' daughter Aphrodite kept them off him night and day, and anointed him with ambrosial oil of roses that his flesh might not be torn when Achilles was dragging him about. Phoebus Apollo moreover sent a dark cloud from heaven to earth, which gave shade to the whole place where Hector lay, that the heat of the sun might not parch his body.

Aphrodite and Apollo combine their efforts to keep Hector's body supple and intact by removing the risks of dismemberment and decay.[32] This theme of freshness opposed to dryness underpins the entire story of Hector's body in death. The preserving intervention of Apollo is, in fact, mentioned in two other passages of the poem. The god covers the body with his golden aegis (*Iliad* 24.20–21) to protect it from corruption. Even in death, Hector retains the brilliance and freshness of youth (24.419–421):

> You should come yourself and see how he lies fresh as dew, with the blood all washed away, and his wounds every one of them closed though many pierced him with their spears.

---

[30] See the remarks on this passage in Vernant and Gnoli 1982:59–60.

[31] The notion of handling or touching something conveyed by the verb *amphaphaō* becomes even clearer if we consider the other uses of the verb in the *Odyssey*: 8.215 (Odysseus and his bow); 15.462 (a necklace); 19.475 (Eurycleia when she recognizes Odysseus by the scar on his thigh).

[32] In her work focused on Aphrodite, Deborah Boedeker (1974:23–42) clearly shows that whenever the goddess is called *Dios thugatēr* by the poet, it is always her protective attribute that is being underlined; she is the divine agent who rescues. On the other hand, whenever she is *philommeidēs Aphroditē*, it is her function as the goddess of seduction and sexual union that is being referenced.

The reference to vegetation, *oion eersēeis* 'fresh as dew' or, more precisely, 'as if covered by dew', is not without significance. Indeed, the theme of dew, and more generally the theme of freshness and botanical growth, is in the background of the narrative of Hector throughout the final three books of the *Iliad*, from the moment his mother cries out to him from the Scaean gates until she laments over his funeral bed. Hecuba attempts to dissuade Hector from the certain death awaiting him in a confrontation with Achilles by speaking to him of the life she gave and the branch she had grown (22.87). During the exchange, she bares her breast, which "wipes away memories of sorrow" (*lathikēdēs*, 22.83).

When she next sees him, she again employs a similar image of vegetation to describe the freshness of Hector's preserved body (*Iliad* 24.757–759):

> Yet here you lie all fresh as dew, and comely as one whom Apollo has slain with his painless shafts.

The paradox, as pointed out by Charles Segal,[33] is that the adjective *hersēeis* or *eersēeis*—found elsewhere in the *Iliad* only in a passage describing the coupling of Zeus and Hera in Book 14, where a patch of "dew-bespangled lotus" (14.348) sprouts from the earth—is used to describe Hector's dead body. There is, then, a symbolic vegetative, and more broadly erotic, background to the story of Hector's corpse, since the noun and adjective forms of "dew" are closely associated with life, growth, and beauty. Seeing "in the corpse of her son a beauty like that of dew and flowers,"[34] Hecuba, in a certain way, summarizes the ideal heroic death of a warrior: to die, after a great accomplishment, at the height of youth and beauty.[35]

Hector's body passes from being an object hidden and protected by the gods to an object prepared and displayed by his loved ones in the city of Troy. From *Iliad* 22.361 to 24.759, it is as if nothing has happened: we find Hector lying down, this time on "a bed" (24.720), beautiful in death, just as Paris, when lying in bed, was beautiful in love (3.382, 391–392, 447–448).

It is perhaps here that we find the clearest element of the term-for-term opposition between Paris and Hector that was established in Chapter 1 above. The beauty Paris evokes while he plays the lyre and dances in his bedchamber is, in effect, a sign of cowardice.[36] The freshness of Hector's body, so soft to the touch after being struck down by Achilles (*Iliad* 22.373)[37] and later lying intact

---

[33] See Segal 1971b:70, as well as the remarks in Onians 1954:254.

[34] See Segal 1971b:70.

[35] See Vernant and Gnoli 1982:45–76

[36] See pp. 11–12 above.

[37] This line warrants comparison with the words of Andromache at 24.739, "for your father's hand in battle was not tender."

on the funeral bed, is the sign of his heroism: because of his courage, he remains dear to the gods (24.423–424), who allow his beauty to endure beyond his death and who, more importantly, accentuate this beauty at the precise moment he loses his life.

In the preceding examples, I have elaborated several elements that place war at the heart of the opposition between Eros and Thanatos. The contiguous spheres of sleep, erotic exchange, and death in the epic have already been clearly defined.[38] Eros and Thanatos provoke the same physical and psychological transformations. Erotic desire and death both engulf the heart of those they strike;[39] both subjugate their targets by loosening their knees.

Besides the analogies linking the modes of intervention of love and death, the epic mentality envisions erotic exchange and hand-to-hand combat in the same way, or at least with the same words.[40] Beyond the shared vocabulary, a series of associations, comparisons, images, and metaphors that conflate the erotic realm and the realm of death in war have been uncovered. Finally, and most importantly, the beauty of a warrior, which is central in the system of epic values, is never more forcefully evoked and affirmed than at the moment of his death. The young warrior dying gloriously in the epic is at the intersection of the spheres of Eros and Thanatos, where a reversal is carried out: his attractive, seductive beauty is confirmed at the very moment that his life runs out. This "eroticized" death belongs fully to the masculine, heroic sphere; for the beauty of the deaths of Patroclus and Hector, there is no feminine equivalent.

---

[38] See, in particular, Vermeule 1979:145–177.

[39] Eros: *Iliad* 3.442; 14.294; Thanatos: 5.68; 16.350, etc.

[40] Cf. pp. 25–27 above. I would point out again the double meaning of the verb *lilaiomai* 'strongly desire' that applies sometimes to erotic desire (*Odyssey* 1.15; 9.30, 32; 23.334: Calypso and Circe's desire for Odysseus; *Iliad* 14.331: Zeus' desire for Hera) and sometimes to the rage of battle (*Iliad* 3.133), or the "desire" of spears to feed on human flesh (11.573–574; 15.316–317; 21.168).

4

The Feminine and the Warrior

As a poem of war, the *Iliad* places at the foreground an intense focus on friendship between companions, as well as between combatants. Yet it is also true that, while women are considered "others," conjugal love is often evoked in the Homeric epic. Before attempting to locate the imprint of femininity on the heroic figure, we must first consider the ties that normally unite the warrior with the feminine world.

When Masculine and Feminine Meet

Love, *philotēs*,[1] between men and women clearly brings them together as happy complements: in the *Iliad*, men and women are drawn together by love.[2] Agamemnon states this explicitly when he swears that he did not approach the young Briseïs (*Iliad* 9.132–134):

> And I swear a great oath that I never went up into her couch, nor have been with her after the manner of men and women.[3]

Similarly, Achilles and Odysseus emphasize the importance of the feelings and bonds of marriage and the linking of two lovers united by the "pact"[4]

---

[1] On *philotēs* in general, see Benveniste 1969 1:341–346. On the difficulties of defining this concept in Homeric thought, see Finley 1983:156–162, though it is also useful to nuance the dichotomy—which I think is too clear-cut—that Finley sets up between feelings men have for each other (feelings that are primary and valorized in the eyes of the poet) and feelings men have for women (which are secondary, or even "lukewarm").

[2] References to love between men and women are common in the *Iliad*. For example: Agamemnon and his female captives, *Iliad* 2.232; Helen and Menelaus, 3.139–140; Helen and Paris, 3.441–446; Achilles and Patroclus with their female captives, 9.664–669; the father of Phoenix and his mistress, 9.449–451; Achilles and Briseïs, 24.675–676. In the *Odyssey*, we see Odysseus going to bed with Circe, 10.333–335; with Calypso, 5.226–227; and with Penelope, 23.295–296. We also see Menelaus going to bed with Helen, 4.304–305.

[3] The idea is restated by Odysseus at *Iliad* 9.275–276.

[4] On the question of *philotēs* as a public and solemn pact or oath in marriage and a private one between two lovers, see Taillardat 1982:11–13.

of *philotēs*. Achilles, lamenting Briseïs, responds to Odysseus, who is trying to convince him to return to battle (*Iliad* 9.340–343):

> Are the sons of Atreus the only men in the world who love their wives? Any man of common right feeling will love and cherish her who is his own, as I this woman, with my whole heart, though she was only the prize of my spear.[5]

And when Odysseus formulates his best wishes for Nausicaa he describes a good marriage (*Odyssey* 6.180–185):

> May the gods grant you in all things your heart's desire—husband, house, and a happy, peaceful home; for there is nothing better in this world than that man and wife should be of one mind in a house. It discomfits their enemies, makes the hearts of their friends glad, and they themselves know more about it than any one.[6]

The principal masculine figures of each epic are characterized also by the quality of the bonds that unite them with their wives. To the examples of Achilles and Odysseus, Hector must be added. On two occasions, Andromache brings up the profound nature of the connections that join her and Hector. From the love that unites them, they have born a son, which she reminds him by speaking in the first-person plural (*tekomen*) and emphasizing their shared responsibility: "The child, of whom you and I are the unhappy parents, is as yet a mere infant" (*Iliad* 22.484–485 and 726–727).[7]

Hector is even described by Andromache as her *parakoitēs* 'he who shares her bed' (*Iliad* 6.430). The use of the masculine form of this compound is rare in the epic: "It expresses Andromache's tenderness and love for Hector."[8] Indeed, the bonds between Hector and Andromache are often mentioned in emotional terms. Yet the *philotēs* that connects Hector and Andromache is surpassed by the demands of the heroic ethic: unlike Paris, Hector places his duties as a warrior over his connection to his wife.

Shifting temporarily from the *Iliad* to the *Odyssey*, encounters with women are pivotal to the fate of Odysseus.[9] Aside from the daughter of the Laestrygonians (who is a giant), women both mortal and divine help him, more

---

[5]   On the use and meaning of *alochos* 'wife', the term applied to Briseïs here, see Chantraine 1946–1947:223.

[6]   See Stanford 1968:53.

[7]   In addition, the entire goodbye scene between Hector and Andromache in Book 6 evokes with intensity the tenderness involved in fatherhood and motherhood (6.399–493).

[8]   Chantraine 1946–1947:226: "Il exprime la tendresse et l'amour d'Andromaque pour Hector." *Akoitēs*: *Iliad* 15.91; *Odyssey* 5.120, and 21.88. *Parakoitēs*: *Iliad* 8.156.

[9]   On Odysseus' popularity with women, see the remarks in Stanford 1968:64–65.

or less spontaneously, to find his way home. After detaining him, both Circe and Calypso provide judicious advice to help him carry out his voyage. It is primarily thanks to Nausicaa and her mother Arete that Odysseus is rescued by the Phaeacians. And finally, Penelope is the key to his return to humanity. Reconnecting with the male "bread-eaters" and having recovered with his wife the bonds of marriage, Odysseus is able to regain his full status as the king of Ithaca. Furthermore, Penelope does not appear again in the poem after the night of her reunion with Odysseus. Once Odysseus has recovered his true humanity, Penelope's "restorative" function is no longer required.[10]

The Masculine within the Feminine

"Warriors," writes Seth Benardete, "ought to believe that to be a woman is the worst calamity."[11] The play of insults between combatants makes this claim persuasive. However, the use of the feminine to describe the conduct of a warrior is not uniquely pejorative. Two levels of meaning can be identified: one, wholly negative, where a man is compared to a woman trying to fight; the other, more acceptable, where certain positive qualities of women are attributed to men.

Negative inversions

Insults

In the *Iliad* a series of insults uttered by the warriors themselves compare fighters to—or explicitly call them—women. The most significant of these is used by Thersites (*Iliad* 2.235), then Menelaus (7.96), to shame the Greeks in order to reawaken their courage; each speaker shifts from the masculine to the feminine form of the word "Achaeans":

> "Weakling cowards, Achaean women rather than Achaeans [*Achaïides, ouket' Achaioi*]"

> "vain braggarts, Achaean women, not Achaeans [*Achaïides, ouket' Achaioi*]"

The inversion could not be clearer.

Wanting to return home to moan like children and widows (*Iliad* 2.289–290); treating one's enemy like a woman ignorant of war (7.235–236);[12] being

---

[10] See Foley 1978:20–21.

[11] Benardete 1963:1.

[12] The emphasis is clearly women's characteristic ignorance in matters of war. In this passage, Hector, who is insulting Ajax, presents himself in contrast as one who is knowledgeable.

transformed into a woman; being no longer anything but a cowardly young girl (8.162–163);[13] scratching an opponent with one's arrows, as a simple woman would (11.389);[14] being like a "little girl that comes running to her mother, and begs to be taken up and carried" (16.7–8);[15] shouting insults at an enemy like an enraged woman instead of fighting with bronze (20.252–254);[16] being "as though I were a woman, when I had off my armor in battle," that is, without armor, shield, helmet, or spear (22.124–125)[17]—all are considered forms of weakness that classify the warrior among the feminine and the cowardly.

To this list must be added the passages where an unskilled fighter regresses toward childhood. Arguing like children in the middle of the fray[18] or fleeing the battlefield to throw oneself into the arms of a spouse[19] also signifies an absence of masculinity. The warrior who flees to his wife for safety is rapidly diminished to the level of a child rushing into his mother's arms.

Finally, and this is continuously characteristic of Paris, the man who is more "woman-crazed" (*gunaimanēs*, *Iliad* 3.9; 13.769) than he is a fighter is often likened to a young girl.[20] In any case, this man has no recognized place in the masculine world of the warriors in the *Iliad*, where there is only one possible course of action: to bravely confront one's enemies on the field.

All of these references to feminine attitudes are the exact antithesis of the masculine conduct celebrated and valued by heroic ethic. In this context, femininity is negative, fundamentally inadequate to the world of a warrior; it would do well to be removed from the battlefield.

---

[13] Thus Hector insults Diomedes. The use of the verb *antiteuchō* 'to make in opposition to', which appears only here, is significant: it echoes *antianeirai* (both 'equal to males' and 'enemy of males'), which is used to describe the Amazons; on this point, see Carlier 1980–1981:11. The following line, where Hector calls Diomedes a "miserable doll" before he leaves the battlefield, only reinforces Hector's ironic transformation of Diomedes.

[14] "I care no more than if a girl … had hit me," Diomedes responds to Paris. Here, the archer is explicitly associated with a woman; on this passage, see pp. 9–10 above.

[15] This is Achilles' reproach of Patroclus, when he sees him desolate and crying over the losses of the Greeks. It seems appropriate, however, to see these words more as encouragement to remain strong, rather than as an actual insult.

[16] "Like women who when they fall foul of one another go out and wrangle in the streets" (Aeneas addresses Achilles before their single combat). Here again, masculine conduct is clearly defined: on the battlefield, it is the clash of bronze not words that counts (*Iliad* 20.256–258).

[17] See Redfield 1975:158, who draws a parallel between this passage, where Hector, terrified by the dazzling site of Achilles and his weapons, feels as vulnerable as a woman, and the earlier episode where Hector himself frightens his son with his helmet (6.467–469).

[18] *Iliad* 20.244–245: "And now let there be no more of this prating in mid-battle as though we were children"; Achilles' words to Aeneas echo lines 20.200–201.

[19] Helenus advises Aeneas to rally his companions before "they … fling themselves into the arms of their wives" (*Iliad* 6.81–82).

[20] See Chapter 1, pp. 9–10 above.

Comparisons to female animals

Women and the feminine in general characterize the inadequate warrior. Therefore, the most degrading comparisons to animals are those that include the female dog, the doe, the ewe, or the dove.

The comparison to the ewe is particularly meaningful because it functions on two levels. First, as females, these are weak animals; then, their bleating accentuates the impression of panic, disorder, and an absence of strength that the poet wishes to highlight. This is indeed the case in the following presentation of the two armies (*Iliad* 4.431–436):

> It seemed as though there was not a tongue among them [the Greeks], so silent were they in their obedience; and as they marched the armor about their bodies glistened in the sun. But the clamor of the Trojan ranks was as that of many thousand ewes that stand waiting to be milked in the yards of some rich master of flocks, and bleat incessantly in answer to the bleating of their lambs.[21]

The contrast is striking between the silence of the Greeks and the "bleating" of the Trojans. Here, silence is synonymous with masculinity and muddled noise with femininity.[22] In all of these instances, the females that are chosen are not distinguished by their courage. Having the heart of a doe, being dog faced, cowering like a dove: these, among others, are frequently used insults when the warriors are railing at each other. They are a far cry from the heroic lion.

Parallel to what has already been considered, a segregation exists, then, inside the animal world as well: the female can never serve as the heroic model. During the chariot race, for example, Antilochus excites the energy of his horses, wanting to pass Menelaus, who is racing with Aethe, Agamemnon's mare (*Iliad* 23.408–409):

> You must overtake the horses of the son of Atreus and not be left behind, or Aethe (a female!) who is so fleet will taunt you. Why, my good men, are you lagging?[23]

---

[21] Masculinity and war are in opposition throughout with femininity and nurturing maternity. For the Greeks, the vocabulary of war is predominant; for the Trojans, however, the clamoring and vulnerable nature of the female animals is emphasized.

[22] The same idea is apparent in the simile of the cranes (*Iliad* 3.1–5), well known for the sound of their cries.

[23] The use of *thēlus* in this passage is significant and refers to a functional aspect of the female animal: *thēlus* = 'milk bearing'; Benveniste 1969:1.22–23, 33.

In the human sphere as in the animal sphere, roles are clearly attributed to males and females.[24] Thus the place for females, both human and animal, is inside, where their role is to raise offspring.[25] The place for males is outside, in combat during times of war. In this sense, the feminine gender, when it is applied to men in combat, whether in human or animal form, is an insult marking weakness.

Even beyond the heroic comparison *par excellence*—that of the lion—it is the comparison to the male animal, the stud, that glorifies the warrior (*Iliad* 2.480–483, referring to Agamemnon):

> As some great bull that lords it over the herds upon the plain, even so did Zeus make the son of Atreus stand peerless among the multitude of heroes.

The symbolic background of power relations between the sexes[26] therefore determines the male exchange of insults on the battlefield. While denying the masculinity of the adversary, the insult also detracts from his value.

Overly sophisticated armor

There are few references to men leaving for war with the wrong equipment. A hero's armor might be more or less beautiful or prestigious (his father's weapons, weapons made by a divine hand), but it is usually essentially the same.

One passage from the *Iliad*, however, mentions a warrior whose armor is not fit for use in battle. His armor is like a woman's dress. Too sophisticated, more decorative than functional, it is as useless, when facing the bronze of Achilles, as jewels for stopping a bronze spear (2.872–875):

> [Amphimachus] came into the fight with gold about him, like a girl; fool that he was, his gold was of no avail to save him, for he fell in the river by the hand of the fleet descendant of Aeacus, and Achilles bore away his gold.

Amphimachus' excess, linked with the delicate and refined nature of a woman's adornments, is presented as explicitly feminine. The "weapons" of women are ineffective and inadequate in the context of war. In Aphrodite's misadventure in

---

[24] The Cyclops and Eumaeus keep female animals inside with their young; males are left outside: *Odyssey* 9.237–239 and 14.13–16.

[25] In Homer, *mētēr* can refer to a woman or a goddess with children or a female animal with offspring (for example, *Iliad* 2.313). Cf. Chantraine 1946–1947:238. *Patēr* is not used to refer to animals. This detail was underlined by Redfield 1975:119: the father is the "social" and "cultural" parent. His role only exists among humans. The mother has a much greater role in the natural realm.

[26] See Guiraud 1978:105.

Book 5, the brilliantly adorned goddess is immediately driven off by Diomedes. Is there, in Amphimachus, a pale reflection of the eminently feminine figure Aphrodite? One thing is for sure; when Amphimachus dies at the hand of Achilles, the gold in his armor is restored to the normal channels of war: the victor will claim the armor of his adversary. When armor takes on the literal qualities of women's finery, the man who wears it can no longer remain a part of the community of warriors.

Positive comparisons

Positive comparisons to women are, of course, less common. The heroic ethic, closely centered upon the notion of masculinity, clearly shies away from favorably comparing men to women.

The undaunted tenacity of the Achaeans and the courage of the Trojans, who clash without either army being able to gain an advantage, are compared only once to the qualities of a woman (*Iliad* 12.433–435):

> And as some truthful woman weighs wool in her balance and sees that
> the scales be true for she would gain some pitiful earnings for her little
> ones, even so was the fight balanced evenly between them.

This is an extraordinary comparison: the woman is labeled as *alēthēs* 'truthful' rather than careful, and the relationship between the balance and the truth is underlined. Commenting on this passage, Marcel Detienne writes: "If the female worker in the *Iliad* is described as *alēthēs*, it is almost certainly because she is holding a balance, the symbol and instrument of justice. This is further evidence of the close and fundamental association between the balance and the truth."[27]

Furthermore, this woman holding the balance is associated with Zeus, who uses a golden scale to decide the fate of the two armies (*Iliad* 8.69–72); and beyond the relationship between the balance and the truth, it is also important to note the specific relationship that seems to exist between women and the truth.[28] It is significant that the woman of the simile occupies the position of judge and arbiter, acting as a kind of magistrate.[29]

The other undeniably positive aspect of women—their maternal nature—provides a second level of comparison that valorizes the warrior.

---

[27] Detienne 1973:39n57: "Si l'ouvrière de l'*Iliade* est qualifiée d'*alēthēs*, c'est très vraisemblablement parce qu'elle tient une balance, symbole et instrument de justice. C'est un témoignage supplémentaire de la complémentarité étroite et fondamentale de la balance et de la 'vérité'."

[28] Cf. p. 72 below.

[29] Detienne (1973:39n57) notes the relationship between the epithet *alēthēs* and the participle *isazousa*.

From the start, one point is worth attention: in the *Iliad*, certain warriors, including some of the greatest, have their mothers near them, close enough almost to speak with them. Obviously, the relationship between a mother and her hero-son is most perfect in the case of Thetis and Achilles. The "the son of lovely-haired Thetis" (*Iliad* 4.512; 16.860) is assisted by his mother from the first through the last book of the poem. On the Trojan side, Aeneas and Hector also meet with their mothers.[30]

The relationship between Aeneas and Aphrodite most resembles that between Achilles and Thetis. Aeneas is the most valiant of the Trojans after Hector. He engages in single combat with the principal Greek heroes: Diomedes in Book 5, Idomeneus in Book 13, and finally Achilles in Book 20. He is honored by the Trojans as Hector's equal (*Iliad* 5.467–468), and even as a god (11.58). And his divine birth further adds to his prestige: his mother is Aphrodite, a goddess superior in rank to Thetis (20.105).[31]

Hector's mother is a mortal. The possibilities for Hecuba to intervene are therefore limited: she can only encourage Hector to seek shelter and rest inside the walls of Troy or beg him to renounce his battle with Achilles.

Maternal love toward the major heroes is addressed almost exclusively in these passages,[32] and it is expressed by gestures that highlight the strong physical connection that unites a mother and her son.

Beyond the words exchanged, the body, in fact, speaks in particularly important ways during conversations between mothers and sons in the *Iliad*. Thus Thetis rushed to be with a weeping Achilles, sat in front of him, and "caressed him with her hand" (*Iliad* 1.361). Later, when he is weeping over the body of Patroclus, she hears his cries (18.35), comes near to assist him (18.70), and holds his head in her hands (18.71).[33] And finally, sitting near him again while caressing him lightly, she persuades him with affectionate words to relinquish Hector's body (24.125–137).

In these three examples, physical closeness is clearly underlined by the poet: Achilles regains the tenderness and softness of a mother's gestures

---

[30] Hector: inside the city of Troy (6.251–285); beneath the ramparts (22.78–79). Aeneas: on the battlefield (5.311–343).

[31] See the remarks in Dumézil 1982:114–117.

[32] The only example of a young infant in the arms of his mother is Astyanax. The poet, however, does not particularly emphasize Andromache's maternal gestures. The child is also carried by a nurse; after cuddling him, Hector himself hands him to Andromache (*Iliad* 6.399–403, 466–474, 482–483).

[33] Here, Thetis makes the initial gesture of the female lamentation ritual (*Iliad* 24.212; Alexiou 1974:10). This anticipatory gesture reinforces the weight of Achilles' statement several verses later asserting that his own fate is attached to Patroclus' death; Achilles is presented as Thetis' future dead child (*Iliad* 18.89).

toward a young child when Thetis is near him. Affectionate words and multiple reminders of parental bonds are also predominant in these dialogues between mother and son.[34]

The same is true for Aeneas, although the context that allows him to meet with his mother is different: Aphrodite is not there to console Aeneas, but rather to save him after he is wounded by Diomedes. Aphrodite's intervention warrants a close examination (*Iliad* 5.311–316):

> And now Aeneas, king of men, would have perished then and there, had not his mother, Zeus' daughter Aphrodite, who had conceived him by Anchises when he was herding cattle, been quick to mark, and thrown her two white arms about the body of her dear son. She protected him by covering him with a fold of her own fair garment, lest some Danaan should drive a spear into his breast and kill him.

First, note Aphrodite's attentiveness as she watches over her son. To protect him, she performs a series of maternal actions: taking him into her arms, holding him against her bosom and navel. The arms of a mother are like a city wall: Aphrodite literally puts herself between Aeneas and the Greeks. She shields him with her arms. Additionally, the fold (*ptugma*, *Iliad* 5.315) in the garment where she hides Aeneas reinforces the idea of the depth in which she enfolds her son. This depth is like the symbolic security of a child near a mother's womb. Aeneas is transformed back into a young child, incorporated within his mother's body, hidden and cradled in her arms. When Aphrodite is, in turn, injured in the arm by Diomedes, she can no longer carry her son; she opens her arms and drops him (5.343).

The initial closeness of mother and son is itself the subtext for the conversations that certain heroes have with their mothers. In this respect, Hecuba and Hector are significant. When she meets him in front of the palace, Hecuba rushes and "[takes] his hand within her own," she forcefully attaches herself to him (*Iliad* 6.254). Later, she will try to dissuade Hector from challenging Achilles by reminding him, through both word and gesture, of the maternal bonds that connect them (*Iliad* 22.80–83):

> ... she bared her bosom and pointed to the breast which had suckled him. "Hector," she cried, weeping bitterly the while, "Hector, my son, spurn not this breast, but have pity upon me too: if I have ever given you comfort from my own bosom ...

---

[34] *Mētēr*: *Iliad* 1.351–352, 357; 18.35, 70, etc.; *pais*: 18.71, 89, etc.; *teknon*: 1.362, 414; 18.73, etc.

Hecuba's gesture is solemn: by showing her breast, a symbol of maternity, and by making reference to its nourishment and protection, she reminds Hector, just before his death, that he was once a young child, and that even the bravest warrior remains, in a certain sense, a child for his mother.

Thus, at the height of the war, the hero is curiously sometimes found in the situation of a child being protected by his mother. His masculinity, however, does not seem to be challenged in this scenario. Rather, a few splashes of femininity upon the heroic figure serve to bring the contours of his masculinity into sharper focus.

The theme of maternity, beyond even the mother-son relationship, functions on yet another level in the *Iliad*: it is used to describe the protection that a warrior can provide to a comrade who is injured or in danger. The hero then becomes a mother to his companion. Ajax and Teucer, like mother and son, fight in this manner (*Iliad* 8.266–272):

> Ninth came Teucer with his bow, and took his place under cover of the shield of Ajax son of Telamon. When Ajax lifted his shield Teucer would peer round, and when he had hit any one in the throng, the man would fall dead; then Teucer would hasten back to Ajax as a child to its mother, and again duck down under his shield. [35]

Ajax's shield here is like the maternal womb,[36] or at least like the garment a mother uses to hide a child. Even if the comparison of the shield and the womb is only suggested, the image, which is clearly maternal, retains its force. In another comparison from Book 5, Ajax's shield has the same function as Aphrodite's *peplos* 'garment'. To protect Aeneas, Aphrodite hides him in the folds of her radiant garments (*Iliad* 5.315); to protect Teucer, Ajax hides him under his radiant shield (8.272). The vocabulary and the movement suggested by these images are identical.

Elsewhere, Menelaus is compared to a mother, an animal here, protecting her young (*Iliad* 17.4–6):

> As a cow stands lowing over her first calf, even so did yellow-haired Menelaus bestride Patroclus.

In this comparison, the poet clearly develops the theme of maternity: Menelaus is a mother, Patroclus a new-born calf. Is this a poetic way to emphasize

---

[35] The comparison, however, is not without ambiguity: Teucer is the bastard brother of Ajax; he is an archer who fights from a hiding place. While the comparison of Ajax to a mother does not diminish his virtue, it is not certain that the same goes for Teucer.

[36] Loraux 1981b:48n60.

Menelaus' concern and the fragility of Patroclus? Or is it simply a way to say that Patroclus has just been cut down at the height of his youth? Patroclus is the only warrior who drifts a little from the purely warlike model of masculinity, without, however, transgressing its limits; Patroclus' gentleness is mentioned both by a woman (Briseïs, *Iliad* 19.300) and his companions in battle (Menelaus, 17.671–672).[37] Without going so far as to claim that Patroclus occupies the place of a woman with Achilles,[38] there are certain peculiar aspects of his character worth pointing out. It is Achilles who calls him a "little girl" (*kourē nēpiē*, 16.7–8)[39] when he sees him lamenting the Achaeans' misfortunes. During the embassy scene in Book 9, Patroclus prepares the libations and instruments of sacrifice, while Achilles cuts the meat (9.201–220). Patroclus also treats Eurypylus' wounds. When the doctors Podalirius and Machaon are absent, Patroclus replaces them, using helpful *pharmaka* 'drugs' (11.844–848). In both the Trojan and Greek camps, women are never shown tending to the wounded. War is strictly the business of men, and in this sense Patroclus, the gentlest of the Greeks, represents the "positive" side of feminine virtues: food preparation, healing, tenderness.

If Patroclus is the less brutally masculine and more tender of the Achaean heroes, he is not likened to a woman (recall his *aristeia* 'accomplishments' in Book 16). Instead, he represents a positive tenderness and cannot at any point be considered a parallel to Paris.

As one final intersection of maternity and war, a mother's suffering serves as a model to describe the endurance of a warrior. There is an intensely feminine suffering for a woman in labor or a mother who loses her children. The physical and mental pains of women appear in the *Iliad* as the extreme limits of suffering and, in this respect, can qualify the resistance of the warrior as positive.

In a recent study, Nicole Loraux shed light on a strange passage from the *Iliad* that compares the pain of the injured Agamemnon to that of a woman in labor (11.267–272):[40]

... but when the blood had ceased to flow and the wound grew dry, the pain [*odunē*] became great. As the sharp pangs which the Eileithuiai, goddesses of childbirth, daughters of Hera and dispensers of cruel pain, send upon a woman when she is in labor—even so sharp were the pangs of the son of Atreus.

---

[37] See Romilly 1979:19–20.
[38] As Beye 1974:88 argues, claiming that Patroclus does for Achilles what women do for others. But can we conclude from this that Patroclus is acting as a woman?
[39] See n. 15 above in this chapter.
[40] Loraux 1981b:54–57.

Odunē should be understood here in the full sense of the term: the word refers to sharp, shooting, heavy, exhausting pain[41]—all characteristics of the pain of childbirth. In this way, "the masculine universe of the Achaean combatants ... attributes the suffering of a woman in labor to the king of kings among the heroes."[42]

In the same way, Achilles chooses to speak of feminine suffering to Priam to encourage him to stay alive. By reminding him that even the inconsolable mother and symbol of maternal suffering Niobe "had to think about eating" (*Iliad* 24.602), Achilles asserts that there is no greater pain than a mother's suffering and presents Niobe as a valid model for men as well. We will return to this point at greater length in the third part of this volume.

₪

The foregoing mapping of heroism allows us to propose three levels of interpretation.

First, on the surface level of the text, there is a maximum separation between the world of warriors and the world of women, a distance clearly illustrated by even the geography of the *Iliad*: the open plain of Troy and the city of Ilion enclosed inside its walls. The young warrior within the ramparts loses his status as a hero if he is unable to maintain an established distance between his original sphere and that of Aphrodite.

Second, if we consider only the battlefield, we see that the feminine, far from being absent, is on the contrary clearly recognizable in more than one passage. On a primary level, femininity obviously serves as a foil: the most significant insults are those that compare the warrior to a woman or female animal, obvious symbols of weakness. On a secondary level, the feminine also emerges as a model in the surprising figure of the maternal warrior, the hero who endures pain like a woman giving birth.

Narrowing the field of observation still further to the heroic site *par excellence*, the body of the warrior, we find a more deeply complex relationship between his masculine nature and what would seem to be its absolute opposite: the world of women and love. There is a permanent slippage between the level of beauty that provokes fear and the level of beauty that awakens desire; the warrior's body does not only emit warlike signals. At the most intense

---

[41] On this point, see the detailed remarks in Mawet 1979:37–51.

[42] Loraux 1981b:56: "l'univers masculin des combattants achéens ... attribue les souffrances d'une accouchée à celui qui, parmi les héros, est le roi le plus roi." While Agamemnon is the only one described by such a comparison, he is also the only one who pushes his cruelty to the point of envisioning the death of Trojans still in their mother's womb: "Let us not spare a single one of them—not even the child unborn and in its mother's womb" (*Iliad* 6.57–58); see Segal 1971b:11.

moments of war, the heroic and the erotic are joined in the hero's body. It is at these moments that, by appropriating portions of positive femininity while maintaining a distance, the wholly masculine ideology of the *Iliad* constructs its heroic specificity.

Part II

Femininity in the Epic

1

Women in the Epic

Be that as it may, there is no mistaking the fact that Homer fully reveals
what remained true for the whole of antiquity, that women were held
to be naturally inferior and therefore limited in their function to the
production of offspring and the performance of household duties,
and that the meaningful social relationships and the strong personal
attachments were sought and found among men.[1]

This assertion by Moses I. Finley needs to be qualified, as the natural inferiority of women is not so clearly confirmed by Homer, nor is it "fully revealed."
A close reading of the text uncovers a certain number of problematic, or at least
ambiguous, features linking the heroism of warriors and feminine virtues. The
preconceived notion that masculinity is exclusively "positive" and femininity
exclusively "negative" does not fully account for the complexity of epic values,
which are certainly not so clear-cut.

Of course, a rapid glance at the activities reserved for women quickly shows
the extent and limitations of their social position and power. Examining the
text closely and considering the symbolic meanings that function in metaphors
and comparisons will show that the role of women is not strictly confined to a
specific domain nor entirely excluded from men's sphere of influence. Let us
then outline the sometimes blurry contours of the female figure in the epic.

Women and Epic Values

Ideological background

If there is an exclusively masculine sphere, one that is portrayed only as masculine, it is surely that of heroism. There, women have no place. The Homeric
warrior effectively has the ability within himself to rise above his ordinary
nature; and when he does transform himself from *anthrōpos* into *hērōs*, the

---

[1] Finley 1978b:132.

combatant in the *Iliad* is situated exclusively and definitively in the masculine sphere. For women, there is no equivalent. They do not possess the duality that would allow them to access a superior state. They remain women, as M. I. Finley writes: "'hero' has no feminine gender in the age of heroes."[2]

Women belong definitively to the category of mortals, the community of *anthrōpoi*. There is not a recognized, celebrated means by which to overcome, through some form of excellence, so as to access an intermediary status between human weakness and the all-powerful gods. For the male, this possibility exists through the path of heroism.[3]

In this way, the delineation of the spaces reserved for men and women, mentioned above,[4] corresponds to the demands of epic morals: war is exclusively the business of men (*andres*); peace is everyone's business, both men and women.

Heroes are the sons of heroes, recapitulations of their fathers; they maintain the masculinity of their ancestors. While a woman might sometimes be the daughter of a hero, she cannot, under any circumstances, maintain the level of glory of her male ancestors. Her only hope, and sole duty, is to be mother to heroes. Moreover, her sons will act as heroes in order to defend her, as well as the other women of the community.[5]

The socio-political system

Even though Helen, Clytemnestra, and Penelope are queens, they do not have any independent power. Their importance comes solely from being the wives of kings. Their status is determined by that of their husbands, just as before their marriages it had been determined by that of their fathers.

Whether legitimate wife or simple concubine of servile origins, a woman exists only in relation to the man to whom she is attached. Agamemnon plans to bring Chryseïs with him to Mycenae; Priam has numerous concubines in his palace; both have an official partner who is more queen than wife.

Whether mistress, mother of children, queen, or "preferred wife," the woman remains always defined by the man with whom she lives: "A woman's status like that of a son, legitimate or bastard, depends in large measure on the

---

[2] Finley 1978b:25.
[3] See Benardete 1963:1–5, who shows clearly that there can be no heroes except among the *andres*. In the same sense, he points out that the divine epithet can only be used for the *andres*, and never for the *anthrōpoi*; Achilles, for example, is *theios anēr* (*Iliad* 16.798). On the battlefield, instances of "be men" (*aneres este*) are frequent: 8.174; 15.487, 561, 661, 734; 16.270; 17.185.
[4] See Part 1, Chapter 1 above.
[5] See Redfield 1975:119–120.

timē, the honor that the head of the family recognizes in her."[6] Contrary to the man, whose status is simultaneously that of king, warrior, hero, and father, the woman can only be a spouse—legitimate or not—and live in the *oikos* 'domain, house' of the man.

War

We have already seen the ways the *Iliad* presents women as ill-equipped for war. Women are both at stake to be defended and prey to be attained. Outside Troy, Hector tries to defend Andromache and the women of Troy, while Achilles tries to take possession of them (e.g. *Iliad* 9.327).[7]

For women and children, slavery is the trade-off for war. Briseïs and Chryseïs, for example, are "taken with the spear."[8] Women figure often as prizes: for example, Agamemnon promises Achilles seven tripods, twelve horses, and seven excellent women workers (*Iliad* 9.264–272). Elsewhere, a woman is "valued ... at four oxen" (23.705). In the *Odyssey*, Eurymedousa, who had been taken from Apeira, is given as a gift to Alcinous (7.8–11). Men are either killed or made the object of ransom, as in the case of Lycaon, whom Achilles sells and sends away to Lemnos (21.40; and see 6.46–50 for Adrastus, and 10.378–381 for Dolon).

For women, the distinguishing characteristic is the potential to be an object of prey; for men, it is the ability to defend themselves or attack. As James Redfield correctly observes, a woman, who might belong to one man and then later to another (the wives of the Trojan commanders will again become companions of choice for the Achaean heroes), is a type of "permanent child."[9] Andromache, for that matter, tells Hector explicitly that he is a father, a mother, a brother, and a husband for her all at the same time (*Iliad* 6.429–430). Insofar as they lack the power and the cultural means to defend themselves, women regress back into childhood in times of war. Women, children, and old men, then, are "marginalized" and excluded from this type of agonistic society.[10]

For the victors, war allows men to earn great *kleos* 'glory' and allows women to preserve their freedom. For the vanquished, defeat leads to death for men, or, in any case, dishonor, and slavery for women. This change in scale, this difference in worldview between male and female, is clearly expressed by Hector

---

[6] Vernant 1974:68: "Le statut des femmes comme celui des fils, légitimes ou bâtards, dépend donc dans une large mesure de la *timē*, de l'honneur qui leur est reconnu par le chef de famille."

[7] See also Mazon 1967:296; Beye 1974:87–88.

[8] There are numerous references in the *Iliad* to slavery of women and children—for example, Andromache and Astyanax: 6.429–430 and 460–465; 22.484 and following; 24.725–774.

[9] Redfield 1975:120; see also Avezzù 1983:87.

[10] See, too, Priam's evocation of the horrifying scene of his fate and that of the women and children of Troy, should Hector disappear: *Iliad* 22.59–76; and see the women, children, and old men on the shield of Achilles: 18.514–515.

and Andromache in Book 6. When evoking Hector's death, Andromache thinks immediately of her own loss and that of her son (6.407–413), while Hector envisions the fall of Troy (6.441–449).

Requirements of a Virtuous Woman in the Epic

Three feminine statuses are frequently mentioned by the warriors at Troy: the mother, the legitimate spouse/concubine, and the mistress. Of course, of the three, the mother seems to occupy the most influential place. One need only recall the importance of Thetis, mother of Achilles, or Aphrodite, mother of Aeneas. Even in the thick of the fray, when the virgin Athena protects Menelaus or Odysseus, she is compared to a mother who watches over her children (*Iliad* 4.130–131; 23.782–783). As Ajax says just after losing the foot race to Odysseus, Athena is the goddess who "watches over Odysseus and stands by him as though she were his own mother" (23.782–782).

The place of women

The primary function of women was to have children and to raise them so that they might later become warriors. As a good mother and wife, the woman had to stay in her place—that is, inside the home, or, when there was no home (in the case of Briseïs, for example), inside the tent. The *Iliad* offers no example of a mortal woman truly leaving her domain, in the strict sense of the term, as a brief look at the movements of the three major women in the poem will verify.[11]

After quarrelling with Achilles, Agamemnon orders his attendants to go to Achilles' tent to apprehend Briseïs (*Iliad* 1.322–323); they do so, and Achilles requests that Patroclus bring the girl out to them (1.337); Patroclus enters the tent and brings back Briseïs (1.346). Briseïs then passes from one interior to another. When Agamemnon later returns her, he swears "she has remained in my tents inviolate" (19.263).

Helen is in the great hall of the palace when Iris comes to arouse in her the desire to see Menelaus (*Iliad* 3.125); she is in her bedchamber when Hector enters looking for Paris (6.321 and 323–324). Her last appearance in the poem shows her crying over Hector in his bedchamber, along with Hecuba and Andromache (24.719–775).

When looking for Andromache, Hector names the places where he is likely to find her: among her sisters, with her sisters-in-law, or in the temple (*Iliad*

---

[11] There are a number of other examples I could cite: *Iliad* 18.495–496: on the shield of Achilles, woman are represented standing in doorways and men in the agora (18.497), or 19.260: the female captives Agamemnon offers as gifts to Achilles are then kept inside Achilles' tent (19.280).

6.376–380)—that is, in the company of women. At the moment of Hector's death, Andromache is "in an inner part of the house" (22.440), occupied with her weaving. The domestic space of the household is, without doubt then, the site to which women are confined.[12]

The Trojan woman, and specifically Hecuba and Andromache, are seen only once outside the city gates: when they surround Priam's chariot, which carries Hector's corpse (24.714). But the funerary rituals take place inside the city walls.[13]

Indeed, the ultimate boundary for the movement of women in Troy is the ramparts.[14] This is where Hecuba begs Hector not to confront Achilles. Moreover, two of the most important scenes of the *Iliad* take place on the ramparts: in Book 3, when Helen names the Achaean commanders for Priam, and in Book 6, when Hector and Andromache part. The ramparts are a privileged site of intersection between the masculine and feminine worlds.

The case of Helen, who meets with the "Trojan leaders gathered on the rampart" (*Iliad* 3.153), is remarkable in this regard. There in the presence of men (*hēgētores* 'leaders'), Helen will relieve the poet.[15] We see in this scene a two-fold disruption of the orthodox distribution of male and female spaces: while the rampart is the seat of the leaders who are too old to fight (3.150), their only possible link to the battlefield, it is also here that a woman portrays the Greek heroes making their way to battle, singing of their courage.

So, too, the only meeting of Hector and Andromache takes place in this intermediary space. The rampart provides the necessary conditions for Hector—the incarnation of the authentic warrior—to have a private conversation expressing his personal feelings (romantic, paternal) while the battle continues on the plains. And here Andromache can intervene in matters of war by giving her husband military advice (*Iliad* 3.433–434).[16]

Are the walls of Troy the only possible meeting place for the world of battle and the "interior" world, a blurred space that, while temporarily suspending the action, merges the masculine and the feminine?

[12] Vernant 1974:160–163.

[13] It is, however, important to point out that women are permitted a relative level of freedom in the epic. Indeed, we see them circulating in the streets: Andromache and Helen go freely to the ramparts, even if accompanied by two attendants.

[14] Cassandra is the exception. She climbs to the top of the citadel, where she sees her father bringing back Hector's body, *Iliad* 24.700.

[15] See Vidal-Naquet 1975:32; see pp. 80–81 below.

[16] See also p. 78 below.

Activities of women

Women were responsible for domestic affairs inside the home, the *oikos*.[17] Their principal activity was spinning or weaving. Throughout the two epics, we see women sitting at their looms. Helen (*Iliad* 3.125–128, and 6.323–324), Andromache (22.440, 510–511), and Penelope (*Odyssey* 19.148–150, among others), as well as Calypso (5.61–62), Circe (10.221–223), and Arete (6.306, 7.234–235) are described with distaff in hand. Weaving is truly the essential activity for women; in a way, it defines them as such. Thus Polites, a companion of Odysseus, can exclaim at the threshold of the house of Circe, about which he knows nothing (*Odyssey* 10.226–228):

> There is some one inside working at a loom and singing most beauti-fully; the whole place resounds with it, let us call her and see whether she is woman or goddess.

Other activities incumbent on women include dyeing fabrics (*Iliad* 4.141–142), washing clothing (*Iliad* 22.153–155; *Odyssey* 6.90–95), preparing baths (*Iliad* 22.444; *Odyssey* 3.464–466, 4.252, 5.265, 19.386–392), and preparing food (*Iliad* 11.625–640, 14.5–8, 18.559–560).

Modesty and feminine love

While the primary Achaean commanders are surrounded by numerous female captives who are usually their mistresses (Agamemnon and Chryseïs, *Iliad* 1.112–115; Achilles and Briseïs, 1.184–185, etc.), the two adulterous women of the epic (Clytemnestra and Helen) are condemned because their infidelity is a source of danger, and even war, for the kingdom.

Polygamy is unsuitable for women. They are praised, on the other hand, for their chastity and modesty. Consequently, Penelope has her two attendants at her side when she goes down to the hall where the suitors are feasting, and before appearing in front of them, she always pulls her veil over her cheeks (*Odyssey* 1.330–334; 18.182–184: "[The servants] must be with me when I am in the hall; I am not going among the men alone; it would not be proper for me to do so"). Similarly, the model young woman in the *Odyssey*, Nausicaa, is constantly accompanied by her attendants; two of them even sleep in front of the door to her room (*Odyssey* 6.18–19). Her decency extends to the point of prohibiting her from speaking of her marriage in front of her father (6.66–67).

---

[17] For a comprehensive treatment of this question, see Mossé 1983, Chap. 1: "La femme au sein de l'*oikos*."

Modesty is also required of goddesses: while Poseidon, Hermes, and Apollo delight in laughter at the spectacle of Ares and Aphrodite chained to their adulterous bed, "the goddesses stayed at home all of them for shame" (*Odyssey* 8.324).[18]

Making proper use of sexuality, for women, means above all to obey—the rules of chastity, fidelity, and modesty, in regard to the exterior world and strangers, and, in the end, the desires of their husbands. Helen, who seems hostile to Paris' desire when she chastises him for his cowardice during his duel with Menelaus, ends up submitting and sharing her bed (*Iliad* 3.447). Similarly, Andromache obeys Hector without protest in the famous farewell scene (6.490–492):

Go, then, within the house, and busy yourself with your daily duties, your loom, your distaff, and the ordering of your servants; for war is man's matter ...

The parentheses on the ramparts closes: Andromache returns to her proper place.

The daughter submits to the father, the wife to the husband, and, when the master is absent, the mother submits to the son. Thus Telemachus orders Penelope on two occasions to return to her legitimate sphere and to leave him, the man of the house, to direct the affairs of the palace. In Book 1 of the *Odyssey*, when Phemius, the bard of Ithaca, sings of the "return from Troy," Penelope asks him to stop; but Telemachus says to her (*Odyssey* 1.356–359):

Go, then, within the house and busy yourself with your daily duties, your loom, your distaff, and the ordering of your servants; for speech is man's matter, and mine above all others—for it is I who am master here.

The same thing happens when she intervenes during the contest of the bow. Later in the epic, Telemachus again orders Penelope, in identical terms, to

---

[18] On the meanings of words ending in *-teros* in Homer, see Chantraine 1958–1963 1:254–259; at its origins, the suffix *-teros* was used especially as a way of marking opposition: "Une forme comme θηλύτεραι, θηλυτεράων, etc., dans des formules (θ 234, Θ 520 ; λ 386, Ψ 166 ; λ 434, ο 422, ω 202) précise plus nettement que θῆλυς l'opposition entre les deux sexes ("Forms like θηλύτεραι, θηλυτεράων, etc. in formulas (θ 234, Θ 520 ; λ 386, Ψ 166 ; λ 434, ο 422, ω 202) specify more clearly than θῆλυς the opposition between the two sexes") (257). On feminine modesty and "shame," see Pomeroy 1976:27 and Redfield 1975:118.

return to the house (21.350–353).[19] In both cases, she obeys, submitting to the authority of her son.

In the epic, the virtuous woman remains at home taking care of her weaving, the education of her children, and the management of her husband's *oikos*. In masculine spaces such as war, the assembly, banquets, or during the trials of the suitors, she has no place—except when she herself is put up for auction, a prize for marriage or reward for accomplishments.

If women are so strictly confined to these domains of well-codified activities, it is because they can be the source of trouble, danger, and malevolence. It is because certain vices are inherent in their nature.

The toxicity of women

The different examples of reprehensible feminine conduct all apply, more or less directly, to women who use their powers of seduction and attraction in improper ways, women whose power of erotic attraction is excessively displayed and evil-minded.

In the *Iliad*, one woman (Helen) and two goddesses (Aphrodite, of course, and Hera) are sources of danger and sometimes disaster. The ambivalence provoked by women is fully expressed in Priam's remarks as he looks upon Helen (3.156–160):

> There is no way to wish for retribution that Trojans and strong-greaved Achaeans should endure so much and so long, for the sake of a woman so marvelously and divinely lovely. Still, fair though she be, let them take her and go, or she will breed sorrow for us and for our children after us.

Helen's seductiveness is irresistible, since all men (both Trojans and Greeks) are subject to its law. The only Achaean who seems clearly to condemn the importance granted to Helen is Achilles. But Achilles is a superior hero, a man concerned only with his glory. While his anger does erupt over Briseïs, he feels it less over the loss of a woman than over the dispossession of his honor. Compared to the death of Patroclus, having Briseïs by his side seems not to have any importance (*Iliad* 19.58–60).[20] For Achilles, war and friendship come ahead of love, even sincere love, for a woman. Is it not Helen, a woman whom Achilles

---

[19] If we compare this passage, the preceding passage (*Odyssey* 1.356–359), and the nearly identical passage from the *Iliad* (cf. p. 59 above), we see that the only modifications to the formula used are the substitutions of *muthos* 'speech' (*Odyssey* 1.358), *toxos* 'bow' (*Odyssey* 21.352), and *polemos* 'war' (*Iliad* 6.492), three terms belonging to the masculine sphere.

[20] On Briseïs, see Farron 1979:27–30.

calls "dreadful" (19.325), who ultimately causes the death of Patroclus? This radical rejection of Helen, whom all other men venerate, is unique in the *Iliad*. It is as if Achilles, the irresistible warrior, cannot bear for another figure to exercise power over men, though in her case it be by means of seduction, another irresistible attraction and subject worthy of song.

For here we find the true danger of women: they seduce and they deceive. When Hera wants to temporarily stop the aid that Zeus has been providing for the Trojans, her irresistible weapon is erotic seduction. With the help of Aphrodite, she provokes in Zeus an irrepressible desire for her. The whole account of this divine union is framed by the theme of trickery and seduction.[21] Agamemnon encapsulates Hera's feminine ruse: "Hera, a woman, beguiled him" (*Iliad* 19.97). There is no better way to summarize the duplicity and the power of women.[22]

Of course, Aphrodite is not forgotten: she is the one responsible for Helen's kidnapping; she deceives with her flattering words;[23] she is crafty (*Iliad* 3.405) and dispenses "costly sensual pleasures" (24.30).

Women can be a danger through the erotic attraction they arouse and through the deaths they cause: in war (Helen); through murder directly (Clytemnestra); or through deceptive seduction (the Sirens).

The disappointed woman, having failed to seduce, can exact treacherous revenge: thus the case of Anteia, who fell in love with Bellerophon (*Iliad* 6.160–166). Finally, women who no longer respect domestic order, who "[leave] the house" (*Odyssey* 20.6–8) to sleep with the enemies of their former masters, are treacherous, as in the case of Penelope's maids.[24]

---

[21] Hera wonders "how she might trick [Zeus'] thinking" (*Iliad* 14.160). Later Sleep lets Poseidon know that Zeus is no longer watching, because "Hera has beguiled him into going to bed with her" (14.360). Zeus will end up reproaching her afterwards for her trickery (15.14); see Detienne 1973:64–65.

[22] The use of *thēlus*, rare in the *Iliad*, is particularly interesting here: it suggests the idea of a kind of 'blemish' and feminine inferiority, even among goddesses; cf. p. 41, n. 23 above.

[23] Of the five uses of *ēperopeuō* in the *Iliad*, four are reserved for the domain of sensuality and eroticism (Aphrodite: 3.399, 5.349; Paris: 3.39, 13.769). The only other one describes Antilochus' ruse during the chariot race (23.605).

[24] It must be pointed out that the insult reserved for all these adulterous and immodest women is "bitch." Helen: *Iliad* 3.180, 344, 356 and *Odyssey* 4.145. Hera: *Iliad* 8.483 and 18.396. Clytemnestra: *Odyssey* 11.424, 427. Aphrodite: *Odyssey* 8.319. Melantho: *Odyssey* 19.91. Disloyal servants: *Odyssey* 19.354 and 372. See Loraux 1981c:102n136–105.

2

The Specificity of Women

Is it possible to bring to light the specifics of feminine nature in the *Iliad*? Beyond the apparent oppositions that posit femininity as the simple, if not simplistic, negative of masculinity, does Homeric epic paint a feminine world in and of itself? I will attempt to respond to this question by choosing to consider the physical appearance of women (their bodies, their beauty) and their speech.

Is it necessary to outline that such an approach will stumble, from the outset, upon the problem of formulaic epithets, which have their own distinctive character? That this particular character is encoded within a complex set of values that change, at the discretion of the narrative structure, the scope of a particular epithet within the epic tradition? That sometimes an epithet is used in a line for purely metrical reasons, its proper meaning relatively diminished, which allows for another adjective to be just as easily substituted?[1]

In fact, nothing is more full of meaning in a psychological inquiry than those things that, because they belong to a collective consciousness, seem to have no meaning. It is, therefore, in the repertoire of formulas and epithets representing the most prominent portion of this common stock that we have some chance of finding epic femininity.

The Female Body

While Homer's heroes are not merely outlined but their physical beauty is described at great length,[2] the situation is very different for the female characters. Curiously, the women seem to lack bodies and physical substance, even though they have no other possible way of existing in this masculine world except for their beauty. In her magnificent essay on Homer, Rachel Bespaloff states:

---

[1]   See Parry 1928a:146–181 ("L'épithète fixe peut-elle avoir un sens particularisé?").
[2]   See Part 1, Chapter 2 above.

Homer refrains from describing beauty, as if it were a forbidden anticipation of bliss. We know nothing about the shade of Helen's eyes, the
color of Thetis' locks, the arc of Andromache's shoulder. No specifics,
no unique traits are revealed to us, and yet we see these creatures, we
recognize them, it is impossible to mix them up.[3]

The discrepancy between the amount of description of the physical image of
men and women is absolutely striking in the *Iliad*. Here, then, is what we do
know of women, more or less precisely.

The face

One of the epithets most frequently used to describe women's faces is *kallipareios*
'fair-cheeked'.[4] Briseïs has a "beautiful face" (*Iliad* 19.285), Hera, an "immortal
head" (14.177). Chryseïs has "lively, moving eyes" (1.98), and Aphrodite "sparkling eyes" (3.397). Also evoked are Hera's earlobes (14.182) and the "beautiful
neck" of Aphrodite (3.396) and of Briseïs (19.285). References to the female face
end there.

Hair

Hair, curls, and locks are distinctive features of feminine beauty. Women have
"lovely tresses"; "lovely hair."[5] When Hera is preparing to seduce Zeus in Book
14, the poet emphasizes this point (*Iliad* 14.175–177):

> With this she anointed her delicate skin, and then she plaited the fair
> ambrosial locks that flowed in a stream of golden tresses from her
> immortal head.

To characterize female figures, the poet evokes their hair, and Helen, the emblem
of femininity, is labeled seven times as "lovely-haired Helen" (3.29, etc.).[6] Still,
descriptions of hair are quite imprecise: there is hardly any information about
its color or any criteria for judging what makes it "lovely" (shine, length, etc.).

---

[3] Bespaloff 1943:37–38: "Homère se garde bien de décrire la beauté, comme s'il y avait là une
anticipation interdite de la béatitude. Nous ignorons la nuance des yeux d'Hélène, la couleur des
tresses de Thétis, la courbe de l'épaule d'Andromaque. Aucune particularité, aucune singularité
ne nous est révélée, et pourtant nous voyons ces créatures, nous les reconnaîtrions, nous ne
pourrions les confondre."

[4] Fourteen occurrences: *Iliad* 1.143, 184, 310, 323, 346, 369; 6.298, 302; 9.665; 11.224; 15.87; 19.246;
24.607, 676. Women's cheeks are described specifically during scenes of mourning: while crying,
a woman will "tear her cheeks."

[5] There are a total of thirty uses of epithets referring to hair.

[6] See Bussolino 1962:217.

Arms, legs, and body

Other features of women's bodies are no more precisely described. There is no feminine equivalent of men's broad shoulders, powerful arms, or rapid feet. Other than the "white arms" of the frequent traditional epithet *leukōlenos*,[7] we see the arms and wrists of Aphrodite (*Iliad* 5.339), her fair "skin" (5.354, 357) as well as Hera's (14.175), the "beautiful ankles" of Danae (14.319) and of Cleopatra, Meleager's wife (9.557, 560), and Hera's "radiant feet" (14.186). The chest is often mentioned, but most frequently to describe the postures of women during scenes of mourning; furthermore, the word used, *stēthos*, is used for both men and women.

Here again, it is rather difficult to formulate a conception of the "femininity" of the body in the epic tradition.

Symbols of maternity: The breasts and womb

When Andromache is waiting for Hector on the ramparts, she is accompanied by the nurse of Astyanax, who carries the "little child in her bosom" (*Iliad* 6.400, 467). Several lines later, Hector places his son on Andromache's "own soft bosom" (6.483). These are indeed references to women's bodies, but there is a question as to whether *kolpos* refers here to the corset or to the breast or bosom. The primary idea is that of a sunken space, a fold, and in this sense the term sometimes denotes the crease in an article of clothing—for example, the robes "with deep folds" (*bathukolpos*, *Iliad* 18.122) of the Trojan women. This term is only applied to women and, like the French *corsage* or *décolleté*, can mean both the body part and the corresponding garment. In this case, it obviously indicates, or at least evokes, the idea of maternity (sunken space, cavity): Andromache's maternity and Hecuba's. The same goes for the nurse of Astyanax as well as for Thetis, who nurses the child Dionysus on her breast (6.136).[8] We saw that Hecuba bares her breast to move Hector: she presents her *mazos* to him and points to her bosom while imploring him to return inside the walls of Troy.[9]

And when Priam evokes Hecuba's womb before Achilles, it is to say that nineteen of his sons were born "from a single womb" (*Iliad* 24.496). In other passages, the word *gastēr* refers to women's abdomens, but always in a strict relationship with childbearing.

Each instance where the female body is mentioned specifically—and they are rare—refers then to the reproductive and maternal function of women.

---

[7] For example, Andromache: *Iliad* 6.371, 377; 24.723; Helen: 3.121.

[8] Chantraine 1968–1977:558 s.v. κόλπος, and Nawratil 1959.

[9] *Iliad* 22.80–83; see pp. 45–46 above on this passage.

The female body appears very rarely, and never for itself, never in its distinct morphology. It is mentioned during maternity (Hecuba, Penelope, and by extension Eurycleia and the nurse of Astyanax), in scenes of mourning (women pulling out their hair, pounding their chests, tearing their cheeks),[10] or in relation to divinity: it is Hera and Aphrodite who provide the rare details about feminine beauty.

The eclipsing of the female body, then, is one of the remarkable features of the *Iliad*, one of its grand paradoxes. The Trojan War takes place because of Helen, the most beautiful woman in the world. Yet this woman is never specifically described; her beauty is only asserted, never detailed. She always appears beneath long veils. Is this not a deeply rooted sign of a masculine ideology that only bestows excellence on men's abilities and bodies and that only considers men worthy of mention? A body must be used to wage war; yet women have no access to battle. Is it appropriate to advance the idea that, since women do not make war, they are not entitled to a complete body, but are limited to a womb?

Feminine beauty

One of the conventions of the epic is to describe and praise the power of heroes and their beauty in exceedingly laudatory terms: each great hero, during his *aristeia* (the series of feats he accomplishes), is always the greatest of all. This literary convention also applies to descriptions of feminine beauty.

For this beauty to exist, for it to be worth mentioning, it has to be altogether exceptional. The notion of competition, of rivalry, of *eris*, seems to be mandatory, as if women—in their sphere—must rival each other in beauty. When the poet presents a women, she is almost always "the fairest" or "of surpassing beauty."[11]

Is there a symmetry between the exploits of the warrior, sung by the poet, and the exceptional beauty of a woman (a kind of accomplishment), also celebrated by the poet? Any symmetry would be limited, since for women there is no *aristeia*.

Women's attire

We have seen how the poet is reticent in detailing the appearance and charm of women; the same is true concerning their attire.[12]

---

[10] Cf. p. 124 below.

[11] For example, "Laodice, the fairest of Priam's daughters," *Iliad* 3.124; 6.252. The same goes for Alcestis (2.715) and the Lesbians offered by Agamemnon to Achilles are "all of surpassing beauty," 9.130, etc.

[12] See Lorimer 1950:377–390. Only a few objects worn by women are mentioned: golden clasps (*Iliad* 5.425; 14.180), belts (for example, 14.181), earrings and jewels (14.182–183; 18.400–402), a headband for tying up hair (22.469).

The women that appear outside of their homes all wrap themselves in veils. Helen, to go to the ramparts, "threw a white mantle over her head" (*Iliad* 3.141); similarly, when admonished by Aphrodite and seized with fear, "she wrapped her mantle about her and went in silence, following the superhuman force and unnoticed by the Trojan women" (3.419–420).

The veil seems to be for women what armor is for men.[13] In both cases, it is "attire" that is worn to go outside the home; it is also a means of protection—from the blows of the adversary, from the gaze of others. The veil can also be, more interestingly, a "woman's armor," which a woman puts on when heading out to conquer a man or god. This becomes clearer when considering the episodes in which three goddesses use, in different ways and with varying degrees of success, their finery. The respective relationships of Athena, Aphrodite, and Hera with their attire-armor are significant.[14]

Athena, like a warrior preparing for combat, recalls her "ardent valor" (*Iliad* 5.718) and arms herself to assist the Greeks (5.733–744):

> Meanwhile Athena, daughter of aegis-bearing Zeus, flung her pattern-woven *peplos*, made with her own hands, on to her father's threshold, and donned the *khiton* of Zeus, arming herself for battle. She threw her tasseled aegis about her shoulders, wreathed round with Rout as with a fringe, and on it were Strife, and Strength, and Panic whose blood runs cold; moreover there was the head of the dread monster Gorgon, grim and terrifying to behold, portent of aegis-bearing Zeus. On her head she set her helmet of gold, with four plumes, and coming to a peak both in front and behind decked with the emblems of a hundred cities.

This long citation makes clear that for combat with men it is not the *peplos* 'dress' but the cuirass that is required—*khiton,* aegis, and helmet, not ribbon and diadem. Here, Athena, brilliant in her armor, is located entirely within the masculine sphere of war.

In contrast stands Hera, who, after lengthy preparation of her clothing and jewels, will be able to confront Zeus and make him succumb to her charms (*Iliad* 14.178–188):

> She put on the wondrous robe which Athena had worked for her with consummate art, and had embroidered with manifold devices; she fastened it about her bosom with golden clasps, and she girded herself with a girdle that had a hundred tassels: then she fastened her

---

13 Identical vocabulary: "fitted" armor or clothing (for example, *harmozō*: 3.332–333 and Hesiod *Works and Days* 76); cf. pp. 21–22 above.

14 See the detailed analysis of this passage in Nagler 1974:55–59.

earrings, three brilliant pendants with much charm radiating from them, through the pierced lobes of her ears and threw a lovely new veil over her head. She bound her sandals on to her feet, and when she had finished making herself up in perfect order, she left her room.

There are correspondences to be identified between the scene where Athena arms herself and the scene where Hera dresses herself. Hera puts on her *peplos* and fastens it in the manner of a warrior who latches the buckles on his belt (*Iliad* 4.132–133): her belt is tightened (*araruian*) like that of a warrior (4.134; 11.234, etc.);[15] on her head shines her gleaming veil like a hero's glistening helmet. Hera, though, is situated entirely within Aphrodite's feminine sphere while preparing herself this way for a sort of lovers' combat.

The intersection of the two planes—the bronze of war and the maternal *peplos* of feminine dress—operates with Aphrodite. When faced with the bronze of Diomedes' spear, she intervenes on the battlefield with the grossly inadequate weapons of a mother (unprotected arms, folds in her robes of fine fabric).[16] Unarmed, Aphrodite has truly ventured into a domain that is not her own. Her two enemies in the *Iliad*, Hera and Athena, refer derisively to the scratch, rather than the wound, that she suffers during her misadventure with Diomedes. Aphrodite should only be scratched by the clasps of her feminine attire, not by the point of a spear (5.424–425);[17] her place is not on the battlefield and her golden *peplos* cannot protect her from the weapons of the male warriors.

Colors

Just as a helmet shines, bronze gleams, or a shield possesses "a splendor as of the moon" (*Iliad* 19.373–374, the shield of Achilles), robes and veils also glisten.[18]

This light color, especially bright, situates female adornments on the side of the divinity of the Olympians. Darkness and black—rarely used to describe women[19]—lean, on the contrary, toward the chthonic deities, toward death. In the *Iliad*, black and darkness often refer to boats, sorrow, blood, war, and death.[20] Shining, glistening, and gleaming are reserved for the weapons of heroes, their hair, and feminine or masculine beauty.

---

[15] On the doubling of the belt, masculine and feminine, see Schmitt 1977.

[16] See p. 42–43 above. Aphrodite wounded at *Iliad* 5.337–340.

[17] Nagler 1974:23n31.

[18] For example, Helen's "white" veil (*Iliad* 3.141 and 419); Aphrodite's "fair garment" (5.315); the veil Hecuba offered to Athena that "glittered like a star" (6.295), etc. All these descriptions recall the brilliant white robe and veil of Pandora, Hesiod *Theogony* 574–575.

[19] The veil of Thetis at the end of the poem is dark blue—*kuanos* (*Iliad* 24.94); on the meaning of this epithet, see Rowe 1972:346–353.

[20] See, principally, Moreux 1967 passim.

Here, again, it seems the radiance of feminine beauty and attire corresponds to the radiance of the bodies and weapons of warriors.

Cosmetics and perfume

In Homer, there is little to no trace of embellishment of feminine beauty through "make-up" or other artifice. The only substance used seems to be a kind of ointment for the body, or scented oil, used by men and women alike.[21] Hera, after cleaning her body with ambrosia, anoints herself with "olive oil, ambrosial, very soft, and scented specially for herself" (*Iliad* 14.171–172).

References to scents and odors are inscribed in a context associated with divinity and femininity. Scented oils are used to embalm bodies: Apollo rubs Sarpedon with ambrosia (*Iliad* 16.680); Aphrodite, when watching over Hector, "anointed him with ambrosial oil of roses" (23.186–187).[22] Perfumes are associated with Zeus, surrounded by a "fragrant cloud" (15.158), and with the ground where he lies with Hera (14.347–349):

> With this the son of Cronus caught his wife in his embrace; whereon the earth sprouted them a cushion of young grass, with dew-bespangled lotus, crocus, and hyacinth, so soft and thick that it raised them well above the ground.

Paris and Helen's bedchamber is "scented and perfumed" (*Iliad* 3.382); in Lacedaemon, Helen's *thalamos* is perfumed, smelling of cedar (*Odyssey* 4.121). Her clothes are perfumed also, as are those that Calypso offers to Odysseus (*Odyssey* 5.264).

Colors, scents, and softness are closely associated to suggest erotic union, charm, and beauty, spheres in which the woman occupies a prominent place.

The Voices and Words of Women

The *Iliad* depicts very few women and, of those mentioned, even fewer speak. Among the women of the epic, who speaks, when, and in what way?

Which women speak? When?

The very first woman to speak in the *Iliad* is Helen, and the words she pronounces are not insignificant. Responding to Priam's questions on the ramparts, Helen tells stories of the Achaeans' feats and bravery. Her "poetic word" informs Priam

---

[21] Grillet 1975:90–91.
[22] See Bounoure 1983:17–18.

and the Trojans; it is the truth. At the moment when she mentions Odysseus, Antenor—one of the elders seated on the wall who had offered his hospitality to Odysseus—interrupts her to say: "Madam, you have spoken truly" (3.204).

The proximity of Helen and the bard is already underlined in her first appearance in the poem. She does not yet speak, but Homer depicts her as occupied with the weaving of "the struggles between Trojans, breakers of horses, and bronze-armored Achaeans" (*Iliad* 3.126–127). Her weaving is like a foreshadowing of the words she will pronounce on the ramparts. In both cases, she is joining in the affairs of men, of heroes.

Helen speaks on four occasions in the *Iliad*. On each occasion, she speaks in her name, in an autonomous manner. She responds once to the questions of a man, becoming herself the poet of Troy, and three times she takes the initiative to speak.

She shouts at Paris and reprimands him for his cowardice (*Iliad* 3.428–434):

> "So you are come from the fight," said she; "would that you had fallen rather by the hand of that brave man who was my husband. You used to brag that you were a better man with might and spear than warlike Menelaus. Go, then, and challenge him again—but I should advise you not to do so."

Later, when Hector is in the city, it is she who first addresses him, expressing regret over both the suffering she is causing for the Trojans and her husband's cowardice. Once again, the comparison between the valiant warrior and the hesitant coward is explicit in Helen's words; Hector is the one she would have preferred to have as a husband in Troy (*Iliad* 6.350–353):

> But, since the gods have devised these evils, would, at any rate, that I had been wife to a better man—to one who could smart under dishonor and men's evil speeches. This man was never yet to be depended upon, nor never will be, and he will surely reap what he has sown.

And finally, she is the third woman to weep over Hector's body and the last woman whose words are heard in the *Iliad* (24.760–775).

Helen initiates feminine speech, and she has the privilege of being the last woman to speak. Her words are not plaintive, even if she wishes three times for her own death.[23] Contrary to the wailing women in the poem, she cries only once, in a final address to Hector lying on his deathbed. She converses with

---

[23] *Iliad* 3.173–175; 6.345–348; 24.764; it is her union with Paris, cause of so many deaths, that she regrets. At 3.173–175, there is suggestive wavering between *thanatos/thalamos*: "'Sir [Priam],' answered Helen, shining among women, 'father of my husband, dear and reverend in my eyes,

Priam, Hector, Paris, and Aphrodite. In the *Iliad*, Helen is a woman who could be man's equal, whose words could meaningfully intervene in a masculine world. She has the ability to speak for herself, without systematically referring to her husband. Helen's "discourse" is independent.

This is not the case for Andromache. She addresses Hector three times, crying each time, always evoking her own loss and affirming her vulnerability, her lack of existence without her husband.[24]

Hecuba is the woman who speaks most often in the poem.[25] Her discourse might be considered a model for women. She does not try to dissuade Hector from going to battle (*Iliad* 6.254), but only demands that he be prudent; she remains entirely in the maternal sphere (somber speech, the symbolic gesture of baring her breasts; *Iliad* 22.82 and following). She weeps for her dead child, even envisioning life to be impossible without him.[26] Just as the most fully described maternal body in the *Iliad* belongs to Hecuba, she is also the only woman clearly characterized by her piety: she is the one who goes to pray to Athena (6.305 and following), and she is also the one who, with her speech, persuades Priam to offer libations to Zeus before leaving for the Achaean camp (24.287–298).

Briseïs, who figures prominently in the first two thirds of the poem, speaks only once, and never to Achilles. Her only words are addressed to the dead Patroclus on the day she is returned by Agamemnon. In her voice, only weeping and regret can be heard.[27]

The feminine voice oscillates between two poles: powerlessness, with its share of cries and moans of painful awareness, but also clairvoyance, truth, and poetry.

How do women speak?

From muddled whispers to repellent barking, a wide register of feminine voices is identifiable in epic.

---

would that I had chosen death [*thanatos kakos*] rather than to have come here with your son, far from my bridal chamber [*thalamon*].'"

[24] At *Iliad* 22.477, Andromache, seeing her husband dead in front of the gates, calls him "Hector." When his corpse is inside Troy, she addresses him as *anēr* (24.725), asserting once again her dependence on a man.

[25] Is this because she is the mother of the main Trojan hero or rather because she is the wife of the Trojan king? She speaks with Hector: *Iliad* 6.254 and following; begs him to return to the city: 22.82 and following; weeps: 22.431 and 24.77; prays to Athena: 6.305–310; and advises Priam: 24.201–208 and following.

[26] Cf. Anticlea, who dies of sorrow from waiting for Odysseus' return: *Odyssey* 11.202–203.

[27] *Iliad* 19.295–299. These words are analogous to Andromache's (6.410 and following). In tears, both moan over their destiny; see Beye 1974:87–88; Farron 1979:29–30.

Young people, boys and virgin girls, converse tenderly, whispering between themselves (*Iliad* 22.128).[28] Women, on the contrary, sometimes quarrel, squealing at each other in the streets (20.251-255). However, most often in the *Iliad*, women wail, cry, and scream in pain (e.g. Hecuba at 22.407).[29] The *Odyssey*, as well, is filled with the sound of Penelope's sobs as she cries throughout Odysseus' entire journey and return to power.

But a woman's voice can also be prophetic, as in the case of Cassandra: while Priam is gone to Achilles' tent, "she went about the city saying" that Priam was on his way back to Troy with Hector's body. She is the only one who sees Priam and his attendant from the walls (*Iliad* 24.697-699):

No one neither man nor woman saw them, till Cassandra, fair as golden Aphrodite standing on Pergamon, caught sight of her dear father.

In the *Odyssey*, two women make prophecies: first Helen, who predicts (*manteusomai*, 4.172) the return of Odysseus, then a servant in the palace in Ithaca, who renews this prediction before the contest of the bow: "a miller-woman from hard by in the mill room lifted up her voice" (20.105). Her words are a "sign to her master" (*sēma anakti*, 20.111).

Close proximity exists between prophetic speech,[30] truth, and femininity. But this all-powerful feminine voice can be as dangerous as it is beneficial. In women's speech the same feminine duality can be found as has been previously discussed.

In the supernatural world of the *Odyssey*, the power of women's voices and of the female beings Odysseus encounters is clearly indicated. These voices alternate between horror (Scylla, a hideous monster who "yelps") and infinite charm and maleficent seduction. The voice of the enchantress Circe, the alluring songs of the Sirens, and the forgetfulness-inducing words of Calypso are all dangerous temptations for Odysseus.[31] Marcel Detienne points out:

As *Peithō* or *Apaté*, speech in mythical thinking has a dual power, positive and negative, and in this sense, it is perfectly analogous with other ambiguous powers. There are, in a certain way, equivalences among

---

[28] This theme is developed in Hesiod *Theogony* (205-206): the privileges of Aphrodite are "the amorous converse of maidens, their smiles and wiles, their sweet delights, their love, and blandishment"; see Detienne 1973:64n91.

[29] See pp. 105-106 below.

[30] One might consider another type of ritual, feminine chant—the *ololugē* of women—by examining Eurycleia who, seeing the suitors' dead bodies, prepares to let out the *you-you* of victory. On this point, see Gernet 1983:250-253 and Rudhardt 1958:178 and following.

[31] Circe: *Odyssey* 10.136, 221; 11.8. Calypso: *Odyssey* 5.56-57, 61; 12.449. Scylla: *Odyssey* 12.85-86. Sirens: 12.44, 183, 187, 192, etc.; cf. Kahn 1980:123-124.

them: ambivalent speech is a woman, it is the god Proteus, it is a multi-colored cloth.[32]

Helen seems to be the only woman whose speech is acceptable for men: she does not moan or try to hold them back from combat; she does not deceive them or destroy them through seduction; she speaks without shouting or crying. She is situated at the fringe of masculine "discourse" and the feminine "voice."

Through this examination, we have seen that the radiance of feminine beauty corresponds with the radiance of masculine achievements and that—aside from Helen—confused and subordinate feminine voices correspond to the organized discourse of men. Is there a specific feminine nature here? It may lie in a sort of absence. In the *Iliad*, the feminine appears fantasized in a way that prevents it from being truly evoked.

---

[32] Detienne 1973:66 "En tant qu'elle est *Peithō* ou *Apaté*, la parole est dans la pensée mythique une puissance double, positive et négative, qui, sur ce plan, est parfaitement analogue à d'autres puissances ambiguës. Il y a en quelque sorte une équivalence entre elles: la parole ambivalente est une femme, elle est le dieu Protée, elle est un tissu bariolé."

3

Virile Women ... or Heroines?

If there were an attempt to perform an analysis of women parallel to the one offered above for men, an admission would have to be made that there are no masculine traits that become derogatory when applied to women. Quite the contrary, in fact. Two levels of masculine conduct in women can be identified: first, when women engage, more or less confusedly, in the affairs of men; second, when comparisons of masculinity directly describe the three main feminine characters in the epic—Penelope, Andromache, and Helen.

Traces of Masculinity in Women

Several times, Hector mentions the importance of the Trojan women. Their judgments matter in his eyes; whether they are related to the way he wages war (*Iliad* 6.441–443):

> Wife, I too have thought upon all this, but with what face should I look upon the Trojans, men or women, if I shirked battle like a coward?

or to the consequences of failure (*Iliad* 22.104–105):

> Now that my folly has destroyed the army, I dare not look Trojan men and Trojan women in the face.

Trojan women are always associated with their spouses (see again, *Iliad* 7.297–298); Hector's leadership affects them as much as the men. And the council that Priam and the elders of Troy form has its feminine counterpart: the group of women gathered around Hecuba (6.270, 287, 296). This is the group of women in whom Hector entrusts the mission of imploring Athena's mercy (6.269–270). In their sphere also, women have a form of proper authority, and their requests have an individualized character: the prayers addressed to Athena are related, strictly speaking, to the world of women—wives and young mothers. They pray that Athena "will have pity upon the town, with the wives and little ones of the

Trojans" (6.276, 310). There is then a recognized domain reserved for women: relations with the goddess. But it is scant indeed.

In the story of Meleager, who refuses to defend his city and withdraws from combat, there is a certain form of feminine power, or more precisely that of a wife: a persuasion that will make even the most obstinate yield. Whereas the leading authorities of the city (the elders of Aetolia and the most important priests), the representatives of familial authority (first his father, then his mother), and even his dearest battle companions fail (*Iliad* 9.574–587), his wife alone succeeds in convincing him to go fight: "His heart was stirred when he heard what bad things will happen. He got up and went off" (9.595–596).

In the *Odyssey*, the political authority of Arete, who reigns with king Alcinous over the Phaeacians, is clearly emphasized. She is the first to address Odysseus—as if he must, first and foremost, be accepted by the queen. It is she who ultimately decides to welcome Odysseus (*Odyssey* 6.304–305, 312–315), a point that is underlined by Moses I. Finley, who notes "her strange unwomanly claims to power and authority."[1] We will not dwell on the obvious fact that in the *Odyssey* the three queens, Penelope, Helen, and Arete, maintain privileged relationships with royal power. Penelope in Ithaca, Helen in Sparta, and Arete in Scheria embody authority just as their husbands do.

Penelope: A Heroic King For Ithaca?

A certain number of descriptions depict the figure of Penelope with masculine, always prestigious, traits. These refer to the world of combat, but with a discrepancy that distinguishes the *Odyssey* from the *Iliad*.

Even after the massacre of the suitors, Penelope's caution and suspicion remain intact: wanting to test Odysseus again, she provokes the indignation of Telemachus, then of Odysseus himself. She is criticized for having a heart "as hard as a stone" (*Odyssey* 23.103), a heart that nothing can soften (23.167), and a will of iron (23.172). These images recall metaphors of combat in which the warrior has a heart of iron (*Iliad* 22.357; 24.205). The inversion is even more striking considering that, in the moments when these descriptions are applied to her, her femininity is confirmed, even heightened: "to you beyond all women" (*peri soi ge gunaikōn thēluteraōn*, *Odyssey* 23.166).[2]

Another of Penelope's distinguishing features is that she is, with Athena, the only female character in the epic to be characterized by her "strong hand" (*cheiri pacheiēi*, *Odyssey* 21.6; of Athene at *Iliad* 21.403, 424). The epithet applied

---

[1] Finley 1978b:132.
[2] See Loraux 1981c:76–79.

here to Penelope, which has intrigued commentators, is that granted to a warrior clutching a spear with his broad hand (*Iliad* 7.264; 8.221, etc.). It is significant that this feature is accorded to both the most warlike of the goddesses and the heroine of the *Odyssey*.

To interpret this "strong hand" as a symbol of Penelope's power inside the home, it must, of course, be placed in context: Odysseus is about to take up the royal bow, and only his hand will be strong enough to string it. This is not the only case where twinning between Odysseus and Penelope occurs.

Beyond this type of scattered evidence, two comparisons warrant particular attention. When Penelope fears for Telemachus' life, she is compared not to a lioness, as we might expect, but to a male lion who fears for his young. A heroic comparison, doubtless, even though Penelope is likened, not to the formidable lion, but rather to the cornered and threatened one (*Odyssey* 4.791–792). It is as if she has reached the very limits of a woman's heroism.[3]

In another passage, Odysseus says of Penelope (*Odyssey* 19.108–110):

For truly your glory reaches the wide firmament of the sky itself—like the glory of some faultless king who, godlike as he is, and ruling over a population that is multitudinous and vigorous, upholds acts of good *dikē*.

The references to glory (*kleos*), justice (*eudikias*), and royalty (*basilēos*) establish a network of values closely linked to masculinity. This kind of *aristeia* for Penelope does not acquire its full meaning unless we stop to examine the circumstances that provoke this praise. Odysseus, who had proclaimed his own glory in similar terms (*Odyssey* 10.19–20) while with the Phaeacians (here again confirming the twinning of Odysseus and Penelope), is now in a completely reversed situation: "do not seek to know my lineage and family" (19.116), he responds to his wife, who has not yet recognized him. The king, like the male lion, falls into the category of masculine heroism. It is because she is an exceptionally wise and faithful wife that she can—in the absence of a man—convey royalty and assume for a while the role of the kingdom's regent.

However, Penelope's response to Odysseus is significant (*Odyssey* 18.124–128):

Stranger, the immortal gods robbed me of all excellence, whether of face or figure, when the Argives set sail for Troy and my dear husband

---

3   Foley 1978:10 does not take into consideration the fear of the lion, but retains the image of the besieged warrior, an image directly likened to Penelope; for a more nuanced interpretation, see Schnapp-Gourbeillon 1981:61–62.

with them. If he were to return and look after my affairs I would have more fame and would show a better presence to the world.[4]

It is important that Penelope herself refuses the usurped *kleos*—demonstrating once again that her fidelity is the basis for her true glory.[5] When Odysseus returns, at the moment he recovers his status as mortal and king, she will recover her true place, her true function as a woman.

Andromache: A Double of the Warrior Hector?

Andromache, the name of the paradigmatic woman of the *Iliad*, contains roots meaning both 'man' and 'war'. There is very little basis for the idea that she is "an unrecognized example of matriarchy."[6] A careful examination of the lines dedicated to Andromache will perhaps determine the reality—and the limits—of her contact with the war.

Three times Andromache encroaches into a domain reserved for men, and particularly into that of war. She tends to Hector's horses and feeds them; she would have received the prestigious armor of Achilles from Hector, had he been victorious; and, finally, she makes a more marked incursion into the world of men when she takes it upon herself to give Hector tactical advice (*Iliad* 6.433–434):

As for the army of warriors, place them near the fig-tree, where the city can be best scaled, and the wall is weakest.

Of note is, first of all, that the advice is defensive; it is about the best way to protect the city, that is to say, the women and children. The strangeness of this initiative is underscored by Hector, who sends Andromache back to her loom (*Iliad* 6.490–492).

Weak evidence, certainly, but all three cases are related to the practices of war. Andromache's proximity to combat is clarified, however, by Charles Segal's analysis of *Iliad* 22.437–476.[7] Through a very attentive study of formulas and expressions applied to Andromache's suffering, Segal brings to light the complex play of similarities and differences that the poet uses to prioritize Andromache's pain by slightly distorting formulas ordinarily reserved for warriors.

---

[4] Like Odysseus, Penelope speaks of her *kleos* in the first person, cf. p. 99 below.
[5] *Odyssey* 24.196–198: "Thus the glory will never perish for him, the glory that comes from his merit, and a song will be created for earth-bound humans by the immortals—a song that brings beautiful and pleasurable recompense for sensible Penelope."
[6] Pomeroy 1975 makes this claim, without providing any proof.
[7] Segal 1971a.

His analysis will allow for an examination of the physical manifestations of Andromache's pain at the moment of Hector's death (*Iliad* 22.447–448 and 451–453):

> She heard the cry coming as from the wall, and trembled in every limb; the shuttle fell from her hands.
>
> *Iliad* 22.447–448

> I heard the voice of my husband's honored mother; my own heart beats as though it would come into my mouth and my limbs refuse to carry me.
>
> *Iliad* 22.451–453

> Over her eyes a dark night spread its cover, and she fell backward, gasping out her life's breath. She threw far from her head the splendid adornments that bound her hair—her frontlet, her snood, her plaited headband, and, to top it all, the headdress.
>
> *Iliad* 22.466–470[8]

> But when she recovered her breathing and her life's breath gathered in her heart, she started to sing a lament in the midst of the Trojan women.
>
> *Iliad* 22.475–476

With a prescient sense of her coming misfortune, Andromache's body is struck like that of an injured warrior: her limbs vibrate and the shuttle slips out of her hands like the weapon of a man who is collapsing (*Iliad* 8.329; 15.465). Her heart shakes violently like the spear brandished in the hand of a combatant (3.19; 16.142); her knees stick in the ground like a spear in a helmet (4.460). A black night spreads over her, a synonym of the warrior's death in combat (5.659; 13.580); and immediately afterward, she collapses. Catching her breath, as a hero does during an effort to fight (5.697; 11.359, etc.), she comes to (*apo de psuchēn ekapusse*, 22.467: literally "she breathes out her life's breath"). Her pain is analogous, in every detail, to that of an injured or slain warrior, and this extraordinary scene confers upon her suffering a particular character.

---

[8] See also pp. 29–30 above.

While Segal's analysis undoubtedly proves that Andromache is acquainted with war and combat, it does not, however, make it possible to see in her the form of a warrior. Indeed, it seems that her relationship with war is essentially transmitted through Hector. As if she feels the impact of Achilles' spear, which pierces Hector's body, she totters and collapses. This is, perhaps, a way of expressing the closeness that exists between her and Hector, their absolutely interwoven fates, which make them, like Odysseus and Penelope, more than a couple. Andromache figures as Hector's double: "Woe is me, O Hector; woe, indeed, that to share a common lot we were born" (*Iliad* 22.477–478). Andromache suffers as Hector dies, and it is here perhaps that she reaches her limit. The "heroic" pain of Andromache ceases to be heroic when the man that acted as its referent disappears. She then reinstates her entirely feminine personality and weeps for her dead husband as a wife.[9]

Helen: A Double of Achilles?

Just as Achilles exceeds all other warriors in bravery, Helen is the most beautiful among women. However, their resemblance extends beyond their excellence. Both of divine heritage, their fates have been determined by the gods, and this destiny creates around them a kind of isolation.[10] Like the strength of Achilles, the beauty of Helen is irresistible. It also brings about death, and her character is closely associated with the balefulness of war.[11]

Her "bitchiness," which is underlined several times, calls to mind the scavenging dogs that roam the battlefield: "Poor brother! I am nothing more than a dog and a malicious frozen heart," she says to Hector (*Iliad* 6.344; see also 3.180, 6.356; *Odyssey* 4.145). In this single verse, three descriptive elements contribute to the concentration of the threats of war and violent death around her character: the carnivorous dog, the battle or grievance that freezes the heart (*Iliad* 9.464, 24.524; *Odyssey* 11.212, etc.), and the horror of fighting (*Iliad* 9.257). She is also *stugerē* 'detestable', like death (8.368). And, finally, she has the power to make men shiver (24.775) from fear or horror (19.325), like the lion (11.383). These many qualities, while they might bring her into the world of men and war, do not erase her eminently feminine nature.

If Helen is associated with death, she is also, in a certain manner, the one who bestows immortality. This works in two ways: by the war she has provoked, where men will distinguish themselves as heroes; and in her capacity as a bard, again like Achilles. Sitting at her loom, she works on "a great web of purple wool,

---

[9] See pp. 107–108 below.
[10] On the "resemblance" of Achilles and Helen, see Reckford 1964:18–20.
[11] See the detailed remarks in Clader 1976:16–23.

on which she was pattern-weaving the struggles (*aethlous*) between Trojans, breakers of horses, and bronze-armored Achaeans, that Ares had made them fight for her sake" (*Iliad* 3.125-128),

She is spinning, a wholly feminine activity, but on this purple cloth, which is the color of death,[12] Helen diverts the poet and tells of great feats: the suffering and death endured for her. Poet at her loom, she is later the one who points out the Achaean leaders to Priam, associating each of them with her own destiny (*Iliad* 3.178–235).

She also possesses this gift of clairvoyance in the *Odyssey*, since she can immediately recognize and name Telemachus (4.141–144). Like the bard, she helps people forget their sorrow with *nē-penthes*, a drug that "made one forget all bad things" (4.220–226).[13]

If in the *Iliad* Achilles is the champion of masculine values, Helen embodies the essence of femininity. But, again, the symmetry between the two figures is complex. It is not a coincidence that these two characters, who occupy the primary roles in the epic, are also the ones that best succeed at integrating elements typical of the opposite sex without altering their masculinity/ femininity in the least. Despite having his mother nearby and always accessible, even on the battlefield, Achilles remains the greatest among the warriors. Helen, who intervenes in the affairs of men to distribute death and immortality, is not rendered any less feminine for doing so. Helen's beauty is the cause of the Trojan War, and the war reveals the beauty of Achilles.

While it is fair to suggest that the close relationship and consubstantial status of Andromache and Penelope with their husbands allow for a certain circulation of masculine values, Helen is the only heroine who does not owe her renown to her husband. In the *Iliad*, Helen is situated beyond the conjugal relationship, and this is, perhaps, what makes her a heroic figure.

---

[12] See Moreux 1967:263–268 (on *porphureos*).
[13] See below, pp. 104–105.

Part III

Sobs of Men, Tears of Women

1

Crying in the Heroic Space of the *Iliad*

> Then we should be right in doing away with the lamentations of men
> of note and in attributing them to women and not to the most worthy
> of them either, and to inferior men, in that those whom we say we are
> breeding for the guardianship of the land may disdain to act like these.
>
> Plato *Republic* III 387e–388a

In Books 2 and 3 of the *Republic*, Socrates and Adeimantus discuss the program
of education that would be implemented in their ideal city. The idea is proposed
that the legislature should control the fables and myths of the poets, that they
should "edit" a sort of orthodox Homer whose heroes do not cry. This conception of crying as a manifestation of weakness, vulnerability, and cowardice,
while it is clearly formulated during the classical period, does not appear to be
applicable to the world of epic.

The heroes of the *Iliad*, in particular, are very often presented in tears,
suffering grief and pain. The tears of Achilles, just as his military exploits, are
present throughout the poem, from his first appearance to his last. When he
is not fighting, he is crying. All signs suggest that for an epic hero crying was
not simply the expression of momentary distress, but rather a form of conduct
that was a constituent part of his nature. On the other hand, how are the tears
of exceptional warriors to be interpreted with regard to the crying of women,
which might be expected? Why are intrepid warriors not called "women"
(*Achaiides, Iliad* 2.235; 7.96) when they weep, as they are when they flee?

We have already observed the complex play of opposition, interference,
alterity, and the blurring of the masculine and feminine in the *Iliad*. Is it possible
to locate a similar oscillation in the expression of an emotion like suffering?
Pain is indeed a cause, if not the only cause, common to the masculine and feminine spheres. It is therefore necessary to examine the details of tears in the epic
and their distribution among the sexes to verify whether or not a discrimina-
tory distribution of the type made by Plato exists.

If war is a necessary condition for men to prove themselves to be heroes through their exploits, it is nonetheless a source of fear and pain, given that it is specifically by falling in combat while still young that a warrior ensures his *kleos*.

War is thus the path to heroism and simultaneously the "source of tears" *par excellence*, since it results in death. The descriptions of war (e.g. *Iliad* 3.165; 5.737; 8.388; 17.512; 22.487; *Odyssey* 11.383), combat, and defeat (*Iliad* 11.601; 13.765; 16.436; 17.192; 16.568) all point in this direction.

Tears are not reserved for the families of warriors slain in combat; the heroes themselves cry, and the leaders first among them. Their nature is such that, even while accepting the outcome of a struggle, they are no less sensitive to the loss of a friend or merely the failure of a confrontation. With the exception of Diomedes, all the great heroes of the *Iliad* cry, most of them on the battlefield.

Diomedes is the only hero, in fact, to cry in a context outside of war. It is neither cruel combat nor the loss of his companions that causes him to shed tears, but his defeat at the chariot race during the funeral games in honor of Patroclus. At the moment when he is going to pass Eumelus, Apollo knocks the whip out of Diomedes' hand. His failure is assured at that point, and "tears of anger fell from his eyes" (*Iliad* 23.385). These are tears of rage, mixed with frustration and anger.[1] For Diomedes, unlike the other heroes, the tears of grief seem inaccessible, as if his ambivalent nature, more savage than heroic,[2] desensitizes him to the spectacle of death.

This is not the case for the principal warriors of the poem. Ajax cries over Patroclus, who has just died (*Iliad* 17.648); Agamemnon appears often with tears in his eyes: when he sees Menelaus wounded (4.153), when the Trojan advances are becoming a threat (8.245; 9.14–16), or the evening following a Trojan victory, when the festivities in Troy fill him with grief (10.9). In the same way, Patroclus weeps profusely at the sight of the wounded Eurypylus (11.815; 15.398) or when he wants to rescue the Greeks who are poorly positioned (14.320). Hector also cries when, injured, he is carried away from the battle by his companions (16.423).[3]

But of all the heroes, the greatest, both in bravery and in the extent of his tears, is naturally Achilles. If the *Iliad* is the song of Achilles' anger, it is also, and

---

[1] Discussing the verb *chōestai* in the epic, A. W. H. Adkins compares this passage with *Iliad* 22.291, where Hector is frustrated to see his spear miss its target. *Chōestai* describes a state of mind related to the inability to hit a target; Adkins 1969:13 and following.

[2] See the remarks in Schnapp-Gourbeillon 1981:95–131.

[3] A number of other warriors cry in the *Iliad*: for example Antilochus (17.596, 700; 18.17, 32), Teucer (8.334), Deiphobus (13.538), the Trojans all together (22.408–409; 23.1; 24.664, 714, 740, 786), the Greeks (1.42; 2.288–289; 4.154; 13.88; 18.315–316, 355; 23.154, 211).

especially, the extraordinary tale of his grief. On this point, a recent study by Gregory Nagy has explained extensively how the theme of grief underpins and frames the character of Achilles.[4] His anger toward Agamemnon prompts his withdrawal from combat: near the ships, he ruminates on his resentment and walks away from his men to be alone and cry at the shore (*Iliad* 1.349–350). His tears at this point seem to be more a manifestation of spite and irritation than real pain. "Agamemnon, son of Atreus, has done me dishonor, and has robbed me of my prize by force," he says to his mother while crying (1.355–356; tears over Briseïs: 1.347, 357, 364).

It is Achilles' honor that is at stake here; his distress must be understood from the perspective of the code of heroic values. Embittered, he withdraws from combat; the woman being only a pretext, what matters is the affront that has just been inflicted upon him. It is quite different than the excruciating pain he feels when Patroclus is killed: at that moment, his tears overtake him entirely. From that point forward, forgetting his oath never again to fight the Greeks (*Iliad* 1.233), his only reason to live is to kill Hector. Killing and weeping then characterize Achilles as he returns definitively to his role as the central character in the poem.

Iliad 18 and 19 are largely devoted to the story of Achilles' tears (*Iliad* 18.35, 55, 78, 235, 318, 323, 354; 19.5, 304, 338, 345, etc.). Fighting no longer takes place, as if Patroclus' death marks a gap in the progression of confrontations. Instead, the focus of the plot tilts and inverts. The tears of Achilles are followed immediately by reconciliation in the Greek camp and preparations for combat—with the magnificent interlude of Hephaestus' crafting of Achilles' armor in Book 18 (463–617). Achilles stops weeping to start a fight. Once Hector has been killed, he returns to camp to look after the funeral preparations for Patroclus; crying over his friend becomes the only conduct possible according to the logic of his character (after killing Hector: *Iliad* 23.9–10, 11, 14–17, 60, 98, 108, 153, 172, 178, 222, 224–225; with Priam: 24.9, 123–128, 507, 512–513, 591).

The "best of the Achaeans," then, is also the one who most often experiences grief, the one who seems most inclined to tears and weeping. And this feature, far from being paradoxical, is, on the contrary, deeply rooted in his nature. The hero is not simply a killing machine; he is a hero as much for his courage facing death as for his close relationship with pain.

The tears of Achilles are inscribed well within the requirements of epic morality: a sense of honor and friendship, of fidelity toward his fellow soldiers—requirements that, for Achilles, take on a distinctive scope and proportion.[5]

---

4 Nagy 1979; see, in particular, Chap. 5, "The Name of Achilles," 69–83.
5 We will see below (pp. 125–133) the details of the physical manifestation of Achilles' tears, and the specific connections that attach him to Patroclus.

When Achilles weeps over Patroclus, he is also weeping for himself. Given that Patroclus is his "second self" (*Iliad* 18.81–82), the death of his closest companion obviously foreshadows his own. Returning to combat, he knows that he will die there and win great glory, as did Heracles, the archetypal Greek hero whom he chooses to evoke at the moment he becomes fully aware of his destiny (18.114–118):

> I will go; I will pursue Hector who has slain him whom I loved so dearly, and will then abide my doom when it may please Zeus and the other gods to send it. Even Heracles, the best beloved of Zeus—even he could not escape the hand of death.

Heracles, when he appears in the *Iliad*, is also presented weeping: "He would weep till his cry came up to the sky" (8.364), Athena says of him, describing his pain and exhaustion during the labors imposed upon him by Eurystheus.

From this first level of analysis, it appears that the valorized figure of the crying and suffering hero is radically different from the model of masculinity in place in the classical era. If, in the *Iliad*, Heracles can be evoked with tears in his eyes without it affecting the image of his valor in the least, the story is quite different in tragedy, where on several occasions mention is made of his legendary inability to cry as a way to better mark his decline and agony. "But I have tasted of countless troubles, as is well known;" the Heracles of Euripides says, "never yet did I faint at any or shed a single tear; no, nor did I ever think that I should come to this, to let the tear-drop fall" (*Heracles* 1353–1356; trans. Coleridge); Sophocles further specifies this characteristic in his *Trachiniae*, "And pity me, for I / am pitiful indeed as I lie sobbing / and moaning like a virgin [*parthenos*]" (1070–1072; trans. Torrance 1966).[6]

Tears are not reserved for warriors, as great as they may be; the gods also cry: Zeus and Ares lament their sons, who are killed in combat.[7] The space of war is thus the only place where it is permissible, if not compulsory, to shed tears. In this respect, the episode involving Thersites marks well the boundary between acceptable, noble tears and tears of weakness, which are admonished and derided. When Thersites, after quarrelling with the Achaean commanders, is beaten by Odysseus, his tears are a subject of mockery for all in attendance (*Iliad* 2.266–270):

---

[6] Another significant example of the gap that separates the epic mentality from tragedy is found in Euripides' *Helen* (947–949), where Menelaus says: "I could not endure to fall at your knees, or wet my eyes with tears; for if I were cowardly, I would greatly dishonor Troy" (trans. Coleridge).

[7] Zeus cries over Sarpedon: *Iliad* 16.450; over Hector: 22.169. Ares cries when he is injured by Diomedes: 5.871; and by Athena: 21.417; he laments the loss of Ascalaphus: 15.114.

Then he beat him with his staff about the back and shoulders till he dropped and fell weeping. The golden scepter raised a bloody welt on his back, so he sat down frightened and in pain, looking foolish as he wiped the tears from his eyes. The people were sorry for him, but they laughed heartily.

His tears have nothing to do with heroic pain. For the law of war is entirely different; it contains within itself this *condition*: glory and pain. Tears are the complement of *kleos*; one is not possible without the other. In this sense, there is nothing about crying that demeans or emasculates the hero.

Achilles, the model of masculine courage, expresses himself the hard law of the heroic condition, where glory and pain are inseparable: "I can take thought of nothing save only slaughter and blood and the rattle in the throat of the dying" (*Iliad* 19.214).

2

Tears in a Different World
The *Odyssey*

The "world of Odysseus" presents us with the disorder in Ithaca, a kingdom without a king, ruled in the interim by a woman, and the strange universe of the journey where "from the Lotus-eaters to Calypso, passing by way of the Cyclops and the Underworld, Odysseus does not encounter a single human being, technically speaking."[1]

In this radically different context from the *Iliad*, the act of crying seems to be situated, through a shift in meaning, to another plane. Nowhere in the *Iliad* is it ever stated that tears must be contained or controlled; things are different in the *Odyssey*. Tears are at times forbidden and at times allowed. What are the criteria for making this distinction? Focusing on the character of Odysseus, I will try to clarify the discrepancy between the *Odyssey* and the *Iliad*.

When and Why Does Odysseus Hold Back Tears?

Though Odysseus cries often, he does not do so the same way in every case. A prisoner of Calypso, he spends his days apart, crying over the impossibility of his return. Far from the nymph's cave, "on the shore of this island where, with a word, he could become immortal, sitting on a rock, facing the sea, Odysseus wails and sobs all day long."[2] Not until nightfall does he return to Calypso (*Odyssey* 5.154–155).[3] The first *appearance* of the character Odysseus in the poem is thus placed under the sign of grief. The essence of his character, the *polutlas* 'he who has suffered greatly', resides as much in his suffering as in his heroism.

---

[1]   Vidal-Naquet 1981:47: "des Lotophages à Calypso, en passant par la Cyclopie et le pays des morts, Ulysse ne rencontre pas un seul être humain à proprement parler."

[2]   Vernant 1982a:17: "sur la rive de cette île où il n'aurait qu'un mot à dire pour devenir immortel, assis sur un rocher, face à la mer, Ulysse tout le jour se lamente et sanglote."

[3]   For his tears, see *Odyssey* 5.82–84, 151–153, 156–158. Like Achilles, he goes off alone to express his despair; see J. B. Hainsworth's commentary *ad loc.* in Hainsworth and Privitera 1982.

While with the Phaeacians, when the bard Demodocus is singing, he raises his mantle over his head to hide his tears from the audience:

> Thus sang the bard, but Odysseus drew his purple mantle over his head and covered his face, for he was ashamed to let the Phaeacians see that he was weeping. When the bard left off singing he wiped the tears from his eyes, uncovered his face, and, taking his cup, made a drink-offering to the gods.
>
> *Odyssey* 8.83–89[4]

After each of Demodocus' performances, Homer emphasizes Odysseus' desire to hide his tears. Even in his sorrow, Odysseus practices dissimulation, as if the act of hiding—literally behind a mantle or figuratively behind lies and ruses—were a defining characteristic of his nature.[5] At other moments in the narrative, the need to refrain from crying and to hold back tears is emphasized. For instance, Odysseus orders those of his men who escaped the wrath of the Cyclops not to cry: this is a matter of not wasting enthusiasm or the time needed to embark (*Odyssey* 9.468–469).

Once he has returned to Ithaca, we see him struggling against the emotion that overtakes him upon seeing his son and holding back his tears as long as possible. Odysseus only yields to his weeping afterwards, when on the order of Athena he reveals his true identity to Telemachus. Transformed by Athena's golden wand, he regains his stature and beauty; the "long-suffering hero" can then cry:

> As he spoke he kissed his son, and a tear fell from his cheek on to the ground, for he had restrained all tears till now.
>
> *Odyssey* 16.190–191[6]

Later, transformed for the needs of the plot into an unrecognizable old beggar, Odysseus himself expresses the idea that tears are useless and improper, during a conversation with Penelope. Crying too much in someone else's house

---

[4] The same image is applied to Telemachus who, hearing Menelaus tell the story of his father's exploits, hides behind his purple mantle to cry, *Odyssey* 4.115–116.

[5] See *Odyssey* 8.532. We see the same idea, but from another perspective, when he hides his tears (*lathōn*) from Eumaeus after seeing his old dog Argos, 17.304–305. At other moments in the plot, an extensive field of associations with the hidden and the invisible is constructed around the character of Odysseus, a specialist in the art of dissimulation: He is disguised in rags as an unrecognizable beggar (in Troy, 4.245 and following; in Ithaca, 13.429 and following); hidden inside a wooden horse (8.502 and following), etc.

[6] The expression *nōlemes aiei* 'obstinately, without respite' shows the extent to which Odysseus held back his emotion before the revelation of his identity.

can easily be compared to another type of excess, drunkenness (19.118–122).[7] Holding back tears is the best form of conduct for a man, as is made clear in the last exchange between Odysseus "the stranger" and Penelope (19.209–211):

> ... even so did her cheeks overflow with tears ... Odysseus felt for her and was for her, but he kept his eyes as hard as horn or iron without letting them so much as quiver, so cunningly did he restrain his tears.

It is worth lingering a bit on these three verses, since several notable layers of meaning can be observed, especially if we digress and connect them with another crucial passage from the *Odyssey*: the contest of the bow in *Odyssey* 21. There, horn and iron are also associated: the great bow of Odysseus is made of horn (*kera*, 21.395), and the arrows must pass through iron axes (21.81, 97, 114, 328).[8] The emphasis is placed on the hardness and solidity of these elements.

In the *Iliad*, we observe parallel, but inverted, play on the value of horns as a theme. Two characters draw our attention: Paris and Pandarus, both archers. Pandarus' bow is described precisely: it is made from the horns of a wild ibex (*Iliad* 4.105). And Paris is the target of insults that have been interpreted in various ways since antiquity: "Archer [*toxota*], you who without your bow are nothing, you who take pride in your locks [*kerai aglae*], slanderer and seducer" (11.385).[9] The expression *kerai aglae* could refer to a particular hairstyle in the shape of a horn,[10] to the bow, or to Paris' immoderate use of his sexuality. In any case, these different themes are interlaced around the figure of the archer, who in the *Iliad* might sometimes be a *gunaimanês* 'womanizer' (3.39; 13.769), but who is always a coward or a traitor.

To the extent that horns have a value as a "symbol of vital masculine energy,"[11] there is a clearly drawn boundary in the epic between good and bad masculinity—associated, obviously, with a heroic and anti-heroic way of fighting. In this respect, the Odysseus of the *Odyssey* belongs, without any doubt, to the first category.

"He kept his eyes as hard as ... iron": if the value of horns is inscribed in the semantic field of sexuality, iron itself is associated with war. Achilles, in the middle of the fray, possesses a *menos* equal to blazing fire (*Iliad* 20.372), a heart of iron (22.357), and a voice of brass (18.222). From the glimmer of armor to

---

[7] The man who is "heavy" (19.122) with wine and whose moistened eyes "swim with tears" (*dakruplōein*).

[8] Amory 1966:43–47.

[9] See the detailed remarks on the possible meaning of this line in Onians 1954:242–243.

[10] As P. Mazon's French translation suggests: "homme fier de sa mèche" ("the man who takes pride in his locks").

[11] Amory 1966:56; see also Onians 1954:238–244.

the inflexible determination of a brave heart, it is as if there is no difference in register: iron and bronze are the obligatory referents of war and masculinity.[12]

Odysseus holding back his tears in front of Penelope is then doubly characterized by words with connotations of masculinity: horn and iron. The joining of these two terms of comparison is reinforced further by the adverb *atremas* 'immobile, without even a tremble'. Ultimately, his eyes, like the horn and iron, play a role similar to that of his mantle when he is with the Phaeacians: in both cases, Odysseus is hiding behind something to cry (*Odyssey* 8.83–89).[13] Hiding his tears behind the appearance of a hard and horned exterior, which resembles weapons and armor, Odysseus, the true Odysseus, i.e. the one who is hiding, is crying *in the interior* of his heart. The time has not yet come for him to surrender to tears; his apparent impassivity only underlines his *andreia*, his masculine bravery.

This self-mastery in the *Odyssey* is indeed the mark of a superior quality, of a valorous essence. The poet on two other occasions reprises this image of a man able to contain his emotion and handle the fury in his heart. These deal with the sons of the two principal heroes of Homeric epic.

As he endures the spectacle of his father's mistreatment by the suitors, Telemachus is able to contain his emotion: "No tear fell from him, he shook his head in silence and brooded on his revenge" (*Odyssey* 17.490–491).

In the Underworld, Odysseus recalls for Achilles the bravery of his son Neoptolemus: his ardor exceeded that of all others, never was he afraid, never did emotion take hold over him. Odysseus recounts the ruse of the wooden horse:

> Though all the other leaders and chief men among the Danaans were drying their eyes and quaking in every limb, I never once saw him turn pale nor wipe a tear from his cheek.
>
> *Odyssey* 11.526–530[14]

₪

The absence of trembling, the hardness of horn or iron, impassivity—all are qualities that mark the difference between an ordinary nature and a superior

---

[12] Aeschylus, in his *Seven against Thebes* (50–53), summarizes this remarkably. If the seven leaders cry when thinking of their families "no piteous wailing escaped their lips. For their iron-hearted spirit heaved, blazing with courage, as of lions with war in their eyes" (trans. Smyth 1926).

[13] See pp. 91–92 above.

[14] "Quaking" is cowardly and not masculine. On the *tresas*, see Loraux 1977:108–114.

soul.[15] In the world of the *Odyssey*, where the external war is over, imposing the necessary hardness to hold back tears is, perhaps, a way for a man to remember what it is to be a hero.

When Tears Are Uncontrollable

Just as Achilles' grief appears throughout the *Iliad* from beginning to end, the suffering, hardship, and sorrow of Odysseus are central motifs of the *Odyssey*. The situations Odysseus confronts push him time and again to the limits of human suffering. His unwavering resistance and active resignation ("Heart, be still," *Odyssey* 20.18; also 10.153) make him a model of endurance, the *polutlas*, who has suffered greatly. During all his wanderings, his primary, inescapable adversary is death, against which he struggles desperately. One cannot fail to note that, when Odysseus falls prey to his tears, he is among non-humans, where the values of human society are not operative. The moral of the *Iliad*—die in combat or return victorious—is no longer in place in the supernatural worlds that Odysseus traverses. While he is, indeed, one of the victorious heroes of Troy, the terms of his return are clouded. And it is no small paradox in the poem to see this model of bravery, this champion of virility, become the prisoner of women in worlds where a warrior's values are no longer strictly relevant.

The *Iliad* constantly evokes the hard necessities of the feminine condition during times of war: the woman, more often with her children, is taken prisoner by the man who has overcome her husband. She becomes his slave. This is a bit like what happens to Odysseus; unable to return to his native land, he is the captive of Circe, then Calypso. His life has been suspended, and it is precisely his weeping and sobbing that preserve him from the hand of death, that are the mark of his humanity.[16] When his return to Ithaca is finally set by the gods, Calypso requests that he put an end to his tears (*Odyssey* 5.151–158):

> She found him sitting upon the beach with his eyes ever filled with tears, his sweet life wasting away as he wept for his homecoming; for he had got tired of Calypso, and though he was forced to sleep with her in the cave by night, it was she, not he, that would have it so. As for the daytime, he spent it on the rocks and on the seashore, weeping, crying aloud for his despair, and always looking out upon the sea.[17]

---

[15] Remember, for example, Odysseus' companions who spend their time crying; it is very often Odysseus who puts an end to their sobbing. See the comparison that presents him as a "mother" for his companions in tears, *Odyssey* 10.410–414.

[16] On Odysseus' predisposition to tears, which was condemned by the Stoics, see Stanford 1968:121–122 and 265–266n9.

[17] On the *aiōn* being shed along with his tears, cf. p. 119 below.

Certain details further specify the strangeness of Odysseus' situation. Calypso and Circe are described in specific gold and silver clothing that they put on at sunrise (*Odyssey* 5.230–232 = 10.543–545). The bright clothing, the breaking of the day, and the love of the two goddesses are themes that recall the affairs of Aphrodite and Eos with their mortal lovers.[18] Odysseus, in his own way, is also a victim of abduction, as Orion and Tithonus are. He is virtually the prisoner of Calypso. For purely erotic reasons, the brave warrior Odysseus is in turn the prisoner of a nymph and of a magician. The reversal is total: the reasons for and conditions of his detention with Circe and Calypso are the antithesis of the ideal warrior. Thus, as a complete "anomaly," the prisoner of a goddess in a super- natural land, Odysseus can no longer avoid being invaded by extreme suffering; no longer having masculine recourse, he can only abandon himself to tears.

Nor is it a surprise to find Odysseus in tears and terrified in the Under- world. In fact, "the extreme point of this exploration where Odysseus encoun- ters different degrees of inhumanity is precisely what lies beyond death, the other side of the world from those living under the light of the sun."[19] This exceptional ordeal, which by itself would broadly justify the tears of the hero, brings about new sorrow for Odysseus: seeing his mother among the other shadows, he learns at that moment of her death (*Odyssey* 11.87).

Throughout his travels, Odysseus is, in the end, only facing a single adver- sary: death, whether it be peaceful (the inhuman love of Circe or Calypso, forgetting in the land of the Lotus-eaters), violent and wild (the Laestrygonians, the Cyclops, the Sirens, Scylla and Charybdis), or dramatically immediate (the Nekyia). The sobs of Odysseus are a sign of the superposition of fabulous but terrible worlds, a "muddling" in which mortal man has neither place nor possible response.

The raging seas, cannibalistic monsters, and overly loving goddesses are not the only sources of tears that Odysseus experiences. His stay with the Phaeacians, the final stage in nonhuman lands, also brings its share of sorrow.

It is significant that during his time in Scheria Odysseus plunges back into a context that reminds him more of the world of war than of peaceful times suit- able to the bonds of hospitality. With Alcinous, Odysseus reconnects completely with his past and his warrior's nature. The restoration of his hero status becomes possible only because a bard, Demodocus, sings the epic of Troy.

---

[18] For an overview of the question, see Boedeker 1974:64–84.

[19] "Le point extrême de cette exploration où Ulysse rencontre différents degrés d'inhumanité, c'est précisément l'au-delà qu'est la mort, l'envers du monde des vivants sous la lumière du soleil" (Frontisi-Ducroux 1976:544).

Mediation by the Bard:
The Tears of Odysseus, Hero of Troy

Scheria represents, as Pierre Vidal-Naquet has observed, a hinge between the inhuman world of stories and the real world of Ithaca.[20] The manner in which this episode functions as a passage or transition is implied on all levels of interpretation.

From the reputation of the Phaeacian sailors to the location and configuration of their island, everything in Scheria indicates that this is a place and moment of essential passage in the destiny of Odysseus. He is far from indifferent to whether the songs of the Phaeacian bard recover his heroic identity as conqueror of the Trojans; his tears act to reveal his identity. The three songs of Demodocus illustrate perfectly the two functions of the epic: to sing of warriors made famous for eternity by great deeds of war, and to entertain aristocrats at banquet[21] in a prosperous society at peace.

After the first banquet given in honor of Odysseus, the bard thus rises (*Odyssey* 8.73–75):

> ... the Muse inspired Demodocus to sing the glories of heroes. In particular it was something that had a *kleos* that reached all the way to the sky in its full breadth. It was the quarrel between Odysseus and Achilles.

While this story delights the Phaeacians, it immediately provokes tears in Odysseus (*Odyssey* 8.86, 92): it is his identity as the hero of Troy that he retrieves here, because he remembers. The song of the bard places him, in a sense, back in heroic circumstances: after all of the strange adventures that he has known in supernatural lands, he relives at this moment the siege of Troy and the suffering of war. His tears are as much a sign of his current plunge back into the world of warrior's exploits as of his setting aside this heroic world of men, specifically because it fails to return the victor to his homeland.

In the same way, when he hears Demodocus celebrating the ruse of the Trojan Horse, he can no longer hold back his tears:

> So these were the things that the singer most famed was singing. As for Odysseus, he dissolved into tears. He made wet his cheeks with the tears flowing from his eyelids, just as a woman cries, falling down and

---

[20] Vidal-Naquet 1981:60 and following.

[21] *Odyssey* 8.248: "We are extremely fond of good dinners, music, and dancing," Alcinous says to Odysseus. In his commentary on the *Odyssey*, J. B. Hainsworth (Hainsworth and Privitera 1982) shows that this verse is modeled, though in inverted form, on *Iliad* 1.177 and 5.891, verses addressed to Achilles and Ares.

embracing her dear husband, who fell in front of the city and people he was defending, trying to ward off the pitiless day of doom that is hanging over the city and its children. She sees him dying, gasping for his last breath, and she pours herself all over him as she wails with a piercing cry. But there are men behind her, prodding her with their spears, hurting her back and shoulders, and they bring for her a life of bondage, which will give her pain and sorrow. Her cheeks are wasting away with a sorrow that is most pitiful. So also did Odysseus pour out a piteous tear from beneath his brows.

Odyssey 8.521–531[22]

As Pietro Pucci has correctly observed, the song of heroic exploits "brings forth irresistible tears," [23] and it is at this point that the actual metamorphosis of Odysseus takes place. Through his tears, Odysseus regains his past; the song of the bard pulls him again toward the realm of war, of the *Iliad*. What Gérard Genette calls the "oblique relationship" between the *Odyssey* and the *Iliad*[24] can be clearly observed in this passage. In memory of Ilion, Odysseus sheds the tears of a hero, tears significant on two levels: first, it is when the bard sings of Odysseus' victory over Deiphobus (*nikēsai*, *Odyssey* 8.520) that his crying interrupts the story. On this first level, Odysseus is the "ransacker of cities," the *ptoliporthos*[25] hero. On a second level, the tears of Odysseus and the comparison that they cause bring about the end of the interrupted story.[26] The mention of the hero who fell outside the walls of the city while defending his people and the widow taken off into slavery clearly refer to the story of Hector and Andromache. The female Trojan prisoners, implicitly evoked in Demodocus' song ("He sang how the steep citadel was destroyed by different men [the Greeks] in different places," 8.516),[27] can be found in the comparison to the anonymous woman sobbing over her husband.

The structure of this passage, however, remains highly complex, "as if swirling:"[28] in fact, from Demodocus' story to the comparison that associates Odysseus with a widow, there is a double shift in perspective: from the Greeks destroying Ilion (plot) to the Trojan perspective (comparison: the Trojans are the vanquished in question); and from men in combat to a woman in tears.

---

[22] On the meaning of *tēkō* 'dissolve', see p. 113 below.
[23] Pucci 1979:126.
[24] Genette 1982:200.
[25] See the remarks in Clay 1983:103–104.
[26] Nagy (1979:101–102) has demonstrated this in detail.
[27] See Hainsworth and Privitera 1982: ad loc.
[28] Genette 1982:201: "comme tournoyante."

Nevertheless, in order to describe great pain, the poet chooses once again to refer to a woman who is suffering. But the tears, so abundant that they justify this extreme comparison where Odysseus is himself likened to the most vulnerable of victims,[29] give Odysseus the full dimension of his heroic figure, illuminated by the reminder of his painful exploits.

On the other hand, when Demodocus entertains the audience with the love story of Ares and Aphrodite, Odysseus, like the Phaeacians, takes pleasure in the bard's song. The poetic words are also entertaining:

> Thus sang the bard, and both Odysseus and the seafaring Phaeacians were charmed as they heard him.
>
> *Odyssey* 8.367–369[30]

In a sense, the song of the bard sweeps away Odysseus' time adrift at sea. By way of poetry, Odysseus returns to his identity as a great warrior;[31] having been, for the duration of two of the bard's songs, a spectator to another version of himself celebrated by men, he can now return to Ithaca.

Odysseus the Bard

The song of the bard restores a trajectory of possible return for Odysseus. But the ties that the hero maintains with poetry are much more profound and essential. He is one of the Achaeans most celebrated by the bards (*Odyssey* 8.74–75), and at the same time, once his identity has been revealed, he occupies the place of the bard himself, telling his stories in the hall of Alcinous (9.19–20 and 37–38):

> I am Odysseus son of Laertes, renowned among humankind for all manner of subtlety, so that my *kleos* ascends to the sky ... I will tell you of the many hazardous adventures which by Zeus' will I met with on my return from Troy.

The Sirens evoke this same glory of Odysseus, the hero of Troy, using terms from the *Iliad*.[32] Odysseus also, while with Alcinous, tells his story, which is an

---

29 Foley 1978:7; see also Schadewaldt 1965:382–383.
30 For an inversion of this scene, we could compare it to *Odyssey* 8.90–92 (Odysseus weeps, while the Phaeacians are delighted by Demodocus' verses); cf. Diano 1963:418–419; Burkert 1960:136.
31 The *kleos* of the Achaeans sung by the bards is, especially, the tale of their painful trials; Odysseus states this explicitly to Demodocus (*Odyssey* 8.489–490): " ... in such good order do you sing the fate of the Achaeans with all their sufferings and adventures."
32 On this point, see Pucci 1979.

exceptional occurrence:[33] Odysseus is the only character in the epic to tell the tale of his own *kleos*,[34] his own glory.

Just as Achilles, withdrawn from combat, enjoys playing the cithara and singing the deeds of heroes (*Iliad* 9.189), Odysseus is both the hero and the bard of the *Odyssey*. The connections between the figure of the bard and of the hero become still more specific if we take into account where Achilles obtains his cithara: the very instrument of the bard is "part of the spoils that he had taken when he destroyed the city of Eëtion" (9.188). It is as if, between the hero ransacking cities and the bard at the lyre, there exists an obligatory complementarity.[35] It is not irrelevant that Achilles has *struggled to obtain* (the verb is *arnumai*) the lyre specifically, which he plays like a bard. When singing, "[Patroclus] sat in silence, facing him" (*Iliad* 9.190), just as the Phaeacians are attentive to Odysseus' story (*Odyssey* 11.333–334; 13.1–2). The Phaeacian audience is charmed by Odysseus, and Alcinous praises him in these terms: "there is a style about your language as artful as a bard which assures me of your good disposition" (11.368).[36] Great heroes are also singers: "The supreme exploit is then to master language, the gift of poetry ... the only true hero is the one who knows how to speak."[37]

In this other world—the city of Scheria—which is not one of war, Odysseus regains access to his heroic path thanks to poetic song; his tears are those of a hero who remembers. It is as if, among the Phaeacians, his tears are another way for him to recall the valor in his limbs, a means to rediscover his identity. The art of the bard—first hearing it and then practicing it himself—is an obligatory transition from the complete, non-heroic anonymity to which he had been reduced in his wanderings to the all-powerful state he embodies at the end of the *Odyssey*, when he lands in Ithaca as much conqueror of Troy as king.

For Menelaus, another veteran of Troy, even when filled with all the prosperity of his kingdom, does he not cry? Specifically over his memories of Troy and his comrades in arms? "I often grieve, as I sit here in my house, for one and all of them. At times I cry aloud for sorrow" (*Odyssey* 4.100–101), he says to Telemachus.

Heroes, then, through their ability to remember, or more immediately through the powers of *epos* 'poetry', reunite with the essence of their heroic

---

[33] See Segal 1983.

[34] Segal 1983:24 points out that *Odyssey* 9.20 is the only passage in Homer where *melō*, often used in the third person, is used in the first person.

[35] On the lyre and the bow, see Ramnoux 1962:102; Carlier 1981.

[36] See also *Odyssey* 18.518–521 where Eumaeus tells of how Odysseus entranced him with his stories in the manner of a bard.

[37] Frontisi-Ducroux 1976:543: "L'exploit suprême, c'est donc la maîtrise du langage, le don de la poésie ... le seul vrai héros est celui qui sait dire." See also, from a more strictly philological perspective, Di Donato 1969:270–271.

nature by way of their tears. In times of peace, the ability to cry while under the influence of poetic song acts, for the hero, like an extension of his ability to fight during times of war.

The Tears of Odysseus, King of Ithaca

Odysseus' path to winning back his power is fraught with difficulties and hardships, yet, until he is fully reinstated as king, no tears fall from his eyes.[38] It is only after the contest of the bow and the massacre of the suitors, which marks the final transition of his return to royalty, that, with Penelope close, he ceases to contain his emotion and his tears:

> Then Odysseus in his turn melted, and wept as he clasped his dear and faithful wife to his bosom.
>
> *Odyssey* 22.231–232[39]

By the feats he has accomplished, Odysseus has proven himself worthy of royalty and worthy of his wife; in the context of heroic qualification, his tears are possible. In a similar way, he is unable to hold back the emotion that overtakes him when confirming his identity to Laertes; Odysseus cries when reuniting with his father (*Odyssey* 24.234, 318–319).[40]

At the moment when Odysseus accomplishes the feat that confirms his heroism, the comparison that expresses his talent and ability refers once again to his close ties with the art of poetry (*Odyssey* 21.406–411):

> But resourceful Odysseus, when he had taken it up and examined it all over, strung it as easily as a skilled bard strings a new peg of his lyre and makes the twisted gut fast at both ends. Then he took it in his right hand to prove the string, and it sang sweetly under his touch like the twittering of a swallow.

The figure of Odysseus is, in this moment, at the height of his power: handling the agonistic bow with ease, as the bard handles his cithara, making the string "sing" (*aeise*), he completes the act that definitively establishes his preeminence and restores order in Ithaca.[41] He is about to inflict great suffering upon the suitors, and only the bard Phemius will be spared (*Odyssey* 22.344–347).

---

[38] With one exception: when he sees Telemachus at *Odyssey* 16.216–217; see p. 92 above.

[39] Note the contrast between this passage and *Odyssey* 19.209–211 (cited above, p. 93) Odysseus cannot cry when disguised.

[40] When thinking of Peleus, Achilles also cries, *Iliad* 24.511.

[41] Segal 1962:51.

This episode should be compared with the passages in *Odyssey* 8 and 9 where Odysseus reveals his true identity to the Phaeacians. In both cases his status changes: the stranger and guest becomes the lauded hero; the beggar mistreated by the suitors rises to the top of the social ladder in Ithaca. In Scheria, the song of the bard is a source of sorrow for him and a source of pleasure for the Phaeacians (*terpsis*, *Odyssey* 8.91, etc.); in Ithaca his skill, similar to that of a bard, leads to agony (*achos*) for the suitors and joy (*gêthêsen*, 21.414)[42] for himself. In the first case, under the effect of *epos*, he cries and then reconnects with his heroic past; in the second, the archer-bard and the bow-lyre permit a similar movement from anonymity to "recognition."

---

[42] On the alternation of joy and sorrow while under the effect of epic song, see Segal 1983 passim.

3

The Tears of Women

Women do not have it in their nature to compete with the virtue and the greatness of men. On this point, Greek epic does not contradict a universally recognized tradition. Contrary to men, who, through their courage and great deeds, pass from an "ordinary" to a heroic state, women belong, once and for all, to a species that definitively carries within it its own limitations: those of the "race of women."[1]

Therefore, it is no wonder that an examination of the tears of women in one epic poem leads to the other without any difference in perspective. With the exception of a few nuances, the reasons women shed tears are all more or less identical.[2]

The tears of Helen

The figure of Helen, both in the *Iliad* and the *Odyssey*, is situated in the margins of conventional femininity. We have seen that through a number of her characteristics she goes beyond the traditional limits applied to women.[3]

Her tears are not those of ordinary women; they are the manifestation of a more individualized, more personal sentiment, due less to distress and

---

[1] See Loraux 1978 passim and pp. 56–60 above.

[2] In order to be exhaustive, this examination would need to take into account two episodes in the *Iliad* where the poet presents goddesses in tears: Aphrodite wounded by Diomedes in Book 5, and especially Artemis beaten by Hera during the theomachy in Book 21. I will limit myself to pointing out J.-P. Vernant's conclusions on Artemis. Vernant examined this question at length during his 1980–1981 course at the *Collège de France*: an ambiguous figure, Artemis can be a terrible goddess within her legitimate sphere—the *agros* and wild animals, the world and the affairs of women, and more specifically child birth—and at the same time, she is a fragile and weeping virgin when she ventures out onto the battlefield. In this sense, the tears of Artemis in the *Iliad* are a sign of regression back into childhood; rescued by her mother and consoled affectionately by her father, she cries like a little girl (21.493–513). On the meaning one can ascribe to the "error" Aphrodite makes when she goes outside her domain, see Saïd 1978:287–289.

[3] See pp. 80–81 above.

helplessness than to feelings of guilt and shame.[4] In this respect, the fact that each time she speaks in the *Iliad* she wishes for her own death is worthy of note.[5]

Helen cries both while thinking of Menelaus[6] and over the body of Hector, her only friend in Troy whom she has now lost. She also plays an important role in the lamentation at the end of the poem. One may ask[7] why it is Helen, and not a sister—Cassandra, for example—who closes out the lamentations of the women around Hector and the wailing of the people gathered there (*Iliad* 24.776). She is the last of the women to lament, the last woman to speak, and, in a certain sense, the *Iliad* ends with her words: "all shrink and shudder as they go by me" (24.775). The moment she loses Hector, who died for—because of—her, she ceases to be a character in the story and becomes the figure of "Helen, cause of the Trojan War."

Unlike the other women who cry over the loss of a husband or a son, Helen cries for herself, over the pain that her passion has provoked. She bemoans not her condition but her error and its consequences. Helen, like the heroes, sobs over the struggles, the *aethloi*, that she has set in motion. She cries over the human experience of the Trojan War. This makes her the only feminine character in the epic to have such autonomy of emotion: these psychological categories—remorse, guilt—are reserved in the epic for masculine figures.

Conversely, in the *Odyssey*, Helen has the power to stop tears that she has ultimately caused. When Telemachus is the guest of Menelaus in Sparta and the latter evokes memories of Odysseus, everyone begins to cry (*Odyssey* 4.184–186). Using the drug *nē-penthes*, she puts an end to their tears:

> She put a drug into the wine from which they drank. It [= the drug] was against *penthos* [*nē-penthes*] and against anger [*a-kholon*]. It made one forget all bad things. Whoever swallowed it, once it was mixed with the wine into the mixing bowl, could not shed a tear from his cheeks for that day.
>
> *Odyssey* 4.220–223[8]

---

[4] *Iliad* 3.142, 176; 24.773. From the top of the ramparts, surprised not to see her brothers among the Achaeans, she blames their absence on herself: she tells Priam they have not come because of "the shame and disgrace that I have brought upon them" (3.242).

[5] *Iliad* 3.173–175; 6.345–348; 24.764; in these three instances, it is the consequences of her shameful love of Paris that provokes this feeling in her.

[6] Moved by the idea that she might see him on the plains of Troy (which does not happen), she came out of her room "weeping as she went" (*Iliad* 3.142).

[7] Clader 1976:11.

[8] Some commentators think this is opium, since it comes from Egypt; see Stanford 1948 and Hainsworth and Privitera 1982 *ad loc.*

A much later tradition attributes to Helen the origin of a plant with properties similar to *nē-penthes*—those of dissipating melancholy and sorrow: this plant, helenium, is said to be born from her tears.[9] Here again, her duality appears: Helen has the power to both cause and remedy suffering.[10]

The sobs of women

The *Iliad* resonates with the crying and sobbing of Trojan women; the *Odyssey* is made wholly from the tears of Penelope, as if all of femininity were summarized by her crying. In this world of war, each woman cries for a father, brother, or son fallen in combat. As both at stake to be defended and prey to be attained, women can only cry once their defenders have fallen. The death of Hector, protector of Troy, will set off a flow of tears from Hecuba, Andromache, Cassandra, and the Trojan women as a whole.

Andromache weeps from her first appearance in the poem to her last.[11] The theme of tears underpins her entire story. By studying the play of formulas (variations or modifications, certain particular meanings) and the uses of non-formulary language, Charles Segal has shown that the motif of Andromache's grief runs throughout the *Iliad*.[12] Her tears, mentioned while she is on the ramparts, intensify when she returns to the palace. Later, at the moment of Hector's death, she begins a sort of preliminary lament: "she started to sing a lament in the midst of the Trojan women" (22.476). Finally, the scene of great mourning in *Iliad* 24 shows her leading the public lamentation at Hector's funeral. In other words, Andromache is preparing, from her first appearance in the poem, for the final scene of lamentation. In *Iliad* 6, her tears are a sign of things to come: the death of Hector. Her famous "laughing amidst tears" (*dakruoen gelasasa*, 6.484)[13] represents the ultimate commingling of happiness and grief, her final moment of joy shared with Hector. She laughs for the last time, and already her tears irreparably shroud her destiny. Back home, accompanied by her maids, she laments for the living Hector—who is already virtually dead—in a scene that foreshadows the great lamentation at the end of the *Iliad* (6.499–502):

---

[9] Cf. Vellay 1957:105–107, who cites Theophrastus *History of Plants* 2.1.3, etc., and Pliny *Natural History* 21.33 and 91.

[10] See p. 81 above.

[11] Whether her tears are "real" or envisioned: *Iliad* 6.373, 405, 455, 459, 484, 496, 499; 22.87, 476; 24.723, 745–746.

[12] Segal 1971a; see pp. 78–80 above.

[13] On the tradition of this theme in Western literature, see Antin 1961.

[she] ... bade them all [the servants] join in her lament; so they mourned Hector slayer of men in his own house though he was yet alive, for they thought that they should never see him return safe from battle, and from the furious hands of the Achaeans.

The absence of Odysseus and the departure of Telemachus explain why Penelope always appears with tears in her eyes in the *Odyssey*.[14] Like Andromache, she is consumed by the tears of grief for a husband whose death has not been confirmed. Sobbing and wailing are second nature to her.[15] Even in her sleep, she is tormented by sorrow. The vision of her sister, sent by Athena, says this explicitly:

You are asleep, Penelope: the gods who live at ease will not suffer you to weep and be so sad.

Odyssey 4.803–805[16]

Penelope cries without ceasing, as if from the departure of Odysseus her tears are the only way to resist forgetting, the only way to preserve a memory of her husband and, through this memory, to preserve her status as Odysseus's wife. This is her way of refusing to allow, in a word, Odysseus to be replaced.

By her endless tears, it is as if Penelope is "out of bounds"; she abstracts herself in a certain sense from the reality of Ithaca to live, via her sobbing, near her absent husband. Her tears are like a screen that preserves the personal, private memory she has of Odysseus, while, at the same time, preventing the public celebration of his heroic memory. Indeed, she, refuses to hear the bard when he sings "the homecoming of the Achaeans" (*Odyssey* 1.326) to the suitors (1.337–344):

Phemius, you know many another thing that charms mortals, all about the deeds of men and gods, to which singers give glory. Sing for them some one of those songs of glory, and let them in silence drink their wine. But you stop this sad song, this disastrous song, which again and again affects my very own heart in my breast, wearing it down, since an unforgettable grief comes over me, more than ever. I feel this way because that is the kind of person I long for, recalling his memory again

---

[14]   *Odyssey* 1.336, 363; 2.376; 4.110, 705, 719, 721, 749, 758, 800–801, 805–806, 819, 828; 11.183; 13.338; 14.129–130; 16.39, 332, 450; 17.8, 33, 38, 40, 102–103; 18.172–173; 19.204–213, 249, 251, 264, 268, 513, 517, 541, 543, 596, 603; 20.58–59, 84–92; 21.56–57, 357; 23.33, 207, 351–352; 24.295.

[15]   Thus M.-M. Mactoux 1975:21–23.

[16]   See also *Odyssey* 19.541–543. On Penelope's sleeping, see Segal 1967:327–329.

and again, the memory of a man whose glory extends far and wide throughout Hellas and midmost Argos.

Jesper Svenbro has shown that, while the theme of Phemius' song is "return," the song is original in relation to the tradition of *Nostoi*: "It is only in the 'Phemios version,' as we are able to reconstruct it, that the hero dies before making it back to his island."[17] Obviously, the disappearance of Odysseus serves the interests of the suitors; by prohibiting the singing of this "disastrous song," Penelope is refusing the death of Odysseus.

In the *Iliad*, few scenes are as pitiable as the one in which Hecuba, while weeping and baring her breast, begs Hector not to fight Achilles outside the city walls (22.79–85).[18] Having lost her son, in her motherly grief she refers to Achilles as "that terrible man on whose liver I would fain fasten and devour it" to avenge Hector (*Iliad* 24.212–213).[19] Because she has just seen her son die before her eyes, she is momentarily capable of rising to the same level of savagery as Achilles, the "carnivore" (*ōmēstès*, 24.207) whom she so despises.[20] No longer is it possible for her to take part in the reconciliation scene of *Iliad* 24; as a mother, she cannot forgive her son's murderer.

During Hector's funeral, the lamentations of the women are of primary importance, and furthermore, the poet conveys only their words to us. The lamentations of Andromache, Hecuba, and Helen restate in a way the principal themes of the *Iliad*.

Andromache speaks of the suffering of war, the pain of the Trojan people, the impending fall of the city, and its consequence, the enslavement of the Trojan women (*Iliad* 24.728–730):

[Before Astyanax reaches manhood] our city will be razed and overthrown, for you who watched over it are no more—you who were its savior the guardian of our wives and children.

Hecuba makes ample room for the gods in her lamentation, remembering that Hector has always been well loved by them, who, even in death, protect him from affronts by preserving and enhancing his beauty (*Iliad* 24.749–750):

[17] "C'est seulement dans la 'version de Phémios', telle que nous pouvons la reconstruire, que le héros meurt avant d'avoir regagné son île" (Svenbro 1976:20).
[18] See pp. 45–46 above, and Griffin 1980:25.
[19] This scene can be compared to *Iliad* 22.347 (Achilles threatening Hector). On the "avenging cannibalism" of mothers, see Hirvonen 1968:28.
[20] This is the only passage in the *Iliad* where *ōmēstès* is used to describe a human being; see Segal 1971b:61–62 and 68, and Schein 1970:74–75.

So long as you were alive the gods loved you well, and even in death they have not been utterly unmindful of you.

Finally, Helen recalls the qualities of Hector's heart, the aristocratic conceptions of courage and strength, saving room for his gentleness (*Iliad* 24.774–775):

... for there is no one else in Troy who is kind to me.

These three lamentations correspond to the three conversations Hector has while in Troy. In *Iliad* 6, Hector feared the enslavement of Astyanax and Andromache: here, the realization of that threat is approaching and Andromache herself takes up the theme (*Iliad* 6.454–463; 24.731–735). Hecuba had suggested that Hector offer a libation to Zeus, and now, before his deathbed, she recalls the favor the gods showed him (6.258–260; 24.749–750). In her bedchamber in Troy, Helen had "tried to soothe" Hector (6.343) and suggested that he sit and forget the troubles she had caused; in *Iliad* 24 she reaffirms this same idea (6.344–356; 24.762–775). And finally, the servants who had cried for him when he was alive lament in this moment his mortal remains (6.499–500; 24.746).

Funerary ritual required the relatives of the dead, particularly the women, to assemble around the bed to contemplate the dead during the *prosthesis* 'laying out of the body'. For a warrior who saw himself as lost, not having his mother and wife near his deathbed was a major fear (Lycaon: 21.123–124; Hector: 22.352–353). For these women, it would be a great source of regret, as Hecuba says from the top of the ramparts to Hector:

Should the wretch kill you, neither I nor your richly dowered wife shall ever weep, dear offshoot of myself, over the bed on which you lie.

Iliad 22.86–88[21]

In each instance, the participation of women (mothers, wives) is stressed; their presence is essential during the private, familial, first days of the funeral proceedings. Women mourn for the dead as well for their own misfortune; without Hector, the Trojan women are now lost. In the three lamentations just described, there is only the question of grief and regret. These mournful wailings of women, these *gooi*, evoke less the glory of the hero who has just died than the changes—disastrous in nature—that his absence entails.[22] It is certainly significant that this type of resigned and pained discourse comes from women. There are, in fact, two groups surrounding Hector's body: the professional singers who intone the dirges in honor of Hector and the women who

---

[21] See also *Odyssey* 14.129–130; 24.294–296.
[22] See Redfield 1975:180

respond with tears to each of the lamentations (*goos*) of Andromache, Hecuba, and Helen.[23] The threnody is sung by the bards, while the *goos*, a wailing moan, is cried out by the mourning women.[24]

The lamentations of Andromache, Hecuba, and Helen elicit, to varying degrees, the reaction of the participants to the funeral. Each lamentation ends with *hōs ephato klaiousa*—"bitterly did she weep the while"—and the second half of the verse introduces an increase in the intensity of the wailing. Andromache moves the women, who respond to her by sobbing as well (*Iliad* 24.746). The long lament of Hecuba (*adinos goos*, 24.750) causes endless moans from the participants (24.760). And finally, after the third lamentation, that of Helen, the entire crowd sobs (24.776).

The preparation of the pyre, the cremation of the body, the removal of the bones, and the construction of Hector's *sēma* 'tomb' are tasks carried out by the Trojans, the *laos* 'people assembled' (*Iliad* 24.790–791).[25] The ceremony ends with the funeral banquet attended by Hector's family members and his companions in arms. The official funeral services for Hector, celebrated by his companions, help to permanently fix his hero status.

Since their meaning is completely emotional—because they are feminine—the tears of women belong to a limited register (the private sphere) that cannot extend into the praise of the dead, which is a masculine concern. Thus, the distinction of masculine and feminine values is, once again, clearly marked: in the epic, a woman does not cry like a man. Her helpless tears attest to the constant potentiality of her enslavement. Deprived of the man who protects her, she is reduced to nothing. Her tears can only be succeeded by destitution without remedy. At funerals, as well, her attitude differs from that of a man, as Jean-Pierre Vernant has explained, stressing that "in mourning there is a different perspective depending on whether the deceased is seen by a close circle of family, particularly women, or seen by a larger group of his battle companions. In the first case, the deceased is evoked in terms of what his passing will cost those close to him in tears, pain, and grief. In the second, mourners recall the costs he inflicted on the enemy in losses and suffering through his skills as a warrior hero."[26]

---

[23] On lamentation, see Reiner 1938:2–59 and Alexiou 1974.

[24] See p. 114 below.

[25] On the meaning of *laos* in the *Iliad*, see Jeanmaire 1939:54–58 and 88–89.

[26] "... dans la déploration, la différence de perspective suivant qu'il s'agit du mort vu par le cercle étroit de ses proches, spécialement les femmes, et le mort vu par le groupe plus large de ses compagnons d'armes. Dans le premier cas, le mort est évoqué en fonction de ce qu'à ses intimes sa fin coûte de larmes, de douleur, de deuil. Dans le second, on rappelle ce qu'il a coûté à l'ennemi comme pertes et souffrances, en sa qualité de héros guerrier" (Vernant 1977:434).

The energetic tears of heroes, who, after their sobs, can go on fighting, counter the pitiful powerlessness and moral torpor of the wailing women. In short, the tears of women are not, strictly speaking, identical in value to those of men.

4

The Language of Tears

His cheeks were soon wet with tears, as his feelings suddenly broke
loose; he would have wept himself away in the distance, that no trace
of his existence might remain. Amid his deep-drawn sighs he seemed
to recover; the soft, serene air penetrated him. The world was again
present to his senses, and thoughts of other times began to speak to
him consolation.

Novalis, Henri d'Ofterdingen

If the *Iliad* is a story of anger and tears, told by an eminent poet and master
wordsmith, the range of representations of sorrow, its extent and its intersec-
tions with other registers, merits mapping out. The vocabulary of grief, the
symbolism of tears, the gestures of a suffering body: these are the approaches
that I have chosen to address the question of suffering in the epic.

Comparisons. Images. Vocabulary.

For men, the *Iliad* provides essentially one comparison that describes the tears
of two heroes, Agamemnon (9.13–15) and Patroclus (16.2–4):

> Agamemnon shed tears as it were a dark-running stream or cataract on
> the side of some sheer cliff.[1]

Black and other dark colors have connotations of death and danger. The
theme of a dark spring with black waters recalls the strange comparison in *Iliad*
16 that presents the Myrmidons as carnivorous wolves who "go in a pack to
lap the black water bubbling from a dark spring with their long thin tongues"

---

[1] On black water and the epithet *dnopheros* used with *melas* for water, see Moreux 1967:257–261.
We are reminded also of the black and destructive water of the Styx: Pausanias *Description of
Greece* 8.17.6 and 8.18; *Iliad* 8.369.

(160–162).[2] Agamemnon weeps intensely at the spectacle of the Achaeans' defeat. The Trojans fail, in this instance, to definitively defeat the Greeks, though only night halts their momentum. "Their princes were all of them in despair" (*Iliad* 9.3), and Agamemnon convenes the assembly where the decision is made to go and ask for Achilles' relief.

In the *Iliad*, black is the color of Agamemnon's wrath (1.103), black the mental anguish of Hector upon seeing a companion struck down (17.83), black the blood of corpses (10.298). Black is very clearly associated with death and pain, more through the fear and revulsion that they provoke than through a reference to the color of blood. "Death is as frightening as 'black' or the night, death is black, death is night," writes Bernard Moreux;[3] and, indeed, adjectives meaning black or dark abound in the *Iliad*, where death is waiting around every turn. The tears of Agamemnon, compared to the water from a black spring, become part of the evidence in the context of the disastrous war; the tears of the Achaeans' chief are dark like the black death he comes into contact with on the battlefield.[4]

The second notable comparison is one applied in the *Odyssey* to Odysseus and Telemachus, in tears at the moment of their reunion (16.216–219):

> They were both so much moved that they cried aloud like eagles or vultures with crooked talons that have been robbed of their half fledged young by peasants. Thus piteously did they weep ...

The poet here operates on a different level: it is not, as in the comparison in the *Iliad*, a sinister context that causes Odysseus to sob, but the memory of his suffering and the emotion that comes over him upon finally reuniting with his son. The comparison evokes relatively powerful and feared birds—at least, in the case of the vulture—predators whose status oscillates between two poles: they can represent a terrible aspect of divinity (Athena and Apollo at *Iliad* 7.59), or, when they are scavenging on the battlefield, the horror of death without burial. The magnitude and the violence of these acute tears (*ligeōs*) is more intense (with the force of the comparative *adinōteron*) than the cries of birds robbed of their young.[5]

---

[2] The comparison is remarkable for the elements of savagery and brutality in the description of the Myrmidons arming themselves for battle; see Schnapp-Gourbeillon 1981:51–52.

[3] "La mort fait aussi peur que le 'noir' ou la nuit, la mort est noire, la mort est nuit" (Moreux 1967:239). See also Mawet 1979:46–47 on the affective value of *melas* 'black' in the context of pain.

[4] We can account for the tears of Patroclus in the same way: Patroclus is also distraught at the moment when the Greeks have just suffered a terrible assault, during which the principal commanders are wounded (cf. *Iliad* 16.21–29) and after which it seems that victory is no longer possible.

[5] Stanford (1948, *ad loc.*) points out that this comparison was borrowed by Aeschylus in the *Agamemnon* (lines 48 and following) who writes of "that wail, / Sharp-piercing bird-shriek"

For women there is more of an emphasis on passivity, the "liquidity" of feminine nature, as if the inadequacy of the maternal body for war and the art of combat is due, in part, to its ability to melt and soften. Consequently, Penelope is presented in the following manner when speaking with the disguised Odysseus (*Odyssey* 19.204–209):

> Penelope wept as she listened, for her heart was melted. As the snow wastes upon the mountain tops when the winds from South, East, and West have breathed upon it and thawed it till the rivers run bank full with water, even so did her cheeks overflow with tears for the husband who was all the time sitting by her side.[6]

The triple occurrence of the verb *tēkesthai* and the double occurrence of the compound *katatēkesthai* clearly convey the idea of liquefaction, melting, and dissolving. Penelope is consumed by sorrow;[7] as a result of crying, her skin withers, and, somehow, her incessant tears wear the life out of her, dissolve her strength. This is evident in another passage when Odysseus encourages her to stop crying: "No longer waste your beautiful skin nor cry your heart out in weeping" (*Odyssey* 19.262–263).

Sobs have the power to ravage the beauty and the lives of women. Consumed by tears, they waste away; their cheeks wither, and their beauty spoils. The poet, by using a partially overlapping vocabulary, indicates that tears have effects on women similar to those that war has on men. To describe warriors who are dying, Homer uses the verbs *phthinuthō* and *enairō*, among others (*Iliad* 17.364; 24.244); he uses these same terms to express the grief of women, as if tears were the double, however distorted, of wounds on the battlefield.

Is this capacity to empty one's energy in a flood of tears strictly a feminine characteristic? It is not entirely certain. However, one can see in this comparison the poet's intention to distinguish between the way men and women cry. The tears of Agamemnon are dark; those of Penelope alter her beauty as they slide down her cheeks, like the flow of melting snow.

(56–57; trans. Browning 1889). Perhaps we should also read this image of vultures with crooked talons as an allusion to the suitors who, every day, are pillaging the goods of Odysseus (*Odyssey* 1.91–92).

6   This comparison responds to the metaphor at *Odyssey* 19.136 (also in relation to Penelope): "But sorrow over Odysseus melts my heart."

7   She "melts"; in Hesiod's *Theogony* (862), the earth melted when struck by Zeus' lightning bolt. *Tēkō* is also used in the vocabulary of love, the other "weakness" of women: thus, in Sophocles' *Trachiniae* (462–463), Iole is "impregnated" and "melts" with passion for Heracles; see also Euripides *Hippolytus* 525; Plato *Phaedrus* 251B; etc. And see the remarks in Onians 1954:201–203 and Komornicka 1981:62–63.

A digression on vocabulary is necessary here. To express suffering, the Homeric lexicon possesses a considerable number of terms, the exact meanings of which are sometimes difficult to gauge with certainty. Quite often, the semantic fields involved are contiguous, and it is often impossible to determine the precise meaning of a given term. Furthermore, as Francine Mawet has judiciously written, "the major difficulty we encounter is the danger of purely and simply transposing into ancient Greek the categories and the structure of the vocabulary of *'douleur* [pain]' from another language—in this case French—which inevitably occurs if we retain indiscriminately all the words that might be translated as *'douleur'* in French."[8]

In this survey, I am only including words that mean cry or shed tears and have chosen to study them in order of prominence.[9]

> *Klaiō* is the verb used most frequently (thirty-eight occurrences): it often describes the sorrow of grief, and most of the time its meaning is intensified by the assertion of tears shed. The verb is almost always preceded or followed by *dakru* 'tear' (*Iliad* 1.360, 362; 3.148, 176; 7.426, 427, etc.).

> *Goaō* is the verb for sobbing; it often introduces or concludes an expression of grief or a lamentation formulated by the protagonist (*Iliad* 6.500; 18.315, etc.). It is almost always used to describe the suffering of a person in mourning. The noun *goos*, qualified by adjectives like *aliastos* 'incessant' (24.760), *adinos* 'abundant' (24.747), and *krueros* 'frozen' (24.524), is the word for lamentation (twenty-four occurrences). During mourning rituals, the verb used to say "lead them in their lament" is *exarchein* or *archein* (18.51, 316; 23.12, 17; 24.721, 723, 747, 761).[10]

> *Dakruō* denotes the appearance of tears in the eyes. The verb is less common than the noun *dakru*,[11] which is always accompanied by verbs that clearly indicate the image of visible, flowing tears. The most common phrasing is *dakrua cheein* or *kata dakrua cheein* (*Iliad* 1.413; 3.142;

---

[8] "La principale difficulté à laquelle on se heurte est le danger de transposer purement et simplement, en grec ancien, les catégories et la structure du vocabulaire de la 'douleur' d'une autre langue—en l'espèce le français—, ce qui se produit inévitablement si l'on retient indistinctement tous les mots susceptibles d'être traduits par 'douleur' en français" (Mawet 1979:18). Mawet's work and especially her long introduction have been of great utility to me.

[9] For details, refer to the compilation in Scarcella 1958:799–834, which provides a meticulous accounting of the vocabulary of tears in Homer. Even though it does not offer any interpretation, this "catalogue" remains useful.

[10] See Martino 1977:195–197; Alexiou 1974:11–13, 131 and following.

[11] There are five occurrences of *dakruō* in the *Iliad* (1.349; 10.377; 16.7; 19.229; 22.491) compared to forty-three for *dakru*.

6.405, etc.). Homer also says *dakrua leibein* or *eibein* (13.88; 18.32, etc.). Less commonly used are verbs like *rheein* (*Iliad* 18.427; *Odyssey* 24.318), *hēkein* (*Odyssey* 23.33), and *ekpiptein* (*Iliad* 2. 266; *Odyssey* 16.16). With the verb *ballein* 'fall' the locations where the flow of tears begins and ends are often specified: tears fall from eyelids, *apo blepharōn*, and onto the ground, *chamai* (*Odyssey* 17.490) or *chamadis* (*Odyssey* 2.114). A very rare but highly significant use describing the violence of sobbing occurs in the expression *dakru' anaprēsas* (*Iliad* 9. 433 and *Odyssey* 2.81—the only two instances of *anaprēthō* in the epic): tears well up to the point of bursting in the eyes of Phoenix and Telemachus.

A second set of verbs remains to be considered: verbs that refer more to the sound, the noise, of sobbing. Between moans, wails, cries of pain, and tears, there is certainly overlap, but it seems that the group *oduromai, olophuromai, muromai, kōkuō, oimōzō, stenachō, stenachizō,* and *stenō* denotes the sound of wailing more than the flow of tears. *Kōkuō* is an interesting verb because it is applicable only to women:[12] it clearly indicates the idea of a piercing cry or shriek. The expression *baru stenachōn*[13]—'heavily moaning'—might be an equivalent, in the masculine sphere, for the cries of suffering women. Here again, adjectives and adverbs that refer to the register of sound are used to provide details about wailing—sobs of men that are 'heavy' (*baru, barea*), 'intense' (*adina*), etc.

A Biology of Tears

How tears arise

For the warrior, the first signs of a crying episode are shuddering and trembling. It is as if the anxiety mounting in the heart of the afflicted hero corresponds physically to a spasm, an emotional thrust that causes a flow of tears (*Iliad* 10.9–10):

> ... even so did Agamemnon heave many a heavy sigh, feeling his sobs mount from deep in his heart, for his spirit trembled within him and his entrails were shaking.

The tremor that characterizes the physical state just before one bursts into tears is similar in nature to the corporeal manifestation of fear.[14] When the warrior

[12] *Iliad*: Thetis (18.37); Brisēis (19.284); Hecuba (22.407; 24.200); Cassandra (24.703). *Odyssey*: Eurycleia (2.361); a group of women (4.259; 8.537); Penelope (19.541; 24.295).
[13] See pp. 121–122 below.
[14] See p. 21 above.

wants to cry or when he succumbs to fear, his eyelids and knees tremble. In both cases, the specific sign for this type of emotion is the trembling of a body part.[15] Nothing like this happens for women; on the contrary, as we have seen, they cry passively, they dissolve almost peacefully. This inversion is still more precise if we recall how Penelope is consumed by tears and melts like snow in the sun,[16] while Agamemnon's grief in the passage cited above is compared to a flood of hail and snow (*Iliad* 10.6–7).[17]

Stinging in the nostrils is another sign. When Odysseus finds his father, old, miserable, shaken, "his nostrils quivered as he looked upon [him]" (*Odyssey* 24.318–319). Odysseus' vitality, his biting *menos*,[18] floods into his nostrils with a forceful surge (*proruptō*). Again in this image, the signs of impending tears belong to the register of masculine energy.

The third notable physiological manifestation is aphasia, or more precisely aphonia. Sometimes, when emotion and grief are too intense, the hero weeps in silence, as Antilochus does, for example, when he learns of the death of Patroclus: "For a long time he was speechless; his eyes filled with tears and he could find no utterance" (*Iliad* 17.694–696).[19]

Before crying, it is as if the Homeric hero is paralyzed: his entrails contract in a muscular spasm that results in the secretion of tears; his vocal cords are occasionally blocked for a time. Tears are a visible, exterior extension of a wave that invades the body of a man in the throes of suffering.

The fertility of tears

Few epithets are applied to tears: *thermon, teren, thaleron*. Tears are warm, tender, delicate, or still flourishing.

Of the eight uses of *thermos* in the *Iliad*, five are for descriptions of tears; three concern baths and the blood of a wound.[20] The five occurrences of the expression *dakrua therma cheontes* 'while shedding burning tears', apply to two particularly dramatic contexts: the funerals that take place during the truce in Book 7 (as the Trojans prepare their dead for burial, 426) and the episode of Patroclus' death.

---

[15] On this double association (trembling/fear and trembling/tears), see p. 94 above.

[16] See p. 113 above.

[17] Is the opposition between masculine and feminine operative even in the choice of climatic comparisons? Are the sobs of Agamemnon, like a winter snowstorm, diametrically opposed to the stream of Penelope's tears, which are compared to the melting snow of spring?

[18] See Mawet 1979:42 who points out that the adjective *drimus* 'acrid, piercing' describes battles (*Iliad* 15.696), the rage of a lion (18.322), and the *menos* of Odysseus; to varying degrees, we are dealing here with a term that has connotations of masculinity.

[19] Other examples: Eumelus (*Iliad* 22.396–397), Eurylochus (*Odyssey* 10.244–299).

[20] Tears: *Iliad* 7.426; 16.3; 17.437–438; 18.17, 235. The hot blood of Agamemnon's wound: *Iliad* 11.266; hot baths: 15.6 and 22.444.

That sequence begins at *Iliad* 16.30, when Patroclus cries over his inability to come to the aid of the Greeks.[21] Begging Achilles to let him leave, he approaches "with burning tears welling from his eyes, as from some dark spring whose black stream falls over the ledges of a high precipice" (16.3–4). This same comparison[22] was examined above characterizing Agamemnon, though that passage did not mention burning tears. Later, when Patroclus has died, Antilochus brings Achilles the painful message of his death while "weeping burning tears" (18.17). The final echo of this theme is found later in Book 18 (235), when Achilles cries in the same way for his friend. The recurrence of the expression *dakrua therma cheontes* underlines the dramatic intensity of the passage. Another element accentuates the pathos of the episode: when Patroclus dies, Achilles' horses, who, like his weapons, accompany him on the battlefield, shed tears (17.434–440):

> ... they stood with their chariot stock still, as a pillar set over the tomb of some dead man or woman, and bowed their heads to the ground. Hot tears fell from their eyes as they mourned the loss of their charioteer, and their noble manes drooped all wet from under the yokestraps on either side the yoke.

The pillar of stone, the hot tears, the "flourishing" mane: beyond the beauty of the image, the interweaving of themes makes use of the vocabulary of suffering—stone/fountain of tears,[23] heat/tears, fertility/tears. The symbolic elements of tears are condensed in the sorrow of Achilles' horses.

The *Odyssey* presents a distribution that is more or less identical: of eight occurrences of *thermos*, three describe tears. The others describe food, blood, and baths.[24] Burning tears in the *Odyssey* are shed on occasions where the emotional and dramatic dimensions are strongly emphasized: Agamemnon crying upon returning to his homeland before dying (4.523), the tears of Eurycleia in the moments before she recognizes Odysseus (19.362), the sobs of the Achaeans during the funeral of Achilles (24.46).

Apart from poetic conventions and metrical requirements, it seems that the "heat" of tears adds a particular quality to the suffering thus determined. With one exception (the group of Trojans celebrating the funeral for their warriors), it is always the Greek heroes, and the most revered among them, who cry in this manner.

---

[21]   See Segal 1971b:25–26.
[22]   See p. 111 above.
[23]   See pp. 129–130 below on Niobe.
[24]   Food: *Odyssey* 14.77; the bloody eye of the Cyclops: 9.388; hot baths: 8.429, 451; 19.388.

A tear can also be delicate and tender, *teren* (*Iliad* 3.142; 16.11; 19.323; *Odyssey* 16.332). In the epic, leaves, tears, the skin of young people, "the flower of youth" are tender, fragile.[25] Between the delicate young sprout and the tender skin of youth—for young girls and warriors—the analogy is obvious. Should the use of *teren* in the description of tears perhaps be considered an allusion to the "life" of tears, to their vitality?

In this respect, the expression *thaleron kata dakru cheontes* warrants close attention. The adjective *thaleros* is used sixteen times in the *Odyssey* and eighteen in the *Iliad*.

Pierre Chantraine indicates that *thallō* means 'to sprout' or 'to be in bloom' and that the original meaning of the verb was related to vegetation;[26] metaphorically, it means to be abundant or prosperous. In Homeric poetry, the distribution of the use of the adjective 'flourishing' falls into four groups: tears, meals, youth and fertility, and plant life.

Tears are described by this adjective in four types of formulas:

- θαλερὸν κατὰ δάκρυ χέοντες [*Iliad* 6.496; *Odyssey* 4.556; 10.201, 409, 570; 11.5, 466; 12.12; 22.447]

- θαλερὸν δέ οἱ ἔκπεσε δάκρυ [*Iliad* 2.266; *Odyssey* 16.16]

- θαλερὸν κατα δάκρυον εἶβεν [*Iliad* 24.9; *Odyssey* 11.391]

- θαλερὸν δὲ κατείβετο δάκρυ παρειῶν [*Iliad* 24.794]

'Flourishing' tears occur more often in the *Odyssey* than in the *Iliad*. Of the sixteen occurrences of the adjective, ten are specifically related to tears and one, connected to *goos*, is implicitly associated (*Odyssey* 10.457). In the *Iliad*, *thaleros* is most frequently used in its literal sense: it describes fruitful unions, husbands or "flourishing" wives, and men in the prime of their lives (3.53; 6.430; 8.156; 3.26; 4.474; 10.259; 11.414, etc.).

However, as Steven Lowenstam has shown,[27] there is a relationship between *thaleros* and tears that, while indirect, is nevertheless remarkable. In fact, in three of the crying scenes, the epithet is applied not to tears, but rather to thighs, a mane, and a voice. When Ares laments over his dead son, he strikes "his two sturdy thighs with the flat of his hands" (*Iliad* 15.113–114) as a sign of grief. There is a displacement of *thaleros*—usually used as an epithet for *dakru* 'tear'—onto *mēros* 'thigh'. When Antilochus learns of the death of Patroclus, "his

---

[25] Foliage: *Iliad* 13.380; *Odyssey* 12.357; flowers: *Odyssey* 9.449; skin: *Iliad* 4.237; 13.553; 14.406; Hesiod *Works and Days* 522.

[26] Chantraine 1968–1977, s. v. θάλλω.

[27] Lowenstam 1979:125–135.

eyes filled with tears and he could find no utterance" (*Iliad* 17.695–696).[28] Finally, when the time comes for Achilles' horses to cry for their charioteer, the tears flow and soil their abundant manes (17.437–439). The context of weeping thus induces the transfer of the epithet *thaleros* onto another part of the body, a part that is also involved in the pain: the throat, the thighs, the mane. By association, the flourishing character of tears is communicated to another part of the person who is crying.

The majority of commentators[29] interpret this adjective to mean simply 'abundant' or 'humid' when applied to tears, which would correspond to the French expression *"pleurer à chaudes larmes"* [literally, "to cry hot tears")].[30] However, Greek traditions following epic have extensively made use of the theme of the fertility of tears. Whether they are shed by gods, men, or trees, tears give birth to a variety of substances and plants;[31] the most famous example is the amber born of the tears of the sisters of Phaethon: "… in grief for Phaethon, [they] drop the amber radiance of their tears" (Euripides *Hippolytus* 740–741, trans. Kovacs)[32] Furthermore, the eye was often considered to be one of the areas of generation. As Aristotle explains, "the region about the eyes is, of all the head, that most nearly connected with the generative secretions" (*On the Generation of Animals* 747a13, trans. Platt). Undoubtedly, there is considerable difference between Homer's poetic metaphor, the mythical tradition of the creative eye, and Aristotle's theory of bodily fluids. Yet among these elements, each belonging to a different epoch and level of thought, there seem to be points of contact, which do not arise by chance, and which must at least be pointed out.

The association of the ideas of heat, growth, and fertility is thus in the background of the biological conception of tears: tears are alive, "flourishing" even, as the young warriors are. From the adjective *thaleros*, which belongs fully to the vocabulary of plant life, this hypothesis can be further clarified: just as the existence of men is commonly associated with plant growth—and in the specific case of war, the death of a warrior is like the death of a tree or a flower[33]—tears of

---

[28] An identical expression (*thalerē … phōnē*) at *Iliad* 23.396–397; *Odyssey* 4.704–705; 19.471–472.

[29] From Eustathius (*ad Iliad.* 2.206) to Leaf 1900, Stanford 1948, and Willcock 1970 (*ad loc.*)

[30] Translator's note: In French, *"pleurer à chaudes larmes"* is a common idiomatic expression that corresponds roughly to the English "to cry ones eyes out." The French retains the nuances of heat in a way that is lost in similar expressions for intense crying in English.

[31] Tears of the dawn = dew (Ovid *Metamorphoses* 13.621–622); tears of Helen = helenium (see p. 104 above); tears of the lotus = gum (Herodotus 2.96); tears of trees = *propolis* (Aristotle *History of Animals* 533b28, etc); see Deonna 1965:148–153.

[32] See also Lucian *De astrologia* 19; *De saltatione* 35.

[33] Glaucus states this explicitly to Diomedes (*Iliad* 6.146): "Men come and go as leaves year by year upon the trees."

heroes can be viewed as a vital secretion, like the sap of plants.[34] A dead tree dries up, a dead body stiffens; death is total desiccation, as the poet says of a warrior who has just died.[35] The body of a living man differs from that of a dead man in that it continues to be irrigated by vital fluid, which is composed of several different liquids: marrow, spinal fluid, synovial fluid, sperm, etc. Is it not appropriate to include sweat and tears here, as R. B. Onians does[36] in his interpretation of verses that present the sweat that overtakes the knees of a hero or the tears that consume Odysseus' life? When he cries on Calypso's island, Odysseus pours out and loses a little of this vital fluid, known as *aiōn* in Homer (*Odyssey* 5.151–153):

> ... his eyes ever filled with tears, his sweet life [*glukus aiōn*] wasting away as he wept for his homecoming.[37]

For Odysseus, tears "exhaust his will to live";[38] vitality flows from him in his tears. In Homer, *aiōn* can mean lifespan, vital force, and source of vitality all at the same time, and it is difficult to dismiss, in the example of Odysseus, the idea that his life's essence is escaping from his eyes. This is indeed the conclusion of Émile Benveniste concerning the Homeric conception of *aiōn*: "It is indeed because αἰών is the source of all vigor, and not only the duration of life, that one would say of a youth killed in his prime: ἀπ᾽ αἰῶνος νέος ὤλεο (Ω 725), or even μινυνθάδιος δέ οἱ αἰὼν ἔπλετο (Δ 478 = P 302), referring to Simoeisius flourishing in his youth (ἠίθεον θαλερὸν Σιμοείσιον [Δ 473])."[39]

In his prime, Simoeisius loses his *aiōn*; still intact, Odysseus weeps fertile tears and lets his *aiōn* flow out of him. Could there be, in this echoed image of flourishing tears, a transfer of the warrior's vigor, which is being expressed at the same time that it is escaping? Sweating, having a knee joint that dries out, and crying would all then be synonymous ways for Homer to express a loss of vigor. Tears, just like sperm and marrow, would thus participate in a liquid principle of life, a rather indistinct formulation.[40]

---

[34] The death of a warrior = a falling tree or flower: *Iliad* 4.482–487; 8.306–308; 13.178–180, 389–401, 437; 16.482–484; 17.53–56.

[35] *Iliad* 4.487 (Simoeisius lies like a felled and drying poplar).

[36] Onians 1954:191–192, 202 and following. Sweat is associated with the knee at *Iliad* 13.711; 17,385–386. Passages where life is being wasted away in tears: *Odyssey* 5.152–153, 160–161; 18.204.

[37] Jaccottet does not translate νόστον, Bérard gives: "Perdant la douce vie à pleurer le retour" ("wasting his sweet life crying over his return").

[38] Benveniste 1937: "épuisent le vouloir-vivre" (108); see also Degani 1961:17–28.

[39] "C'est bien parce que αἰών est la source de toute vigueur, et non pas seulement la durée de l'existence, qu'on dira d'un être jeune, tué en pleine force: ἀπ᾽ αἰῶνος νέος ὤλεο (Ω 725), ou encore μινυνθάδιος δέ οἱ αἰὼν ἔπλετο (Δ 478 = P 302) au sujet de Simoeisios florissant de jeunesse (ἠίθεον θαλερὸν Σιμοείσιον [Δ 473])" (Benveniste 1937:108).

[40] This is the general idea of Onians's 1954 interpretation, which remains thought provoking, although it is sometimes overly systematic. Words in Homer do not have only one meaning, and

Should this be the perspective from which to understand the epithet *thaleros*? Before proposing responses, other qualifiers applied to tears and other ways of crying should be noted in order to verify whether tears are inscribed in the semantic field of fertility.

Adinon, or *adina*, is one of the adverbs most frequently used to describe the act of crying. Of the twelve uses in the *Iliad*, all are related to lamentation; in the *Odyssey*, five of the nine total uses describe tears. *Adinon* usually accompanies the verbs *stenachō* and *stenachizō*; it also modifies the verb *goaō* or, in the adjective form *adinos*, the noun *goos*.[41] Does it only mean, as Paul Mazon's translation suggests, *at length*? Its meaning seems richer, considering that other occurrences of the signifier *adinos* describe compact swarms of bees or flies, the strong and muscular heart of a warrior, the oppressed heart of Penelope, or even the vast and wondrous voice of the sirens.[42] In the epic, *adinos* has a sense of depth, darkness, and, at the same time, strength and tightness. The groans of Achilles are resounding, deep, intense, and menacing at the same time; this is the manner in which to understand the expression *adina stenachizōn*, which alludes to both the contraction and dilation that characterize sobbing and the pauses, the moments of respite, that create the rhythm of weeping.[43]

The adverb *puknon* is less common than *adinon*, though it belongs to the same register. When Achilles sobs for Patroclus, his wailing lasts a long time: "groaning again and again" (*Iliad* 18.318);[44] this expression also refers to the dense, "thick" quality of the sobs.[45] The poet employs *puknos* when he wants to stress the thick, heavy, dangerous quality of an object or an attitude: "closely serried battalions" (*Iliad* 4.281; 13.145), a dense forest inhabited by a lion (18.320),[46] a "rain of arrows" that follow one after the other without interruption (11.576).[47] The use of this term is not without significance to the register of grief; on the contrary, it specifies and amplifies the idea of suffering.

The volume of sound also indicates the intensity of weeping: it is in this sense that we should understand the expression *baru stenachōn*, which so often

---

their meanings, at any rate, are not necessarily concrete.

[41] With *stenachō*: *Iliad* 18.124; 23.225; 24.123; *Odyssey* 7.274. *goaō-goos*: 18.316; 22.430; 23.17; 24.510, 747; *Odyssey* 4.721; 16.216.

[42] Bees: *Iliad* 2.87; flies: 2.469; the "dense, muscular" heart of Sarpedon: 16.421 (and why not "dark," since death is already upon him?); the "tormented" heart of Penelope: *Odyssey* 19.516–517; Sirens: *Odyssey* 23.326 (Stanford 1948).

[43] See Stanford 1936:54.

[44] See also *Odyssey* 4.153; 19.516.

[45] On *puknos* 'compact' as opposed to *hugros* 'liquid'—that is, the 'compactness' of men opposed to the liquidity of women—see Demont 1978:373–374.

[46] The "clenched" groans of Peleus are echoed, two verses later, by the image of this dense forest.

[47] Ajax is literally overpowered by the compact rain of arrows.

describes the wailing hero.[48] If sobs are heavy in their intensity, they are in the severity of their sound as well. Only men cry so deeply. While *oxus* 'sharp, piercing' often refers to the cries of the warrior, and especially the clamor that rises during an attack (*Iliad* 12.125; 15.313; 17.88–89, etc.), the sharp lamentation can only come from a woman or a goddess. Achilles cries for Patroclus "sobbing heavily"; Thetis rushes to him "shrieking in sharp cries" (18.70–71). [49] The *baru* (masculine) / *oxu* (feminine) binary is clear.

The hand of a warrior is powerful (*Iliad* 1.219; 11.235; 13.410); his weapon can be cumbersome (5.664) in a dangerous sense; a wound causes a limb to swell and become heavy (11.584; 16.519; 20.480); error (2.111; 9.18), disaster, strife, conflict (20.55), and death ("cruel hands of death," 21.548) are unbearable burdens; all of these are ways of expressing the force of a danger or of masculine suffering.

Finally, adjectives used less often to describe men's sobbing, such as *ligus* 'shrill' and *krueros* 'chilling', render simultaneously the dimension of the sound of crying and the idea of the impact of the jolts of pain or emotion. When a man weeps and lets out piercing cries, the context is always extremely dramatic: Achilles near the corpse of Patroclus (*Iliad* 19.5), the anguish of Agamemnon in the Underworld (*Odyssey* 11.395), the horror of Odysseus' shipmates at the memory of the cannibalistic Cyclops (10.391). *Ligus*, though, is also frequently used for the lamentation of women (*Iliad* 19.284; *Odyssey* 4.259; 8.527; 21.56, etc.).

In the same vein, as if in response to these sharp cries, the statement that lamentation freezes the heart—*krueros goos*—is repeated several times, perhaps with a dual meaning: it causes shudders of pain for the one crying and provokes shivers of horror for those who hear the dreadful moans (*Iliad* 24.524; *Odyssey* 4.103; 11.212). It should also be noted that the adjective *krueros*, in its other uses, characterizes the pursuit represented on the aegis of Athena (*Iliad* 5.740) and a rout during a battle (9.2; 13.48); in any case, death is in the background.[50]

The distribution of connotations attributed to tears is thus complex, almost contradictory: tears exhaust the warrior and drive away his vital force, but they also constitute a privileged sign of the energy that he manifests elsewhere, in combat. It is of note that when the poet describes a character consumed by tears, he is referring to either a woman or to Odysseus, whose situation in the *Odyssey* is no longer that of a warrior.

In the *Iliad*, the hot and flourishing tears of heroes are obvious expressions of their vitality. Through the volume of their sound, their staccato character,

---

[48] Out of thirty-two uses of *barus* in the *Iliad*, twelve describe the groans of men: 1.364; 4.153; 8.334; 9.15, etc. (in the *Odyssey*: there are twelve occurrences).

[49] *Oxu* intensifies *kōkusasa*, a verb that is only used for the cries of women; see p. 115 above.

[50] We could compare this 'dreadful moan' to the character Helen, who makes men "shiver in fear" (*Iliad* 19.325), like war (5.351) or battle (17.175).

and their "living" quality, the sobs of men are a manifestation of their masculine nature.[51] It is as if the hero who cries is divided: his energy and his force are externalized in his tears; the pain of the men in the *Iliad* is active, powerful.

The Sites and Gestures of Grief

The spaces associated with tears differ depending on whether the lamentations are masculine or feminine. Men normally cry outside: Menelaus weeps on the seashore when he is with Proteus (*Odyssey* 4.539); Achilles and his companions wet the sands and their weapons with their sobs (*Iliad* 23.15–16); Odysseus sits at the tip of Calypso's island and soaks his clothing with his tears (*Odyssey* 7.260); the sons of Priam, seated in the courtyard of the palace, do the same after the death of Hector (*Iliad* 24.161–162).

On the other hand, Penelope, the archetypal crying woman in the epic, always sobs inside the palace, and more specifically on her bed, inside her nuptial chamber:

> I will therefore go upstairs and recline upon that bed which I have never ceased to flood with my tears …
>
> *Odyssey* 19.594–596 (see also 16.449–450; 17.101–103; 20.58)

The permanent reminder of her bed, the privileged site of tears, demonstrates the perfect bond that unites a woman with her husband;[52] in the bed in Ithaca, Penelope's tears are like a substitute for Odysseus.

A warrior can cry outside, on his weapons, a wife inside the palace,[53] on the marriage bed; once again, the distribution of masculine and feminine spaces is clearly distinguished.

The gestures of tears

The warrior in the epic cries just as he fights: in both cases, it is his body that is emphasized. Men sob *intensely, actively, vigorously*. By expressing grief through his gestures and cries, the Homeric hero reduces the weight of his suffering. Grief always follows an event that has taken place outside of the one who suffers. It is the interior reaction to the perception of this tragic exterior event.[54] This suffering is expressed first and foremost through gestures.

---

[51] See the section on gestures below in this chapter.
[52] On *lechos* 'bed', as a symbol of marriage, see Vernant 1979a:81.
[53] While the sons of Priam are weeping for Hector in the hall, his daughters are wailing "about the house" (*Iliad* 24.166).
[54] Anastassiou 1973:220.

When he sees Hector dragged through the dust, Priam cannot contain himself: with frenzied gestures he expresses his pain, his need to go out and implore Achilles to return his son to him (*Iliad* 22.412–414):

> Hardly could the people hold Priam back in his hot haste to rush without the gates of the city. He groveled in the mire and besought them ...[55]

When misfortune strikes, the grief that invades the heart as well as the body is expressed in a series of self-directed gestures, immediate and violent, upon the man who is suffering: raising hands, striking the face (*Iliad* 22.33–34: Priam), pacing (*Odyssey* 13.220: Odysseus), rolling on the ground in the sand (*Odyssey* 4.539: Menelaus) or the mud (*Iliad* 22.414), and pulling out hair (*Iliad* 10.15: Agamemnon; 22.77–78: Priam; 24.711: Hecuba and Andromache); all are reactions dictated by suffering.

On one level, there is nothing apparent that distinguishes feminine gestures of grief. Women also rip out their hair and beat their chests (*Iliad* 18.30–31, 50-51; 24.710–711). However, they claw "their beautiful cheeks" (11.393; 19.284–285), a gesture that belongs to them alone. The male equivalent of this deface-ment takes on various forms: ash, dust, mud, manure; nothing is too dirty for destroying the radiance of a young body or the majesty of an older man.

One thing is clear: for women, the register for expressing emotion is more limited than for men. This restriction makes sense when we realize that women's grief is always expressed as part of a ritual, in the strict sense: lamentations take place in certain circumstances according to a specific code, which leaves them no room to maneuver.[56]

Without a doubt, the expression of men's grief is also determined on two levels: by the gestural code belonging to Homeric society and by the poetic conventions specific to the epic. But a convention is not necessarily a ritual.

Compared to the feminine expression of suffering, which is fixed by a hyper-ritualized code, the grief of men fits into a broader register. Feminine grief, restricted only to ritual, is set in opposition to the suffering of men, who are free to express themselves using the entire gestural language of epic society.

---

[55]   Cf. Schadewaldt 1965:327.
[56]   See Reiner 1938:42 and following; Neumann 1965:85–89; Anastassiou 1973:22.

5

The Weeping Body of Achilles

Achilles embodies all of the main heroic qualities that are accorded singly to other heroes.[1] He is beauty, strength, and excellence all at the same time. If, in a certain way, the *Iliad* exalts human energy during times of misfortune,[2] it is not surprising that Achilles embodies, by himself, almost all of the suffering in the poem. "Achilles is among the Homeric figures who experiences the most pain. And it is important to make clear that the 'eternally striving youth', with the radiance of his power and beauty, is also for us, on the threshold of Western culture, the figure who felt the most pain, a figure who is capable of great suffering," writes Walter Schadewaldt.[3] And while the *Iliad* is indeed the story of Achilles' anger, it is also the song of his sorrow.

    Iliad 16.162 marks the close of a sequence: Achilles puts an end to his anger[4] and authorizes Patroclus to go into battle with his armor. His fate from then on is upended, and the last third of the poem especially paints the image of his grief. The fiction of an Achilles *adakrutos* 'without tears', which Thetis dreams for an instant, is impossible. "Would indeed that you had lived your span free from all sorrow at your ships,"[5] says his mother. It is precisely because he is the "best of the ... Achaeans"[6] that he cannot be "without tears"; the lot of the

---

[1]   Benardete 1963:1

[2]   Thus Bespaloff 1943:47–48; see also the more decidedly clear-cut opinion of Weil 1953:28, who asserts that the warriors in the *Iliad* only have one single future: the death affixed to them by their "profession."

[3]   "Achilleus ist unter den Gestalten Homers die schmerzensreichste. Und es ist bedeutungsvoll, sich klarzumachen, dass in dem 'ewig strebenden Jüngling', auf dem der Glanz der Kraft und der Schönheit ruht, uns an der frühen Schwelle des Abendlandes auch die Gestalt des dem Leiden Überantworteten, zum grossen Leid Befähigten begegnet" (Schadewaldt 1965:336). On the other hand, Méautis 1930:11, presents Achilles as no more than a "romantic hero."

[4]   Watkins 1977:187–199 demonstrated the gruesome and dangerous character of *mēnis* 'anger' and detailed the linguistic taboo that surrounds the word in Homer.

[5]   1.415–416. I'm grateful to Nicole Loraux for pointing out this important passage.

[6]   Evoked three verses earlier (*ariston Achaiōn*, 1.412).

heroic Achilles is necessarily bound to tears. His destiny is misfortune and the adjective *apēmōn* 'he who knows no pain'[7] reinforces *adakrutos*.

In leaving his anger behind, Achilles finds grief. Before examining the expression of his suffering in the *Iliad*, note the degree to which the death of Patroclus and the pain of Achilles are inextricably interwoven, if not equivalent.

A certain number of paradoxes and permutations warrant attention as well. In a gesture identical to the one Patroclus makes before convincing the son of Peleus to let him fight—that is to say, let him die—Achilles "struck his two thighs" (*Iliad* 16.125 and, for Patroclus, 15.397); this gesture always comes just before the death of the person who makes it.[8] Then, when he sobs upon the announcement of Patroclus' death, it is he who, in a sense, occupies the place of the corpse. The real Patroclus is still on the battlefield, surrounded by the Trojans, and yet the gesture that Thetis makes toward Achilles is one reserved for the deceased: "She laid her hand upon his head and forced out a shrill cry, saying ..." (18.71–72). She weeps for her living son with the gestures and words of funerary lamentation (18.54–60).[9]

One final note on a last analogy between the dead Patroclus and the suffering Achilles: the corpse of Patroclus is protected by Thetis, who instills nectar and ambrosia into his nostrils (*Iliad* 19.38–39); it is also nectar and ambrosia, poured by Athena into Achilles' chest, that preserve his strength and energy (*Iliad* 19.347–348, 353–354).

The Body and Tears

As in our approach to courage, we will consider the question of the expression of heroic suffering from the standpoint of the warrior's body,[10] focusing on the case of Achilles, since in the *Iliad* Achilles embodies the perfect warrior. In sobbing as well the hero's body is enhanced, and qualities similar to those that are exalted in the practice of combat are used to describe the crying warrior.

The correspondences, however, are not so simple. Suffering in the epic is situated at the intersection of different categories of thought: biological necessities like food, rest, or sleep, psychological notions like erotic desire or courage, and aesthetic and moral values like the ideal of a beautiful heroic death are tightly interwoven by the poet when he presents heroes in the throes of pain. An attentive reading will determine the operational similarities between these

---

[7] Cf. Mawet 1979:140–141. I would point out that at 3.160 Helen is described as a *pēma* 'a plague or a misfortune'.

[8] Lowenstam 1981:31–38 sees this gesture as one of the signs in a "typological sequence."

[9] Compare this passage to *Iliad* 22.431–436, where Hecuba addresses Hector after his death.

[10] See Part 1, Chapter 2 above.

different themes, but also—and more interestingly—the moments of interference where these different symbolic planes collide, as if the activity of weeping were a specific form of life, an autonomous physical and psychological condition, sufficient unto itself, that temporarily fuses together the different moments in the life of the epic hero.

Similarities in methods of intervention

Recalling the observations on the limbs of warriors, the knee, in particular, is a key component of the hero's body. The joint of bravery, the knee—depending on whether it is stiff or flexible, firm or loose—expresses several of the warrior's states of being.

> When a goddess wants to give renewed warlike vigor to a hero, "she [makes] his limbs supple and [quickens] his hands and his feet" (*Iliad* 5.122), she puts strength into his knees (18.569).

> Erotic desire buckles the knees of the suitors who contemplate Penelope's beauty: "the suitors were so overpowered and became so desperately enamored of her their knees buckled" (*Odyssey* 18.212)

> Hunger takes hold of the knees: it makes limbs heavy and hobbles knees (*Iliad* 19.165–166).

> Sleep takes possession of the hero by relaxing the limbs: "While Odysseus was thus yielding himself to a very deep slumber that eased the burden of his body and his sorrows" (*Odyssey* 20.56–57; 23.342–343).

> The formula for when a warrior dies is "have his knees loosened" (*Iliad* 4.469; 5.176, etc.).

> And finally, sorrow also causes the knees to falter (*Iliad* 18. 31; 22.448); Achilles, lying in the dust, mourns for Patroclus (18.27).

The fusion of tears with the major stages of life

Living with tears

Grief manifests as a slowing down of physical and social life.[11] When Achilles is grieving, he no longer participates in meals: he is separated from the social life of the banquet. He does not eat until he kills Hector, refusing meals each time they are offered by the Achaeans (*Iliad* 19.205, 209–210, 304, 306–307, 319–321,

---

[11]   See Granet 1922:104 for similarities between ancient Greece and China's classical age.

346). Once he is in possession of his new armor, his only concern is to rush to the battlefield (19.206–210):

> Let the sons of the Achaeans, say I, fight fasting and without food, till we have avenged them; afterwards at the going down of the sun let them eat their fill. As for me, Patroclus is lying dead in my tent, all hacked and hewn, with his feet to the door, and his comrades are mourning round him.

Achilles does not need to be comforted with meals; he burns with a desire for revenge and a suffering stronger than hunger: "if any comrade will hear me, bid me neither eat nor drink, for I am in great heaviness, and will stay fasting even to the going down of the sun" (19.306–307). In his particular condition, food—the poet says explicitly—is incompatible with his tears and the battle that somehow takes the place of meals. Achilles' suffering isolates him from the rest of the army and makes him lose his common sense, but Odysseus takes it upon himself to offer his wisdom (19.160–163):

> ... bid them first take food both bread and wine by the ships, for in this there is strength and stay. No man can do battle the livelong day to the going down of the sun if he is without food.

Food provides not only strength for the body, but also courage, *menos* and *alkē*.[12] For Achilles, sobbing may be equivalent to having a meal; while the Greeks dine, he cries (*Iliad* 23.3–4, 124–125). In his grief, he oscillates between two extreme attitudes toward food: on the one hand, he falls into an animal-like state when, at the height of his rage, he imagines shredding Hector to pieces and devouring him raw (22.347); on the other hand, he tends toward the divine, as the nectar and ambrosia he receives are not human foods (19.353–354).

The hero who suffers then is in a sort of vegetative state, nourishing himself on pain alone, "eating" his heart and not bread: "My son, how long will you keep on thus grieving and making moan? You are gnawing at your own heart" (*Iliad* 14.128–129).[13] It is in this setting that the active grief of Achilles comes to an end. In fact, after the intervention of Thetis, once the idea of returning Hector's body has been approved, Achilles accepts the second phase of his destiny, and his actions become normalized. Consuming food marks a transitional stage, followed by a reinstatement of the norm.

---

[12] See the remarks in Böhme 1929:31–35.

[13] See also the similar image at *Odyssey* 10.379 (Circe speaking to Odysseus): "why do you sit like that as though you were dumb, gnawing at your own heart, and refusing both meat and drink?" See Anastassiou 1973:77–78 and Nagler 1974:178–179.

When Priam arrives at the camp of the Myrmidons, he finds Achilles who "had but just done eating and drinking, and the table was still there" (*Iliad* 24.475–76). The refusal or the need to eat provides then a tempo for his periods of weeping. Through a beautiful reversal, it is Achilles who invites Priam to share his meal. Like Achilles, Priam fasts at the peak of his heartache; once the ransom for Hector's body is accepted, he can think of eating. Achilles offers consolation[14] and reconciliation to Priam, and this reconciliation passes by way of commensality.[15]

As he remembers the meal, Achilles puts an end to his grief; it is an identical recollection that he offers to Priam when urging him to share his table. The example he selects to convince the old king is worth lingering over (*Iliad* 24.601–604, 610–620):

"... for the present let us prepare our supper. Even lovely Niobe of the lovely tresses had to think about eating, though her twelve children— six daughters and six lusty sons—had been all slain in her house ... Nine days did they lie weltering, and there was none to bury them, for the son of Cronus turned the people into stone; but on the tenth day the gods in heaven themselves buried them, and Niobe then took food, being worn out with weeping. They say that somewhere among the rocks on the mountain pastures of Sipylus, where the nymphs live that haunt the river Achelous, there, they say, she lives in stone and still nurses the sorrows sent upon her by the hand of heaven. Therefore, noble sir, let us two now take food; you can weep for your dear son hereafter as you are bearing him back to Ilion—and many a tear will he cost you."

In this complex sequence, the last major speech by Achilles, it is possible to identify several layers of meaning.[16] First, there is the parallel between the stories of Niobe and Priam. The anger of Apollo is the root cause of the death of Niobe's children, just as Achilles' anger causes Hector's death. If the gods prevent the funerals of the Niobids, whose bloody bodies lie dead, Achilles for his part refuses to return Hector's body and grows more obstinate every day. Niobe weeps nine days for her children before they are buried by the gods themselves; Priam asks Achilles for a truce for Hector's funeral preparations—nine days to weep for him and one day to bury him—and Achilles himself places the

---

[14] On the structuring of *consolatio* (commiseration, example, an offer of food and/or drink, exhorting to be courageous), see Nagler 1974:174–198.

[15] Griffin 1980:14–20.

[16] The helpful observations of Kakridis 1930:113–122 and Nagler 1974:193–195 have guided me here.

body on the bier (*Iliad* 24.589). And finally, Niobe ruminates on her sorrow (*kēdea pessei*), and Priam does the same (*kēdea muria pessō*, 24.639). Grief has the properties of a food: it is cooked and digested (*pessō*).[17]

Niobe's story condenses three principal, inextricably linked themes: maternity, memory,[18] and "self-satiating" grief. Niobe wanted to rival Leto, through the proxy of her offspring. Niobe's "achievement" as the mother of many children diminished the prestige of Leto, who only had two herself. Punished for wanting to compare herself to a goddess,[19] she becomes a symbol of maternal suffering. Her fasting and her rigid inflexibility may be poetic ways of saying that a mother dies a little when her children are gone; thus Niobe is a kind of monument to eternal pain.[20] She is like a funeral stele, preserving the memory of her dead children; the image of a stele also characterizes Achilles' horses when they cry hot tears for Patroclus (*Iliad* 17.434–44).[21] The rigidity of stone, like the continuous flow of tears resembling a spring,[22] suggests the permanence of remembrance, the eternity of memory. Niobe is the symbol of maternal suffering and, in this sense, the ultimate reference for all pain; it is this example that Achilles chooses to urge Priam to end his crying and feed himself.

Achilles eats after avenging and burying Patroclus, Niobe after the funeral for her children, Priam after accomplishing his mission to Achilles (24.641–642):

Now, moreover, I have eaten bread and drunk wine; hitherto I have tasted nothing.

Just as Achilles does not eat, he does not sleep during his suffering: he cries for Patroclus every night "and sleep, before whom all things bow, could take no hold upon him" (*Iliad* 24.4–5). True solace does not come until after the reconciliation with Priam. In fact, Achilles only falls asleep for two—very brief—moments, and each time he is awakened quickly, once by the shadow of Patroclus and once by the Achaeans.[23] His futile attempt to embrace Patroclus' shadow wakes him with a jolt (23.101). After the cremation of the body, he once again spends the night weeping. At dawn, exhausted, he falls asleep (23.232) at the same moment when the Achaeans are noisily gathering around him. His sleep only lasts a few moments (23.235). In both cases, this interrupted sleep

---

[17] Echoing the metaphors describing weapons that devour (see p. 23 above), I would point out that the wound caused by an arrow can be "digested": *Iliad* 8.513.

[18] The entire sequence is framed by the doubled theme of memory: for Achilles and Priam: *Iliad* 24.601, 618; for Niobe: 602, 613.

[19] See Saïd 1978:289.

[20] Pucci 1980:195n33.

[21] See p. 117 above.

[22] Patroclus' tears are compared to a spring falling out of a rock: *Iliad* 16.3–4, see p. 117 above.

[23] See Nagler 1974:170–178

seems to indicate a need to go further into the rituals of mourning: he must burn Patroclus' body and build a monument before returning to sleep. However, Achilles will not return to the normal cycle of his life until he shares a meal with Priam, "reconciles" with him, and recovers both his ability to sleep and, at the same time, his love of Briseïs.

Just as Achilles goes without sleep until the end of the funeral ceremony for Patroclus, Priam is unable to eat or sleep until he recovers Hector's body: "Never once have my eyes been closed from the day your hands took the life of my son," he says to Achilles (*Iliad* 24.637–638).[24]

In the end, Achilles will be cleansed of the blood that covers him only after he lays Patroclus on the pyre and cuts his own hair (*Iliad* 23.44–46).

There are three phases then that clearly establish the end of Achilles' grief and his reintegration into the community of the Achaeans: 1) having killed Hector, he can once again take part in meals; 2) having led the funeral rites, he cuts his hair and is purified (*Iliad* 23.141); 3) he then regains his ability to sleep, and Briseïs sleeps by his side (*Iliad* 24.675–676).

The pleasure of sobbing

When he cries, the hero is entirely within his pain, as if isolated temporarily from the rest of life. He must go all the way through to the end of his aching in order to break free from it. Wholly consumed by his desire to cry, he will be sated by his tears, as the poet's own words show. This vocabulary of sobbing is the same as that used to describe pleasure[25]—pleasure of sleep, of love, of eating, of the song of the bard. Achilles experiences a pleasure in playing the lyre (*Iliad* 9.186), just as he does when he is "sated with grief" (24.513).

The desire for tears can be set off by an external event ("Thetis stirred within them a still deeper desire for sobbing," *Iliad* 23.14), by words (the lament of Achilles makes the Myrmidons cry, 23.108), by a gesture (Achilles leaving a lock of his hair on the body of Patroclus, 23.153); it can be provoked by seeing a loved one (the shade of Patroclus, 23.98; and of Anticlea, *Odyssey* 11.212), or the memory of someone who is absent (Peleus, 24.507).

More significantly, this desire is like hunger: it can be satiated. The formulaic verse αὐτὰρ ἐπεὶ πόσιος καὶ ἐδητύος ἔντο ("as soon as they had had enough to eat and drink," *Iliad* 1.469; 2.432; 7.323, etc.),[26] which so often describes a meal

---

[24] Eating clearly marks the return to normal life. Priam, like Achilles, wore himself out sobbing; after having eaten, he asks for someone to prepare him a bed "immediately" (*tachista*), *Iliad* 24.635.

[25] *Terpō* (*Iliad* 23.10, 98; 24.513; *Odyssey* 4.107, 194; 11.212; 19.213, 251); *himeros* (23.14, 108, 153; 24.507, 514; *Odyssey* 4.113, 183; 16.215; 19.249; 22.500; 23.231); *erōs* (*Iliad* 24.227).

[26] See Chantraine 1964.

in Homer, finds an echo in the contexts of weeping. Before leaving for the Greek camp, Priam speaks of the moment when he will "have taken my son in my arms and satiated my desire for sobbing" (24.227).

This is the pleasure of *consuming* tears: one might say that heroes are sated on sobs, as they are, at other moments, on meat and wine. This is the meaning of the verbs *korennumi* and *aō* 'to be satisfied, gorged, or disgusted by', which are frequently used to depict sobbing. In the *Iliad*, a warrior can "gorge" himself on tears, just as he gorges himself on meat, combat, and war.[27]

But sometimes, when mortally wounded, he will in turn satisfy Ares with his blood and the dogs and birds with his flesh. His parents, in their grief, will then hope to gorge themselves on tears. The death of Hector provokes the following reaction in Priam: "Would that he had died in my arms, for so both his ill-starred mother who bore him, and myself, should have had the comfort of gorging ourselves on tears and mourning over him" (*Iliad* 22.427–428).[28]

A man who cries surrenders to the shuddering of his sobs, is satiated by them, and finally, once he has cried enough, he is liberated from them: the desire for tears, which enters into the body through pain, escapes when the pleasure-suffering has been satisfied (*Iliad* 24.513–515):

> But when Achilles was now sated with grief and had unburdened the bitterness of his sorrow, he left his seat and raised the old man by the hand.

Achilles, seated, and Priam, crouched at his feet, cry at length, the one for Patroclus and Peleus, the other for Hector. Once Achilles has worn out his sorrow, the desire for tears leaves, at the same time, his heart and his body. The fading of the desire to cry sets the body in motion: right away (*autika*, 24.515) the hero passes from a prostrate to a standing position. Though verse 514 may well have been athetized by Aristarchus, this does not seem to pose a problem. We have seen, in effect, that flash, that fatigue, that anger seep into the body of the warrior;[29] on the contrary, the fact that sobbing is incorporated deep inside the hero's limbs confirms our hypothesis. For the warrior, to live out suffering in and through the body is one of the signs of his heroic character. It is this coinciding of emotional pain and its physical expression that controls the gestures of tears.

---

[27]   Meat and wine: *Iliad* 19.167, 307; combat: 13.639, 746; 22.218.

[28]   The same idea is at *Iliad* 24.717. In the *Odyssey* (20.59), Penelope "relieved herself by weeping." Menelaus, after having sobbed and rolled in the sand, wears out his suffering (*Odyssey* 4.541).

[29]   See pp. 20–24 above.

In the *Iliad*, the explosion of emotions is expressed in terms of physical transformation. Observe Achilles at the moment of the announcement of Patroclus' death (*Iliad* 18.22–27):

> A dark cloud of grief fell upon Achilles as he listened. He filled both hands with dust from off the ground, and poured it over his head, disfiguring his comely face, and letting the refuse settle over his *khiton* so fair and new. He flung himself down all huge and hugely at full length, and tore his hair with his hands.[30]

In a sense, Achilles merges with the corpse of Patroclus: he is in the same position, he disfigures himself (with dust); he tears out his hair, a symbol of his youth—and therefore a symbol of life[31]—as if he were participating momentarily in a state of death.

During most of his grief, Achilles remains lying down. Stretched out on the ground he weeps for his friend (*Iliad* 18.26–27, 170, 178 [*keiso*]); lying like him in the dust, Achilles holds Patroclus in his arms (19.4); he turns in all directions, moaning (24.5, 10–11); he paces and crawls around Patroclus' funeral pyre (23.225).

ℿ

Thus, in moments of suffering, foregoing food and sleep, lying down, and temporarily disfiguring the body are ways of mimicking death. This travesty of death in combat—"he now lies in repose stretched on earth in the bitterness of his spirit" Thetis says to Hephaestus, exactly as she would say if Achilles were dead (*Iliad* 18.461; cf. 18.20)—as well as the analogous black cloud of grief that envelopes Achilles (18.22), further tightens the connection between tears and war. Furthermore, the extraordinary violence of Achilles' gestures and the terrible moaning sound as he cries out (*smerdaleon d'ōimōxen*, 18.35)[32] are also reminders of the immense force inside his warrior's body. In his tears, mingled with anger and grief, Achilles is, once again, "like a lion" (*Iliad* 18.318, 323).

---

[30]   On this passage, see now the remarks in Schein 1984:129ff.
[31]   See Vernant and Gnoli 1982:62
[32]   Note the parallel to the Cyclops who, when wounded by Odysseus, lets out an identical cry of pain, *Odyssey* 9.395.

Conclusion

As we arrive at the end of this examination, it appears that heroism is, in essence, an ambiguous concept. At first glance, it seems that masculinity is at the core of heroism, and, further, that the limits of heroism coincide with those of masculinity. Without a doubt, a feminine element is not absent, but it acts as a foil. "Weakling cowards, Achaean women rather than Achaeans," exclaims the military commander to revive his troops' ardor. On this level, femininity appears to be the opposite of heroism.

However, the relationship between masculinity and femininity is not one of simple opposition. At the heart of heroism and hyper-virility, fragments have been taken from the feminine sphere. It is precisely this feminine portion, which enters necessarily into the makeup of the hero, that completes the figure. In effect, it is through first assuming and then surpassing the feminine element carried inside himself that the hero acquires his true dimension. This proximity and separation are best manifested in the body of the warrior: the characteristics borrowed from feminine beauty serve to emphasize and to valorize the hyper-virility of the hero.

Another level of overlap must be retained: that of maternity and war. If a hero acts in a "maternal" fashion, he does so on the battlefield. Here again, there is a simultaneous proximity and separation. It is the tension between these binary oppositions that confers upon the hero his true weight and substance.

For women, it is impossible to play as well on both registers. Their masculine side appears essentially temporarily, as a superimposition. They do not incorporate any share of masculinity itself; rather, it is their close proximity to their husbands that permits them to borrow these provisional, but non-constituent, qualities. Penelope, the "king" of Ithaca, plays a role that external events have imposed upon her, which they then withdraw; Achilles never plays any role other than his own.

It is perhaps in this impossibility of truly integrating a share of the masculine that the profound alterity of women resides. Femininity is not the counterpart to the masculinity of the hero. The hero's excellence is indeed dependent on his beauty and on his virtue; and yet, because beauty is revealed in heroic deeds, the beauty of women, though frequently evoked, is never fully manifested. Furthermore, the virtue of women is relative and not absolute: there are no great feminine figures in the epic—apart from Helen—except through relationships with men.

In the *Iliad*, all the great heroes cry. The expression of pain belongs to men and women in common, and it is this very commonality that has made it compelling to study the interplay of similarities and differences. By studying the language of grief, we have shown that, while appropriating the model of feminine pain (childbirth and the story of Niobe), the masculine ideology of the *Iliad* is radically different, and it creates its own mode for expressing sorrow.

The storms of masculine pain contrast with the slow material loss that consumes the lives of weeping women; the variable register of masculine gestures contrasts with the rigid code of feminine body language strictly circumscribed by the ritual of lamentation. But what is more important: the moans of women lead to nothing; their tears only express a radical powerlessness.

If tears characterize first and foremost the great heroic figures, it is because their suffering is active, energetic, and virile. Suffering is inscribed on their bodies in the same manner that warlike ardor is inscribed. Through this valorization of force—in combat as in sobbing—the masculine ideology of the *Iliad* anchors suffering at the very heart of heroism; by creating its own mode for expressing grief, it establishes a system of values where masculine suffering attains a dimension denied to the tears of women.

Far from being an unimportant accessory to the epic warrior, the gift of tears is, on the contrary, one of the elements that constitute his heroic nature. "Valiant men are always inclined toward tears," as one of the scholiasts of the *Iliad* says (ἀεὶ δὲ ἀριδάκρυες ἀνέρες ἐσθλοί, *ad Iliad.* 19.5). If epic heroes cry, it is first of all because they can—masculine tears are not a sign of weakness—but it is also because they must: their pain is a conspicuous sign of strength and vitality.

If the break is so clean at the classical period, where masculine figures no longer cry, it is perhaps because, once they ceased to think along the lines of heroism, men bestowed upon women the gift of tears ...

Bibliography

Adkins, A. W. H. 1960. *Merit and Responsibility. A Study in Greek Values.* Oxford.

———. 1963. "'Friendship' and 'Self-Sufficiency' in Homer and Aristotle." *Classical Quarterly* n.s. 13:30–45.

———. 1969. "Threatening, Abusing, and Feeling Angry in the Homeric Poems." *Journal of Hellenic Studies* 89:7–21.

Alexiou, M. 1974. *The Ritual Lament in Greek Tradition.* Cambridge.

Amory, A. R. 1966. "The Gates of Horn and Ivory." *Yale Classical Studies* 20:3–57.

Anastassiou, I. 1973. *Zum Wortfeld "Trauer" in der Sprache Homers.* Hamburg.

Antin, P. 1961. "Sur le 'rire en pleurs' d'Andromaque." *Bulletin de l'Association Guillaume Budé* 3:340–350.

Arrowsmith, W. 1967. "Thetis and Achilles, *Iliad* XVIII, 1–147." *Arion* 6:246–261.

Arthur, M. B. 1973. "Early Greece: The Origins of the Western Attitude toward Women." *Arethusa* 6:7–36.

———. 1981. "The Divided World of *Iliad* VI." *Women's Studies* 8:21–46.

Auerbach, E. 1968. *Mimesis. La représentation de la réalité dans la littérature occidentale.* Trans. Cornélius Heim. Paris.

Avezzù, E. 1983. "Stilemi associativi e rappresentazioni della parentela nell' *Iliade*." *Quaderni di Storia* 9:69–97.

Banks, J., and G. Nagy, trans. n.d. *Hesiod. Theogony.* http://www.chs.harvard.edu/CHS/article/display/5289.

Barthes, R. 1978. *A Lover's Discourse: Fragments.* Trans. R. Howard. New York. Orig. pub. as *Fragments d'un discours amoureux.* Paris, 1977.

Benardete, S. 1963. "Achilles and the *Iliad*." *Hermes* 91:1–16.

Benveniste, É. 1937. "Expression indo-européenne de l'Éternité." *Bulletin de la Société de linguistique de Paris* 38.1:103–112.

———. 1966–1974. *Problèmes de linguistique générale.* 2 vols. Paris.

———. 1969. *Le Vocabulaire des institutions indo-européennes.* 2 vols. Paris.

Bérard, J. 1955. "Le concours de l'arc dans l'*Odyssée*." *Revue des Études grecques* 68:1–11.

Bérard, V. 1933. *Introduction à l'Odyssée.* 3 vols. 2nd ed. Paris.

Berman, K. 1974. "A Basic Outline for Teaching 'Women in Antiquity.'" *The Classical World* 67:213–230.

Bespaloff, R. 1943. *De l'Iliade*. New York.

Beszard, L. 1903. "Les larmes dans l'épopée particulièrement dans l'épopée française jusqu'à la fin du XIIe siècle." *Zeitschrift für romanische Philologie* 27:385–413; 513–549; 641–674.

Beye, C. 1974. "Male and Female in the Homeric Poems." *Ramus* 3.1:87–101.

Boedeker, D. D. 1974. *Aphrodite's Entry into Greek Epic*. Mnemosyne 32. Leiden.

Böhme, J. 1929. *Die Seele und das Ich im homerischen Epos*. Leipzig.

Bounoure, G. 1983. "L'odeur du héros. Un thème ancien de la légende d'Alexandre." *Quaderni di Storia* 17:3–46.

Broccia, G. 1957. "Il motivo della morte nel VI libro dell'Iliade." *Rivista di Filologia Classica* 85 (n.s. 35):61–69.

Browning, R. 1889. *The Poetical Works of Robert Browning*. Vol. 13, *Aristophanes' Apology. The Agamemnon of Aeschylus*. London.

Buffière, F. 1956. *Les Mythes d'Homère et la pensée grecques*. Paris.

Burkert, W. 1960. "Das Lied von Ares und Aphrodite." *Rheinisches Museum für Philologie* N. F. 103:130–144.

———. 1962. "ΓΟΗΣ. Zum griechischen 'Schamanismus.'" *Rheinisches Museum für Philologie* N.F. 105:36–55.

Bussolino, P. 1957. "Elena: eterno femminino Omerico." *Rivista di Studi Classici* 5:3–17.

———. 1963. "Omero precorritore della psicologia femminile nei Tragici." *Rivista di Studi Classici* 11:129–139.

———. 1982. "La lingua di Omero in rapporto alla psicologia femminile." *Rivista di Studi Classici* 10:129–139.

Carlier, J. 1980–1981. "Les Amazones font la guerre et l'amour." *L'Ethnographie* 74:11–33.

———. 1981. s.v. "Apollon." In *Dictionnaire des mythologies*, ed. Y. Bonnefoy. Paris.

Chantraine, P. 1946–1947. "Les noms du mari et de la femme, du père et de la mère en grec." *Revue des études grecques* 59–60:219–250.

———. 1958–1963. *Grammaire homérique*. 2 vols. Paris.

———. 1963. "A propos de Thersite." *L'Antiquité classique* 32:18–27.

———. 1964. "Les noms d'action répondant aux verbes signifiant 'manger' et 'boire' chez Homère: ΕΔΗΤΥΣ, ΒΡΩΣΙΣ, ΒΡΩΤΥΣ, ΒΡΩΜΗ, ΠΟΣΙΣ, ΠΟΤΗΣ." *Bulletin de la Société de linguistique de Paris* 59.1:11–23.

———. 1968–1977. *Dictionnaire étymologique de la langue grecque* (A–Y). 4 vols. Paris.

Clader, L. L. 1976. *Helen: The Evolution from Divine to Heroic in Greek Epic Tradition*. Mnemosyne 42. Leiden.

Clay, J. 1983. *The Wrath of Athena: Gods and Men in the Odyssey*. Princeton.

Coleridge, E., trans. 1938. "Euripides, *Helen*" and "Euripides, *Heracles.*" In *The Complete Greek Drama*, 2 vols., ed. J. Oates and E. O'Neill, Jr. New York.

Collignon, M. 1903. "De l'origine du type des pleureuses dans l'art grec." *Revue des Études grecques* 16:299–322.

Cramer, O. C. 1976. "Speech and Silence in the Iliad." *Classical Journal* 71:300–304.

Daraki, M. 1980. "Le héros à menos et le héros daimoni isos: Une polarité homérique." *Annali della Scuola normale superiore di Pisa*, Ser. III 10:1–24.

Degani, E. 1961. ΑΙΩΝ *da Omero ad Aristotele*. Padua.

Delcourt, M. 1966. *Hermaphrodite, mythes et rites de la bisexualité dans l'Antiquité classique*. Brussels.

Delebecque, E. 1958. *Télémaque et la structure de l'Odyssée*. Paris.

———. 1980. *Construction de l'Odyssée*. Paris.

De Martino, E. 1977. *Morte e pianto rituale: dal lamento funebre antico al pianto di Maria*. 3rd ed. Turin.

Demont, P. 1978. "Remarques sur le sens de τρέφω." *Revue des Études grecques* 91:358–384.

Deonna, W. 1939. "Le genou, siège de force et de vie et sa protection magique." *Revue archéologique* 13:224–235.

———. 1965. *Le Symbolisme de l'œil*. Paris.

Detienne, M. 1972. *Les Jardins d'Adonis: La Mythologie des aromates en Grèce*. Paris.

———. 1973. *Les Maîtres de vérité dans la Grèce archaïque*. 2nd ed. Paris.

Diano, C. 1963. "La poetica dei Feaci." *Belfagor* 18:401–424.

Di Donato, R. 1969. "Problemi di tecnica formulare e poesia orale nell' epica greca arcaica." *Annali della Scuola normale superiore di Pisa*, Ser. II 38:243–294.

Dodds, E. R. 1965. *Les Grecs et l'Irrationnel*. Paris. Orig. pub. as *The Greeks and the Irrational*. Berkeley, 1951.

Dumas, G. 1920. "Les larmes." *Journal de Psychologie Normale et Pathologique* 17:45–58.

Dumézil, G. 1969. *Heur et malheur du guerrier*. Paris.

———. 1982. *Apollon sonore*. Paris.

———. 1983a. *La Courtisane et les seigneurs colorés. Esquisse de mythologie*. Paris.

———. 1983b. "*Fougue* et *rage* dans l'*Iliade.*" In *La Courtisane et les seigneurs colorés, et autres essais: Vingt-cinq esquisses de mythologie*, 181–191. Paris.

Evans, E. C. 1948. "Literary Portraiture in Ancient Epic." *Harvard Studies in Classical Philology* 58–59:189–217.

Farron, S. 1979. "The Portrayal of Women in the *Iliad.*" *Acta Classica* 22:15–31.

Finley, M. I. 1973a. *Les Anciens Grecs*. Paris. Orig. pub. as *The Ancient Greeks: An Introduction to their Life and Thought*. New York, 1963.

———. 1973b. *Les Premiers temps de la Grèce*. Orig. pub. as *Early Greece: The Bronze and Archaic Ages*. London, 1970.

———. 1978a. *Le Monde d'Ulysse*. 2nd ed. Paris. Orig. pub. as *The World of Odysseus*. New York, 1951.

———. 1978b. *The World of Odysseus*. Rev. ed. New York.

———. 1983. *Le Monde d'Ulysse*. Paris. Orig. pub. as *The World of Odysseus*, rev. ed. New York, 1978.

Foley, H. P. 1978. "'Reverse Similes' and Sex Roles in the *Odyssey*." *Arethusa* 11:7–26.

Fränkel, E. 1975. *Early Greek Poetry and Philosophy*. Oxford.

Frontisi-Ducroux, F. 1976. "Homère et le temps retrouvé." *Critique* 348:538–548.

Genette, G. 1982. *Palimpsestes: La littérature au second degré*. Paris.

Germain, G. 1954. *Genèse de l'Odyssée*. Paris.

———. 1958. *Homère*. Ecrivains de toujours 43. Paris.

Gernet, L. 1983. *Les Grecs sans miracle*. Paris.

Granet, M. 1922. "Le langage de la douleur d'après le rituel funéraire de la Chine classique." *Journal de Psychologie Normale et Pathologique* 19:97–118.

Griffin, J. 1980. *Homer on Life and Death*. Oxford.

Grillet, B. 1975. *Les Femmes et les fards dans l'Antiquité grecque*. Lyon.

Guiraud, P. 1978. *Sémiologie de la sexualité*. Paris.

Hainsworth, J. B. 1964. "Structure and Content in Epic Formulae: The Question of the Unique Expression." *Classical Quarterly* 14:155–164.

———. 1968. *The Flexibility of the Homeric Formula*. Oxford.

Hainsworth, J. B., and G. Privitera, eds. 1982. *Omero. Odissea*. Vol. 2, *Libri V–VIII*. Milan.

Harkemanne, J. 1967. "ΦΟΒΟΣ dans la poésie homérique: Étude sémantique." In *Recherches de philologie et de linguistique*, Vol. 1, ed. M. Hofinger et al., 47–94. Leuven.

Heubeck, A. 1974. *Die homerische Frage*. Darmstadt.

Hirvonen, K. 1968. *Matriarchal Survivals and Certain Trends in Homer's Female Characters*. Helsinki.

Hölscher, U. 1939. *Untersuchungen zur Form der Odyssee*. Hermes Einzelschriften 6. Berlin.

Ireland, S., and F. Steel. 1979. "Φρένες as an Anatomical Organ in the Works of Homer." *Glotta* 53:183–195.

Jeanmaire, H. 1939. *Couroi et Courètes*. Lille.

Kahn, L. 1980. "Ulysse ou la ruse et la mort." *Critique* 393:116–133.

Kakridis, H. J. 1930. "Die Niobesage bei Homer." *Rheinisches Museum* 79:113–122.

———. 1956. "The Role of the Woman in the *Iliad*." *Eranos* 54:21–27.

———. 1963. *La Notion de l'amitié et de l'hospitalité chez Homère*. Thessaloniki.

Kenner, H. 1960. *Weinen und Lachen in der griechischen Kunst*. Oesterreichische akademie der wissenschaften, Philosophisch-Historische klasse, Sitzungs- berichte 234. Vienna.

Kirk, G. S. 1962. *The Songs of Homer*. Cambridge.

———. 1968. "War and the Warrior in the Homeric Poems." In *Problèmes de la guerre en Grèce ancienne*, ed. J.-P. Vernant, 93–117. Paris.

———, ed. 1969. *The Language and Background of Homer*. Cambridge.

Koller, H. 1958. "Σῶμα bei Homer," *Glotta* 37:276–281.

Komornicka, A. 1981. "Sur le langage érotique de l'ancienne comédie attique." *Quaderni Urbinati di Cultura classica* 9:55–83.

Kovacs, D. 1995. *Euripides.* Vol. 2, *Children of Heracles. Hippolytus. Andromache. Hecuba*. Loeb Classical Library. Cambridge, MA.

Larock, V. 1930. "Les premières conceptions psychologiques des Grecs." *Revue belge de philologie et d'histoire* 9:377–406.

Leaf, W., ed. 1900. *The Iliad. Edited, with Apparatus Criticus, Prolegomena, Notes, and Appendices*. London.

Le Goff, J. and P. Vidal-Naquet. 1979. "Lévi-Strauss en Brocéliande." In *Claude Lévi-Strauss*, ed. R. Bellour and C. Clement, 265–319. Paris.

Lesky, A. 1914-. s.v. "Thanatos." In *Paulys real-encyclopädie der classischen Altertumswissenschaft*, ed. W. Kroll and K. Witte, 1245a-1268b. Stuttgart.

Lessing, G. E. 1964. *Laocoon*. Ed. and trans. J. Bialostocka and R. Klein. Paris.

Leumann, M. 1950. *Homerische Wörter*. Schweizerische Beiträge zur Altertumswissenschaft 3. Basel.

Levin, S. 1949. "Love and the Hero of the Iliad." *Transactions and Proceedings of the American Philological Association* 80:37–49.

Lindsay, J. 1974. *Helen of Troy*. London.

Lévy, E., ed. 1983. *La Femme dans les sociétés antiques. Actes des colloques de Strasbourg (mai 1980 et mars 1981)*. Strasbourg.

Lloyd, G. E. R. 1966. *Polarity and Analogy. Two Types of Argumentation in Early Greek Thought*. Cambridge.

Loraux, N. 1977. "La 'belle mort' spartiate." *Ktèma* 2:105–120.

———. 1978. "Sur la race des femmes et quelques-unes de ses tribus." *Arethusa* 11:43–87. Reprinted in Loraux 1981c:75–117.

———. 1981a. "Le héros et les mots." *L'Homme* 21:87–94.

———. 1981b. "Le lit, la guerre." *L'Homme* 21:37–67.

———. 1981c. *Les Enfants d'Athéna: Idées athéniennes sur la citoyenneté et la division des sexes*. Paris.

———. 1982a. "Crainte et tremblement du guerrier." *Traverses* 25:116–127.

———. 1982b. "Héraclès: le surmâle et le féminin." *Revue française de psychanalyse* 4:697–729.

Lord, A. B. 1960. *The Singer of Tales.* Cambridge, MA.

Lorimer, H. 1950. *Homer and the Monuments.* London.

Lowenstam, S. 1979. "The Meaning of IE *dhal." *Transactions of the American Philological Association* 109:125–135.

———. 1981. *The Death of Patroklos: A Study in Typology.* Königstein.

Maas, P. 1914-. s.v. "Threnos." In *Paulys real-encyclopädie der classischen Altertumswissenschaft*, ed. W. Kroll and K. Witte, 595–597. Stuttgart.

MacLeod, C. 1982. *Homer. Iliad, Book XXIV.* Cambridge Greek and Latin Classics. Cambridge.

Mactoux, M. 1975. *Pénélope: Légende et mythe.* Annales littéraires de l'université de Besançon. Paris.

Magnien, V. 1927. "Quelques mots du vocabulaire grec exprimant des opérations ou des états de l'âme." *Revue des Études grecques* 40:117–141.

Marg, W. 1942. "Kampf und Tod in der *Ilias*." *Die Antike* 18:167–179.

Mauss, M. 1921. "L' expression obligatoire des sentiments." *Journal de Psychologie Normale et Pathologique* 18:80–89.

Mawet, F. 1975. "Épigrammes, thrènes et dithyrambes. Les lamentations funèbres de l'épopée." In *Le Monde grec: Hommages à Claire Préaux*, ed. J. Bingen, G. Cambrier, and G. Nachtergael, 34–44. Brussels.

———. 1979. *Recherches sur les oppositions fonctionnelles dans le vocabulaire homérique de la douleur (autour de πῆμα-ἄλγος).* Académie royale de Belgique. Mémoires de la Classe des lettres, Série 2, t. 63, fasc. 4. Brussels.

Mazon, P., ed. 1937–1947. *L'Iliade.* Paris.

———. 1967. *Introduction à l'Iliade.* Paris.

Méautis, G. 1930. "La tristesse d'Achille." *Revue des Études grecques* 43:9–20.

Merkelbach, R. 1948. "Zum Y der Ilias." *Philologus* 97:303–311.

Moreux, B. 1967. "La nuit, l'ombre, et la mort chez Homère." *Phoenix* 21:237–272.

Mossé, C. 1980. "Ithaque ou la naissance de la cité." *Annali del Seminario di Studi del Mondo classico* 2:7–19.

———. 1983. *La Femme dans la Grèce antique.* Paris.

Mugler, C. 1960. "La lumière et la vision dans la poésie grecque." *Revue des Études grecques* 70:40–72.

Mylonas, G. E. 1962 "Burial Customs." In *A Companion to Homer*, ed. A. Wace and F. Stubbings, 478–488. London.

Nagler, M. N. 1974. *Spontaneity and Tradition: A Study in the Oral Art of Homer.* Berkeley.

Nagy, G. 1979. *The Best of the Achaeans: Concepts of the Hero in Archaic Greek Poetry.* Baltimore.

———, trans. n.d. *Hesiod. Works and Days.* http://chs.harvard.edu/CHS/article/display/5290.

Nawratil, K. 1959. "Βαθύκολπος." *Wiener Studien* 72:165–168.

Neumann, G. 1965. *Gesten und Gebärden in der griechischen Kunst*. Berlin.

Onians, R. B. 1954. *The Origins of European Thought*. Cambridge.

Otto, W. 1981. *Les Dieux de la Grèce. La figure du divin au miroir de l'esprit grec*. Paris.

Packard, D., and T. Meyers. 1974. *A Bibliography of Homeric Scholarship (1930–1970)*. Malibu.

Page, D. L. 1963. *The Homeric Odyssey*. Oxford.

Pagliaro, A. 1948. "Sunt lacrimae rerum." *Maia* 1:114–128.

Parry, A., ed. 1971. *The Making of Homeric Verse: The Collected Papers of Milman Parry*. Oxford.

Parry, M. 1928a. *L'Épithète traditionnelle dans Homère*. Paris.

———. 1928b. *Les Formules et la métrique d'Homère*. Paris.

Pavano, G. 1953. "La Morte degli Eroi nell'*Iliade*." *Rivista di Filologia Classica* 81 (n.s. 31):289–319.

Petersmann, G. 1973. "Die monologische Totenklage der *Ilias*." *Rheinisches Museum für Philologie* N.F. 116:3–16.

Pomeroy, S. B. 1973. "Selected Bibliography on Women in Antiquity." *Arethusa* 6:127–156.

———. 1975. "Andromaque: un exemple méconnu de matriarcat." *Revue des Études grecques* 88:16–19.

———. 1976. *Goddesses, Whores, Wives and Slaves: Women in Classical Antiquity*. London.

Pucci, P. 1979. "The Songs of the Sirens." *Arethusa* 12:121–132.

———. 1980. *The Violence of Pity in Euripides' Medea*. Ithaca.

Ramnoux, C. 1962. *Mythologie ou la famille olympienne*. Paris.

Reckford, K. J. 1964. "Helen in the *Iliad*." *Greek, Roman, and Byzantine Studies* 5:5–20.

Redfield, J. M. 1975. *Nature and Culture in the* Iliad: *The Tragedy of Hector*. Chicago.

Reiner, E. 1938. *Die rituelle Totenklage der Griechen*. Stuttgart.

Renehan, R. 1979. "The Meaning of ΣΩΜΑ in Homer: A Study in Methodology." *California Studies in Classical Antiquity* 12:269–281.

Rohde, E. 1928. *Psyché. Le culte de l'âme chez les Grecs et leur croyance à l'immortalité*. Trans. A. Reymond. Paris. Orig. pub. as *Psyche: seelenkult und unsterblinchkeitsglaube der griechen*. Freiburg, 1890.

Romilly, J. de. 1979. *La douceur dans la pensée grecque*. Paris.

Rowe, C. 1972. "Conceptions of Colour and Colour Symbolism in the Ancient World." *Eranos Jahrbuch* 41:327–364.

Rudhardt, J. 1958. *Notions fondamentales de la pensée religieuse et actes constitutifs du culte dans la Grèce classique*. Geneva.

Russo, J. A. 1963. "A Closer Look at Homeric Formulas." *Transactions and Proceedings of the American Philological Association* 94:235–247.

———. 1966. "The Structural Formula in Homeric Verse." *Yale Classical Studies* 20:219–240.

Russo, J. A., and B. Simon. 1968. "Homeric Psychology and the Oral Epic Tradition." *Journal of the History of Ideas* 29:483–498. Repr. in *Essays on the* Iliad, ed. J. Wright, 41–57. Bloomington, 1978.

Saïd, S. 1978. *La Faute Tragique*. Paris.

Scarcella, A. 1958. "Il pianto nella poesia di Omero." *Istituto Lombardo Accademia di Scienze e Lettere, Rendiconti* 92:799–834.

Schadewaldt, W. 1965. *Von Homers Welt und Werk*. Stuttgart.

Schein, S. L. 1970. "Odysseus and Polyphemus in the *Odyssey*." *Greek, Roman, and Byzantine Studies* 11:73–83.

———. 1984. *The Mortal Hero: An Introduction to Homer's* Iliad. Berkeley.

Schmitt, P. 1977. "Athéna Apatouria et la ceinture: les aspects féminins des Apatouries à Athènes." *Annales. Économies, Sociétés, Civilisations* 6:1059-1073.

Schmitz, A. 1963. "La Polarité des contraires dans la rencontre d'Hector et d'Andromaque (*Iliade* VI 369–502)." *Les Études classiques* 31:129–158.

Schnapp-Gourbeillon, A. 1981. *Lions, héros, masques: Les représentations de l'animal chez Homère*. Paris.

Segal, C. P. 1962. "The Phaeacians and the Symbolism of Odysseus' Return." *Arion* 1:17–64.

———. 1967. "Transition and Ritual in Odysseus' Return." *La Parola del passato* 22:321–342.

———. 1968a. "Circean Temptations: Homer, Vergil, Ovid." *Transactions and Proceedings of the American Philological Association* 99:419–442.

———. 1968b. "The Embassy and the Duals of *Iliad* IX, 182–198." *Greek, Roman, and Byzantine Studies* 9:101–114.

———. 1971a. "Andromache's Anagnorisis: Formulaic Artistry in *Iliad* XXII 437–476." *Harvard Studies in Classical Philology* 75:33–57.

———. 1971b. *The Theme of Mutilation of the Corpse in the* Iliad. Mnemosyne 17. Leiden.

———. 1983. "*Kleos* and its Ironies in the *Odyssey*." *L'Antiquité classique* 52:22–47.

Severyns, A. 1948. *Homère*. Vol. 3, *L'Artiste*. Brussels.

Shorey, P. 1969–1970. *Plato in Twelve Volumes*. Vols. 5–6, *Plato. The Republic*. Loeb Classical Library. Cambridge, MA.

Smith, W. D. 1966. "Physiology in the Homeric Poems." *Transactions and Proceedings of the American Philological Association* 97:547–556.

Smyth, H. 1926. *Aeschylus, with an English Translation*. Vol. 1, *Suppliant Maidens. Persians. Prometheus. Seven against Thebes*. Trans. Herbert Weir Smyth. Loeb Classical Library. Cambridge, MA.

Snell, B. 1948. *Die Entdeckung des Geistes.* 2nd ed. Hamburg. Repr. as *The Discovery of Mind.* Oxford, 1953.

Snodgrass, A. M. 1971. *The Dark Age of Greece: An Archeological Survey of the Eleventh to the Eighth Centuries.* Edinburgh.

Solmsen, F. 1965. "Ilias Σ 535–540." *Hermes* 93:1–6.

Stanford, W. B. 1936. *Greek Metaphor.* Oxford. Repr. New York, 1972.

———, ed. 1948. *The Odyssey of Homer.* 2 vols. London.

———. 1968. *The Ulysses Theme: A Study in the Adaptability of a Traditional Hero.* 2nd ed. Oxford.

Svenbro, J. 1976. *La Parole et le marbre: Aux origines de la poétique grecque.* Lund.

———. 1984. "La stratégie de l'amour: Modèle de la guerre et théorie de l'amour dans la poésie de Sappho." *Quaderni di Storia* 19:57–79.

Taillardat, J. 1982. "ΦΙΛΟΤΗΣ, ΠΙΣΤΙΣ et FOEDUS." *Revue des Études grecques* 95:1–14.

Thomas, C. G. 1973. "Matriarchy in Early Greece: The Bronze and Dark Ages." *Arethusa* 6.2:173–195.

Torrance, R. 1966. *Sophocles. The Women of Trachis and Philoctetes: A New Translation in Verse by Robert Torrance.* New York.

Tronquart, G. 1953. "L'Hélène d'Homère." *Bulletin de l'Association Guillaume Budé* 3:28–42.

Trümpy, H. 1950. *Kriegerische Fachausdrücke im griechischen Epos.* Fribourg.

Vellay, C. 1957. *Les Légendes du cycle troyen.* Paris.

Vermeule, E. 1979. *Aspects of Death in Early Greek Art and Poetry.* Berkeley.

Vernant, J.-P. 1974. *Mythe et pensée chez les Grecs.* 2nd ed. Paris.

———. 1977. "Résumé des cours de 1976–1977." *Extrait de l'annuaire du Collège de France* 77:423–441.

———. 1979a. *Mythe et société en Grèce ancienne.* Paris.

———. 1979b. "ΠΑΝΤΑ ΚΑΛΑ. D'Homère à Simonide." *Annali della Scuola normale superiore di Pisa* 9:1365–1374.

———. 1980. "La belle mort et le cadavre outragé." *Journal de Psychologie Normale et Pathologique* 2–3:209–241. Repr. in Vernant and Gnoli 1982:45–76.

———. 1981a. "L'autre de l'homme: la face de Gorgô." In *Le Racisme: Mythes et sciences,* ed. M. Olender, 141–155. Brussels.

———. 1981b. "Mort grecque. Mort a deux faces." *Le Débat* 12:51–59.

———. 1982a. "Le Refus d'Ulysse." *Le Temps de la réflexion* 3:13–18.

———. 1982b. "Résumé des cours de 1981–1982." *Extrait de l'annuaire du Collège de France* 82:407–422.

Vernant, J.-P., and M. Detienne. 1974. *Les ruses de l'intelligence: la mètis des Grecs.* Paris.

Vernant, J.-P, and G. Gnoli, eds. 1982. *La Mort, les morts dans les sociétés anciennes*. Paris.

Vidal-Naquet, P. 1963. "Homère et le monde mycénien: À propos d'un livre récent et d'une polémique ancienne." *Annales. Économies, Sociétés, Civilisations* 18:703–719.

———.1965. "Économie et société dans la Grèce ancienne: l'œuvre de Moses I. Finley." *Archives européennes de sociologie* 6:111–148.

———. 1975. "L'*Iliade* sans travesti." Preface to *Iliade*, trans. P. Mazon, 5–32. Paris.

———. 1981. *Le Chasseur noir*. Paris.

Vivante, P. 1955. "Sulla designazione del corpo in Omero." *Archivo Glottologico Italiano* 40:39–50.

Von der Mühll, P. 1952. *Kritisches Hypomnema zur Ilias*. Basel.

Wace, B., and F. H. Stubbings, eds. 1962. *A Companion to Homer*. London.

Wade-Gery, T. 1952. *The Poet of the Iliad*. Cambridge.

Watkins, C. 1977. "À propos de ΜΗΝΙΣ." *Bulletin de la Société de linguistique de Paris* 72:187–209.

Weil, S. 1953. "L'Iliade ou le poème de la force." In *La Source grecque*, 11–42. Paris.

Whitman, C. H. 1958. *Homer and the Heroic Tradition*. Cambridge, MA.

Willcock, M. M. 1964. "Mythological Paradeigma in the *Iliad*." *Classical Quarterly* 14:141–154.

———. 1970. *A Companion to Homer's* Iliad. London.

Index Locorum

Subject Index